*The American
Immigration Collection*

The Mingling
of the Canadian
and American Peoples

Volume I: Historical

MARCUS LEE HANSEN

Arno Press and *The New York Times*

NEW YORK 1970

Reprint Edition 1970 by Arno Press Inc.

Reprinted from a copy in
The Kansas State University Library

LC# 78-129400

ISBN 0-405-00553-9

The American Immigration Collection—Series II
ISBN for complete set 0-405-00543-1

Manufactured in the United States of America

THE MINGLING OF THE CANADIAN AND AMERICAN PEOPLES

THE RELATIONS OF
CANADA AND THE UNITED STATES

———

A SERIES OF STUDIES
PREPARED UNDER THE DIRECTION OF THE
CARNEGIE ENDOWMENT FOR INTERNATIONAL PEACE
DIVISION OF ECONOMICS AND HISTORY

JAMES T. SHOTWELL, *Director*

THE
MINGLING OF THE CANADIAN
AND AMERICAN PEOPLES

VOLUME I
HISTORICAL

BY THE LATE
MARCUS LEE HANSEN
UNIVERSITY OF ILLINOIS

COMPLETED AND PREPARED FOR PUBLICATION BY
JOHN BARTLET BREBNER
COLUMBIA UNIVERSITY

NEW HAVEN : YALE UNIVERSITY PRESS
TORONTO : THE RYERSON PRESS
LONDON:HUMPHREY MILFORD:OXFORD UNIVERSITY PRESS
FOR THE CARNEGIE ENDOWMENT FOR INTERNATIONAL
PEACE : DIVISION OF ECONOMICS AND HISTORY
1940

INTRODUCTION

IT is not too much to say that this volume contributes a new and fundamental chapter to the history of North America. The movement of people to and fro across the Canadian-American boundary has been regarded, until recent years, as one of those great natural phenomena which are taken for granted in the lives of the two nations. Canadians manned industries in New England, cleared forests in Michigan, broke the sod of prairies in the Mississippi valley, helped to build towns and cities from the Atlantic to the Pacific, and took a leading part in organizing and operating the web of railways whose center is Chicago; while in somewhat lesser numbers, but with equal freedom of movement, Americans shared everywhere in the exploitation of Canadian farmland, mine and forest, and contributed to Canadian life such technical experts as the builder of the first Canadian transcontinental railroad.

So natural has been this interplay of populations in the North American scene, that although it constitutes what is perhaps the largest single reciprocity in international migration in history, historians have hitherto given it little or no attention. This neglect was bound to be the case so long as history was regarded as a subject limited to political events, for the migration across the "imaginary boundary" had little if any political significance, at least in the eyes of the migrants themselves. While they were loyal citizens of either country during their residence in it, their decisions to migrate were determined, for the most part, by the same kind of non-political considerations as had brought them or their ancestors overseas from Europe or from the Eastern States into Ontario. The call to the settler, the worker, the industrialist or the scholar was that of opportunity; the keynote to his thinking in all these matters was individualism.

The world today can hardly understand this type of nationalism, strong in its loyalties to community life and proud of citizenship in a free country, but basing both pride and loyalty upon an intimate personal sense of the dignity of man himself. It was a genuine American outlook. Although its origin lay for the most part in the traditions and institutions of English liberty, the United States and Canada alike added to it the vital stimulus of frontier life. In this larger commonwealth of ideas and ideals there was what one might almost call a common citizenship of English-speaking North Americans, a common sense of participation in the heritage of freedom.

Viewed in this light, a good deal of the story which Professor Hansen and Professor Brebner tell in these pages is an expansion of the great theme of American history which Professor Frederick Turner opened up in his studies of the history of the Westward Movement. While it is possible to relate much of the movement to and fro across the border to the general lines of expansion over the continent, other parts of it belong to the reverse migrations which were stimulated by the industrialization and urbanization of the eastern half of North America. Unfortunately, the government statistics in both countries furnish only moderately revealing information and that for only part of the long story, and the social historian finds to his surprise that the Anglo-Canadian emigrant settling in the United States joined in with the members of his new community in so intimate and natural a way as to make it often more difficult to keep track of ex-Canadians in the American scene than of transplanted residents of the Eastern States who settled in the Mississippi valley. This could not, in the nature of the case, be equally true of the Americans in Canada because in its smaller population the individual necessarily plays a more distinctive part, but the main principle is equally true on both sides of the border.

The present volume is the historian's contribution to a joint enterprise of historians and statisticians. The measurements of the movements here described are to be set forth in a parallel volume by Dr. R. H. Coats, of the Canadian Bureau of Statistics, and Dr. Leon E. Truesdell, of the United States Census Bureau, with whom other specialists have coöperated. It was originally intended to publish the two studies jointly, but each has grown into a full treatment by itself, following, as was inevitable, the entirely different techniques of descriptive narrative on the one hand and statistics on the other. The student of this subject, however, will find that the volumes complement each other, and that both are essential for a well-rounded view of the subject as a whole.

No one who reads this volume can fail to regret the untimely death of its author, whose last thoughts were given to its unfinished pages. Born on December 8, 1892, at Neenah, Wisconsin, the child of a Danish father and a Norwegian mother who had been brought to the United States by their parents early in the 'seventies, he saw in his own household and in his father's congregations the transition from Scandinavian speech and ways to the new American patterns which were being composed in the trans-Mississippi West. As he himself matured in this changing environment, he set himself the task of describing and explaining the European migration to North America as a dynamic and continuing process both at its source and on the immense continent where its forces found play.[1] Trained in Iowa and Harvard Universities, he brought to his mission a strict sense of historical objectivity, challenging accepted ideas wherever the source material called for new and corrected perspectives, and drawing his own conclusions from the evidence at hand. His years of study in his chosen field of the history of American immigration had provided him with a sure background for his work on this movement within the American continent. But painstaking scholarship was never allowed to lessen his interest in the figures which filled the foreground, in whose lives and fortunes he shared imaginatively. Fortunately Professor Hansen had carried his text so far that it was possible for Professor Brebner to complete it and prepare the volume for publication. Professor Brebner has worked with pious and anxious care to keep the book as nearly that which Professor Hansen had planned and would have desired as was possible under the circumstances. His own contribution has been real and important, as can be seen from the concluding chapter and the maps. But the history, the judgments in it and the suggestions it offers are basically the work of Professor Hansen.

J. T. S.

1. See his *The Atlantic Migration, 1607–1860* (Cambridge, Mass., 1940).

own. Finally, what could be made of the human ebb and flow which

FOREWORD

EVER since French Canadians settled in the Illinois country and
Louisiana during the last quarter of the seventeenth century, and
New Englanders supplanted the Acadians in Nova Scotia about the
middle of the eighteenth, the populations of the regions which are
now the United States and Canada have been spilling great waves of
men and women into each other's territories. Anyone at all inquisitive
about the distribution of human beings in North America cannot
fail to have been struck by the basic American stock of the Maritime Provinces and Ontario in Canada, the millions of French Canadians in New England and New York, the traces of the Canadian in
the American Middle West and of the American on the Canadian
prairies, and the persistent to-and-fro movement of both stocks along
the Pacific coast from Mexico to the Bering Strait. Here is a continent where international boundaries have been disregarded by restless humans for almost two centuries.

Although the general features of the continental migrations which
had had such curious results were known to students, and although
some parts of them had been carefully investigated, until a short
time ago no one had ventured to compose the story as a whole. Indeed, when the Carnegie Endowment's investigation of the relations
of Canada and the United States was being planned, and it was felt
to be imperative that so remarkable and fundamental a matter should
be thoroughly described, the historians who were first consulted were
very doubtful whether it could be done.

The source materials upon which an investigator must depend
were practically unobtainable, they pointed out, for great areas
along the migration routes. How could the Americans who poured
into what is now Ontario after 1783 be distinguished from the Loyalists of the American Revolution whom they had submerged numeri-
cally before the War of 1812? Who had taken the trouble to sort
out the Canadians from the waves of North Americans and Europeans which broke over the pine forests of the Lakes region and the
fat farm lands of the American Middle West? Indeed, would it have
been at all possible to sort them out, either there or when land-wise

North American farmers raced into the Canadian prairies knowing that here was the last great area on the continent of the rich farm land which mere vigor and enterprise could claim and make their own? Finally, what could be made of the human ebb and flow which has been going on along the whole length of the Pacific coast since the end of the eighteenth century?

In the pages which follow, the late Professor Hansen has succeeded remarkably in telling the story and answering these questions, partly because from the beginning, refusing to be deceived by political frontiers, he traced his North Americans on the march in continental terms, and partly because he and his assistants uncovered more and better evidence of what happened in the past than the most optimistic questioner might have expected. In this book and in the other monographs which Marcus Hansen left at his death, students and readers are going to become acquainted with a fine scholar who was too little known in his lifetime. It is to be hoped that his demonstrations of what rich harvests of significant knowledge may be reaped from the study of population movements by insight, intelligence, and hard work will create the school of followers which would certainly have been his had he lived on.

For one thing, the persistent North American intermingling which he has portrayed in this book, startling as it may appear to those who happen upon it unforeseen, is not unique in the world, or even in North America, as those who know its Southwest can point out. For another—and this seems more important—the knowledge that at any time since colonial days what are now the United States and Canada have contained substantial bodies of each other's human stock should make it ridiculous that their peoples today should have such distorted ideas of each other. Where, as in parts of Europe, language and traditional ways of living differ sharply at the very political frontiers, there is reason for such ignorance. It is absurd, however, that the school children of Canadian Windsor and American Detroit, separated by no more than a river, should be shepherded through the study of only their own halves of the continent. Their forefathers revealed and developed it in unison—North Americans all, and eminently capable of allegiance to one country one day and to another the next.

Studies like this one make an excellent foundation for awareness of, and pride in, what our ancestors have done for us, irrespective of whether their political allegiances and ours have been the same. There are North American families today, for instance, some of whose members have changed political allegiance back and forth about once a generation since 1750, as the continental migrations have crossed and recrossed the international boundary. Excellent as the reasons may be for warm American loyalty to the United States and equally warm Canadian allegiance to Canada on the part of the present generation, these sentiments should never be allowed to exclude an equally justifiable pride in descent from the mingled peoples of the past who created the common North American heritage.

The reader of a posthumous publication is entitled to know how it was prepared in the absence of its author. In this case, Professor Hansen had completed the drafts of ten chapters and had left some notes for the concluding one. In the normal course of events his manuscript would have been sent to Dr. J. T. Shotwell, Director of the Division of Economics and History of the Carnegie Endowment for International Peace, who would have submitted it for criticism to one or more readers and have returned it to the author with his comments as to final revision.

I have tried to put myself in what would have been Hansen's place, with the advantage of having shared his enthusiasm for the subject and of having talked and corresponded with him about it at intervals during the two or three years before his death. Members of his family have sent me portions of the materials which he had collected and digested, and I was particularly fortunate in that Miss E. E. McKenzie, his trusted principal assistant, was able to go over the entire manuscript with me in a detailed and very helpful discussion of doubtful points. I also profited greatly from the criticisms of both Hansen's chapters and my own which were generously given by three busy men—Dr. R. H. Coats, the Dominion Statistician, Mr. M. C. MacLean, Chief of the Social Analysis Branch of the Dominion Bureau of Statistics, and Dr. L. E. Truesdell, Chief Statistician for Population of the United States Bureau of the Census. These gentlemen are the authors of the statistical studies of Canadian-American population movements since 1850 which are to be found in the forthcoming companion volume to this one and which Professor Hansen did not live to see. We agree in believing that the double approach, historical and statistical, has benefited both volumes.

Dr. Shotwell and I felt that any apparatus of brackets and asterisks to indicate meticulously the changes made from the original manuscript would be both awkward and unnecessary. My task, on the whole, has been that of supplying the minimum of literary revision required to clarify some outlines, and occasionally to free the flow, of Hansen's exposition in sections where his mortal weariness had hampered him. I have added a little to the works of reference cited and have corrected a few errors of fact, emphasis, or interpretation in the light of evidence which Hansen himself would have considered had he lived. Fortunately he and I discussed the maps about a year before his death and I have carried out his wishes in them. I have also done my best to take into consideration his fragmentary notes for the final chapter, but I must accept responsibility for it and for the title of these two volumes. All in all, readers are asked to accept this book as a piece of pioneering scholarship by Marcus Lee Hansen, prepared for publication by other workers in the field where he was master.

Students may be interested to know that Professor Hansen's notes, maps, and other materials have been deposited in the Widener Library, Harvard University. For various reasons it seemed impracticable to compile a comprehensive bibliographical note to this volume, but the index contains references to the first citation of all monographs under their authors' names. While the index is otherwise confined to names and places, treatments of special topics may be located by using the detailed, paginated table of contents.

Since the customary acknowledgments of aid given and of collections opened to Professor Hansen in the preparation of this book could not be more than partial, it has seemed best to omit them altogether. Those who helped Professor Hansen in various ways and the owners or custodians of the widely scattered source materials in the United States and Canada upon which he drew so wisely will doubtless find reward enough in knowing that his distillation from long-buried knowledge is now available to the public.

I should like to add mention, however, of the tributes paid to Hansen's scholarship in the form of generous aid in preparing the maps. The United States Bureau of the Census and the Dominion Bureau of Statistics, through Dr. Truesdell and Dr. Coats, were continuously helpful, and Professor A. H. Moehlman of Ohio State University arranged for the loan of his unique population maps of the Red River Valley. Mr. A. J. H. Richardson of the Public Archives of Canada contributed not only a great deal of time but also the products of his unpublished researches into the settlement of northeastern North America which make our map treatment of that area before 1815 a distinct contribution to knowledge. Miss McKenzie and Mr. J. H. Thurrott were of great assistance in handling the exacting details of publication.

J. B. B.

Columbia University
  July 1, 1939.

CONTENTS

MAPS

MAPS

ABBREVIATIONS

A.R.F.C. Annual Report on Foreign Commerce (Washington).

B.C.: Sess. Pap. Province of British Columbia Sessional Papers.

C.R.U.S.F.C. Commercial Relations of the United States with Foreign Countries (Washington).

D. C. and T. Reports. Daily Consular and Trade Reports (Washington).

Dom. Can.: App. to Jour. H. of C. Appendix to the Journal of the House of Commons of the Dominion of Canada.

Dom. Can.: Debates H. of C. Debates of the House of Commons of the Dominion of Canada.

Dom. Can.: Jour. H. of C. Journals of the House of Commons of the Dominion of Canada.

Dom. Can.: Sess. Pap. Dominion of Canada Sessional Papers.

J.C.T.P. Journal of the Commissioners for Trade and Plantations (London).

M. C. and T. Reports. Monthly Consular and Trade Reports (Washington).

N.B.H.S. Collections of the New Brunswick Historical Society (St. John).

N.S.: App. to Jour. H. of A. Appendix to the Journals of the House of Assembly of Nova Scotia.

N.S.: App. to Jour. of Legislative Council. Appendix to the Journals of the Legislative Council of Nova Scotia.

P.A.C. Public Archives of Canada, MSS Collections.

P.A.C.R. Public Archives of Canada, Reports (Ottawa).

P.C.: App. to Jour. of Legislative Assembly. Appendix to the Journals of the Legislative Assembly of the Province of Canada.

P.C.: Jour. of Legislative Assembly. Journals of the Legislative Assembly of the Province of Canada.

P.C.: Jour. of Legislative Council. Journals of the Legislative Council of the Province of Canada.

P.C.: Sess. Pap. Province of Canada Sessional Papers.

P.O.: Sess. Pap. Province of Ontario Sessional Papers.

P.Q.: Sess. Pap. Province of Quebec Sessional Papers.

P.R.O. Public Record Office (London), MSS Collections.

R.S.C. Proceedings and Transactions of the Royal Society of Canada.

THE MINGLING OF THE CANADIAN AND AMERICAN PEOPLES

CHAPTER I

INTRODUCTION: THE UNITY OF THE WESTWARD MOVEMENT

SINCE the coming of the white man, the continent of North America has provided a vast arena for the interplay of insistently expanding peoples. Historians have made a familiar story out of the clashes and compromises since the end of the fifteenth century which have gradually brought about the present stable division of the land among Canada, the United States, and Mexico, but they have tended to do so in terms of rival political, economic, and social organizations, with somewhat less regard for the mere dynamics of population. Where the one group of forces begins and the other ends is, of course, impossible to say, but a shift in emphasis, particularly where the United States and Canada are concerned, throws abundant new light on their individual and related histories. It will be seen that these North American men and women, responding to pressures generated by their own numbers, by the proportions of old and young among them, or by new tides of immigration, moved about spasmodically and with little regard for political allegiance, making and breaking by their migrations states and systems of community life.

On the continent of North America, settlement expanded across the three thousand miles from coast to coast in the course of less than three hundred years. During the nineteenth century, in particular, population was mobile. No affection for the acres tilled by his father rooted the farmer in the place of his birth. A British official, in commenting on this characteristic of Americans, declared: "They play at leap-frog with their lands; so soon as they have cultivated a spot that any newcomer likes they sell it and remove higher up in the country. . . . I have known them to remove four times in the space of a few years."[1] Land policies encouraged the clearing

1. W. Knox to Clerk of the Council, 16 June 1806; Historical Manuscripts Commission, *Report on Manuscripts in Various Collections*, VI (Dublin, 1909), 224.

and cultivating of new areas and land laws facilitated the alienation of property from hand to hand. A world-wide demand for the staples that the new regions yielded in abundance in return for determined effort—wheat, cotton, timber, minerals—by assuring the pioneer that his enterprise would be rewarded, encouraged adventurers to move on and on in a never-ending search for easily acquired fortunes. The restless spirit that was in part the product of these migratory experiences grew in intensity as the century progressed, so that it came in time to be the major consideration in interpreting the characteristics of the population which were revealed in the periodic census reports.[2]

Stretching from ocean to ocean lay the international line that marked the boundary between Canada and the United States. By the close of the nineteenth century the Pacific coast of the Dominion as well as of the Republic was peopled in general by settlers who had migrated, either themselves or in the persons of their ancestors, from the states and provinces bordering the Atlantic. The Canadian advance and the American advance are usually considered parallel movements. They were, in fact, not parallel but integral. The settlement of the Pacific area, north as well as south of the forty-ninth degree of latitude, was the product of a westward tide of people that was continental and international in origin and in route. The boundary was disregarded by eager land seekers who thought much of fertility and markets and little of political jurisdiction. In time, transportation systems, land companies, and even governmental officials understood the fundamental character of this unconcern and in adjusting policies to this realistic view recorded their recognition of the unity of the westward movement.

Of this unity the pioneer was not aware. He considered himself in all respects an individual and independent adventurer; and historians strengthened the tradition that he fostered by emphasizing the exploits of the most self-reliant and colorful characters in the great army that conquered the North American wilderness. But a more realistic study reveals that in the course of his migration he followed a beaten path or a marked trail, finally striking off to the left or

2. Rudolf Heberle, *Über die Mobilität der Bevölkerung in den Vereinigten Staaten* (Jena, 1929), 1–30.

right, and only his last few miles were through an untrod forest or over trackless prairie. At his journey's end he might live in an isolation that seemed complete. But if it were broken even so seldom as once a year by the appearance of a peddler or by his own visit to the trading post where furs, skins, or potash were exchanged for salt, powder, and lead, these acts established the fact that, albeit unwittingly, he was part of one of the networks of moving people and goods that together gave unity to the westward movement.

From the confused and incomplete picture that is reconstructed out of a thousand stray items of contemporary information it seems that east of the Mississippi the advancing pioneers were marshaled into several great columns. Along the route that each of them traced there flowed outward the few supplies that were essential for the maintenance of the frontier settlements, and in return the ever-increasing volume of products seeking a market that came from the widening clearings. The exact course of any one of these channels was determined by many factors of topography, resources, politics, and chance. But all wound their way back to the Atlantic coast and to that part of the coast which was the base of expanding population.

The Atlantic coast was not the base in its entirety. It would perhaps be logical to suppose that when Europeans began the colonization of the new continent they would occupy every mile of its eastern shore where a human habitation could be established and then proceed, on a long front of a thousand miles, to sweep inland. Some such idea was in the mind of the British authorities when they sliced up the shore line into a series of colonies whose charters gave them jurisdictions "from sea to sea"; and at all promising and at many unpromising points from Newfoundland to Florida, adventurers and groups of settlers landed families and stock in optimistic attempts to secure the foothold which should be the first step toward fortune. Each of the communities that survived disasters and disappointments looked into the future and foresaw in itself a gateway through which were to crowd throngs of followers.

This, however, did not always or speedily turn out to be the case. Europeans continued to come, in increasing numbers, but after the first groups of vessels (properly designated "expeditions") had discharged their passengers at any colony, the subsequent peopling of that province usually ceased to be a matter of promotional enterprise. Liberal policies in the distribution of land were often adopted, and occasionally subsidies of supplies and equipment were granted. But with that the concern of the authorities was at an end. The colonial planter or employer who wanted labor had to seek it himself, and the Britisher or Continental who wanted to adventure across the Atlantic had to search out opportunities for passage. In both cases the arrangements were usually made with the merchants and ship captains who were building up the framework of Atlantic commerce; and when the demand for labor in the colonies became so steady that it paid ship operators to coöperate in methods by which emigrants could gradually "work off" their passage money (the "redemptioner trade"), this early system was also forced to conform to the prevailing routes of international exchange.[3]

The European commerce of the colonies tended to become concentrated in a limited number of ports. From Florida northward to Cape Hatteras the hindrances to navigation were many: dangerous shoals shifting with every change in winds and currents, sand bars that blocked the mouths of rivers and harbors, and the constant danger of hurricanes rushing up from the West Indies.[4] With the exception of Charleston no port developed extensive trading connections with Europe; and in Charleston negro slaves, not white laborers, were in demand.[5] To the north, Newfoundland was ruled out as a site for extensive settlement after the experiences of Gilbert and Lord Baltimore; and the colonization of the peninsula of Nova Scotia was a French, not an English, venture. Englishmen did come to North America by way of Newfoundland, but these were summer "hands" in the fisheries who devised various schemes for getting farther on to settled New England. By 1640 the sturdy stock that was to produce the prolific race of Yankees was planted in the hinterland of Boston and along the shores of Long Island Sound. During the remainder

3. Cheesman A. Herrick's *White Servitude in Pennsylvania* (Philadelphia, 1921) is a general study of the redemptioner system in the colony in which it attained its widest use.

4. *United States Coast Pilot*, Atlantic Coast, Section D (Washington, 1936), 2.

5. Elizabeth Donnan, *Documents Illustrative of the History of the Slave Trade to America*, IV (Washington, 1935), 241.

of the colonial era, emigrants from New England were more numerous than immigrants from abroad.[6]

New York at the mouth of the Hudson River, Philadelphia and Wilmington on the lower reaches of the Delaware River, and Baltimore, Alexandria, and Norfolk on Chesapeake Bay were the seacoast towns at which incoming Europeans, whether tradesmen, independent farmers, or bound servants, normally disembarked. They filtered into the lands beyond these places, forming patches of settlement that grew together into a bloc of occupied territory which extended southward from Albany through the tidewater region of Virginia. The New Englanders, multiplying township by township, steadily approached the Hudson from the east; and in the meantime in the valley of the St. Lawrence the few thousand French habitants who had been sent to New France were taking possession of the banks of the river. Increasing at a rate that equaled that of their Anglo-Saxon neighbors, they were pioneering in the forests that bordered the tributaries flowing from the south, thereby inaugurating the movement that was ultimately to bring the two nationalities together. Not until the early nineteenth century was the process of population consolidation completed in the region from the St. Lawrence to Cape Hatteras, but the historic function that the region was to perform with regard to the rest of the continent had already been revealed.

Aufmarschgebiet is the suggestive word that has been applied to the region by a German scholar who was impressed by the orderly and coördinated nature of the process by which the settlement of the continent was achieved in spite of the diversity in blood and experience apparent among the pioneers. The term, military in origin, denotes the territory in which troops coming in various contingents from many quarters deploy into line of action, making ready for a concerted advance.[7] In this area, irregular in shape, were to be

6. M. L. Hansen, "The Settlement of New England," *Handbook of the Linguistic Geography of New England* (Providence, 1939), chapter ii.

7. Dr.-Ing. Blum, "Geographie und Geschichte im Verkehrs- und Siedlungswesen Nordamerikas," *Archiv für Eisenbahnwesen,* 57 (Berlin, 1934), 241–286, 553–616. H. Baulig, *Amérique septentrionale* (2v., Paris, 1935–36). M. I. Newbigin, *Canada, the Great River, the Lands and the Men* (London, 1928).

found descendants of four colonial empires—New France, New Netherland, New Sweden, and New England (in the larger sense)— and, during the nineteenth century, immigrants from every nation of Europe. Here they were mustered into the ranks and, when the signal to move forward was given, they marched into the forests, fields, and mines of the undefined empire beyond known as the West. A new generation of children and more recent immigrants appeared as replacements and, by a process that historians have not yet succeeded in explaining, they, in turn, became part of the reserve, available for service when the next advance was under way.

The theme of these introductory pages is not the conquest of the West, but the fashion in which the various geographical regions to which the name was applied have determined the course of the population relations between Canada and the United States. Nevertheless, the nature of the relationship may be emphasized by a brief consideration of the various columns of pioneers that marched out of the great mobilization camp along the coast. Of these columns there were four. Each was fairly distinct, if not in the character of its membership, yet certainly in time, in destination, and in significance. It happened that the route of one of them lay along the great internal waterway that was chosen to serve as a considerable part of the boundary between two countries, with the result that, as it moved forward, it wound over the line and back again, thereby setting in motion some countermarches and provoking some political responses which gave it an international character. Otherwise it would be considered as only another of the grand divisions of the continental westward movement.

In considering these columns of migration, the one which might be designated the first used the Atlantic as its highway. This was more of a drift than a march. Since it was unnecessary to blaze a trail or organize caravans, and since no frontier tales of adventure and Indian warfare made it the subject of romance, this drift has failed to receive the historical recognition that its importance would warrant. But it was nonetheless real. New Englanders early began to move down the coast. Before Massachusetts was a generation old, it had sent a colony to Maryland; and within the same length of time after its first planting, New Haven had lost many of its prominent families to New Jersey.[8] A considerable Puritan colony from New England was established among the first settlers of South Carolina.[9] After the conquest of New Netherland in 1664, Dutch farmers left the valley of the Hudson for more southern colonies and later the authorities complained that many of the young people in the Middle Colonies were departing for some southern destination.[10] The Albemarle region of North Carolina was largely peopled by the "overflow" from tidewater Virginia and for a century after its founding, Georgia, colony and state, received newcomers from the north.[11] Many of the first American settlements on the Gulf of Mexico from Florida to Texas were established by the traders who followed the coastal route.[12]

The second column was led by the frontier heroes of the eighteenth century: the Boones, the Seviers, the Hendersons. Mustered into its ranks were the descendants of the mingled population that had first settled the Middle Colonies and the formerly indentured persons who had landed in Pennsylvania or New York and now, after a few years of bound duty, were free to search out land where it was to be had almost for the taking. As they passed through the valley of Virginia and the back country of Carolina they were joined by farmers from the tidewater and the children of the first pioneers who had located beyond the Blue Ridge. Together they advanced along the valleys of the rivers that cut through the mountains and by a dozen branch trails spread over the meadows and into the open forests of

8. Edward Channing, *A History of the United States*, II (New York, 1918), 47. John L. Bozman, *The History of Maryland*, II (Baltimore, 1837), 411.

9. David Ramsay, *History of South Carolina* (Newberry, S.C., 1858), 5.

10. *Calendar of State Papers, Colonial Series, America and West Indies, 1669–74* (London, 1889), 277, 279, 280, 324, 579; *1689–92* (1901), 201, 266; *1693–96* (1903), 119, 236, 511; *1696–97* (1904), 88, 132, 189, 420.

11. John S. Bassett, "The Influence of Coast Line and Rivers on North Carolina," *Annual Report of the American Historical Association for the Year 1908*, I (Washington, 1909), 58–61. Richard H. Shryock, *Georgia and the Union in 1850* (Durham, N.C., 1926), 79–82.

12. G. W. Kendall, *Narrative of the Texan Santa Fé Expedition* (London, 1845), 6. Jedidiah Morse, *The American Gazetteer . . . with a Particular Description of Louisiana* (Boston, 1804): see "population" under article "Louisiana."

Kentucky and Tennessee. For a generation after the close of the war with France in 1763, this was "the West," the goal of every adventurer, land seeker, speculator, ambitious lawyer, and zealous missionary.[13]

Toward the close of the eighteenth century a new West became the focus of pioneering interest and the third column followed a new highway by mountain trail and river keelboat to new homes. The banks of the Ohio River and its fertile tributary valleys extending northward into the Old Northwest were the destinations of these travelers. They, like the earlier migrants, came principally from the prolific homesteads of the Middle States and the immigrant ports on the Atlantic where increasing numbers of arrivals were continually disembarking. For two hundred miles from the coast they continued along the old roads that had long witnessed similar scenes, but instead of veering toward the south they crossed the mountains of Pennsylvania and took to the westward-flowing waters at the frontier post of Pittsburgh. Even the West that had always seen mankind on the move was startled by the crowds that jostled one another on the narrow roads and ventured down the treacherous streams with little, if any, knowledge of navigation.[14] In particular, during the restless years that followed 1815, when old America seemed to one observer to be "breaking up," the Ohio Valley was the great highway into the pioneer states and territories.[15] The route was never deserted. The keelboat and flatboat gave way to the steamboat, and the Conestoga wagon was replaced by the railroad, but Pittsburgh remained a gateway as long as Americans sought the opportunities of the mid-continental empire.

Not a new West but the opening of a new route called the fourth historic column into being. Although the last to take form, it became the greatest in numbers, the most cosmopolitan in composition, and the most persistent in retaining its identity as it pressed onward into the territory beyond the Mississippi. Into its ranks came Canadians, New Englanders, and new Americans from the immigrant sheds in

13. Archer B. Hulbert, *Soil: Its Influence on the History of the United States* (New Haven, 1930), 174–191.

14. Frederick J. Turner, *Rise of the New West* (New York, 1906), 80–83.

15. Morris Birkbeck, *Notes on a Journey in America from the Coast of America to the Territory of Illinois* (2d ed., London, 1818), 30.

New York, but the three did not mingle until after some century-long preliminary movements had been completed. The small Canadian nucleus had to expand mile by mile through the forests of the St. Lawrence basin; the Yankees had to explore every hilltop and mountain valley of their own Northwest and retain in cultivation every farm that would support a family; and New York, as well as Quebec and Montreal, had to develop the overseas connections in trade and personnel that were essential parts of the complicated system of exchange of men and goods which was the foundation of the nineteenth-century immigration.

Of all the approaches from the seaboard to the interior, that known as the "Mohawk route" was the most favored by nature. For a hundred miles west of its junction with the Hudson the Mohawk River was navigable, with an occasional portage, for canoes and bateaux; and when shallow water and shoals made further progress by boat difficult, the traveler had before him an almost level plain that extended for two hundred miles to the shores of Lake Erie. This valley route was the only break in the wall of the Appalachians other than the mountain passes to the south, and this was not a rugged cleft through inhospitable lands, but a belt of rich soil that was destined to support tens of thousands of people as well as to provide for hundreds of thousands access to no less attractive lands beyond.[16]

But not until the European had been established for almost two hundred years at the gateway from the east did the advancing army of pioneers find the way open. Progress up the Hudson was blocked by the great patroonships surviving from Dutch days, on which the acceptance of land involved a condition of dependence that no liberty-loving and high-spirited settler was willing to acknowledge. Beyond Albany, to the north and to the west the traditional enmity with the French constituted a persistent threat, and the unhappy experiences of the German Palatines who were located on the flats along the Mohawk were a warning that discouraged all but a few of the most adventurous. With the peace of 1763 this danger was removed; then, however, the decrees of the colonial administrators still left an obstacle. For on the headwaters of the Mohawk and about the

16. Albert P. Brigham, *Geographic Influences in American History* (Boston, 1903), 7–8, 155.

"finger lakes" that diversify the central New York plain lay the home villages and cornfields of the Iroquois confederacy of Indian nations. Friendship with these tribes was an essential part of British frontier policy and the would-be settler on or near Indian lands was regarded as an intruder to be removed by force.[17]

The American Revolution not only brought about a new frontier policy: the events of the war destroyed the villages and ruined the political power of the confederacy that had claimed lordship over the natives as far distant as the Mississippi. Defeat scattered the warriors and their families to various refuges in the region of the Great Lakes. For many of the Americans the Indian campaign of General Sullivan in 1779 was the most significant episode in eight years of a revolutionary war. An army of a few thousand frontiersmen turned a punitive expedition against the red men into a land seekers' tour over their abandoned fields. This inaugurated a movement of people that in the course of a decade drove westward a wedge of settlement with its point in the headwaters of the Mohawk.[18]

Beyond this, however, it was difficult to go. A traveler of 1792 found a few farms established on the banks of the Genesee River. But thence, ninety miles to Niagara, he saw "not one house or white man the whole way. The only direction I had was an Indian path which sometimes was doubtful."[19] The replacement of this path by road and canal was ultimately to come, but for the time being large investments and extensive works were out of the question. Men

17. Charles H. McIlwain (ed.), *Wraxall's Abridgment of the New York Indian Records* (Cambridge, 1915), xxxvii–xxxviii.

18. Ruth L. Higgins, *Expansion in New York with Especial Reference to the Eighteenth Century* (Columbus, 1931), 101. The extent of settlement is indicated on the "Area Map of the State of New York, 1790," printed in the Rochester Historical Society, *Publication Fund Series,* VII (Rochester, 1928), following page 224.

19. "Extract of a Letter from a Gentleman upon his Return from Niagara, Dated August 8, 1792," *Collections of the Massachusetts Historical Society for the Year 1792,* First series, I (Boston, reprinted 1806), 284–288; quotation on page 286. P. Campbell, *Travels in the Interior Inhabited Parts of North America in the Years 1791 and 1792* (Edinburgh, 1793; reprinted edition by H. H. Langton, with notes by W. F. Ganong, Toronto, 1937), new ed., 183–190, 207–232.

turned, therefore, to a more roundabout route which required only moderate improvements in order to shorten the time of journeying from the Hudson to Lake Erie. At the village of Rome on the Mohawk a short portage led to the headwaters of Wood Creek. After forty miles of meandering, this creek emptied into Lake Oneida which, in turn, had an outlet into Lake Ontario by the Oswego River. This was one of the traditional canoe routes of colonial times, known to fur traders of all nations and followed by war parties of French, English, and Indians.[20]

The Western Inland Lock Navigation Company, incorporated in 1792, undertook to make of this primitive trail a highway of commerce. At Rome a canal was built joining the Mohawk River with Wood Creek; the watercourses were cleared of obstructions and the channels widened and deepened.[21] This, the first man-made transportation route from the Atlantic to the Lakes, was international in character. For the fort at the mouth of the Oswego River was still in the possession of British troops, and the westward-bound traveler from Fort Oswego skirted the southern shore of Lake Ontario to the Canadian side of the Niagara River and, there disembarking, followed the road across the Niagara peninsula to Lake Erie. Americans journeying to the Old Northwest passed through a corner of Canada and officials of Upper Canada who sought the shortest route to England reached the port of New York by way of these connecting lakes and rivers.

Within a decade, however, a more direct way to the Niagara River was open. Wide advertisement of the western lands and the success of the first settlers there turned the current of New England migration, which was now beginning to flow in large volume over its boundaries, into the state of New York. The Genesee country between the headwaters of the Mohawk and Lake Erie was the favorite choice, but still farther west lay a region less fertile and more broken where lands were cheaper. Those who could not pay New York prices fixed their attention upon this New Connecticut, otherwise known as the Western Reserve. The interest thus centered upon the southern

20. Archer B. Hulbert, *Historic Highways of America,* VII (Cleveland, 1903), 135–150.

21. *American State Papers, Miscellaneous,* I (Washington, 1834), 769–789.

shore of Lake Erie grew and the number seeking a shorter route than that via Oswego increased. Accordingly, in 1800 a road was cut from the Genesee River to the mouth of Buffalo Creek, where the village beginnings of the future city were already in existence.[22] During the following years, this became one of the principal highways of migration; and when a branch was laid out to Lewistown opposite the thriving settlements in Upper Canada, Yankees bound for the Reserve mingled with families moving to the British colony. Western Upper Canada exerted a powerful attraction upon westward migrants who thoughtfully compared the friendliness of the Indians toward the British with their hostility toward the Americans.[23]

By 1812 the eastern half of Lake Erie, Canadian as well as American, was ringed with settlement and there was every prospect that the process would be continued until the line of pioneers moving north of the lake would be joined at the western end by that following the opposite shore. But as a result of the war from 1812 to 1815 almost the whole American current was turned into Ohio, where for a time most of it was absorbed. Detroit, farther on, was an old-established post and into its environs came the advance guard of the column, taking over the farms of the French and establishing themselves as merchants in the ambitious villages in the vicinity. However, the territory of Michigan lay outside the channel that gave direction to the movement. Instead of turning to the north and filling in the peninsula between Lake Huron and Lake Michigan, it continued to the west, reaching by the early 1830's Chicago and the prairies stretching to the Mississippi.

The westward movement, as a whole, or in any of its parts, was never constant or steady. Periods of rapid advance alternated with periods in which progress was slow. But during each pause there took place a filling in of areas that had been left unoccupied, even although this process occasionally involved an almost complete re-

22. James H. Hotchkin, *A History of the Purchase and Settlement of Western New York* (New York, 1848), 20.

23. For two contemporary investigations of comparative advantages, see Michael Smith, *A Geographical View of the British Possessions in North America* (Baltimore, 1814), Preface and *passim;* P. Campbell, *op. cit., passim.*

versal in direction. When the pioneers reached the prairies, hesitation was inevitable. They knew only woodland farming; they were dependent on the forest for wood and game; rivers and lakes were essential links in the lines of communication which tied them to markets. Without the sod plow, coal, and cheap lumber, and above all the railroad, an attack upon the prairie was hopeless. It did not become general until the 1850's.[24]

The preceding fifteen years had been marked by many confusing crosscurrents of population movement. One phase was the entwining of lines of advance that had hitherto been entirely Canadian with those that had been entirely American. All parts of the northern Atlantic coast population base were now for the first time ready to throw their forces into a joint conquest. Settlement that had risen to the top of the New England hills started to recede when the farmers, feeling the competition of the West, joined their competitors. Their French neighbors on the north, forced to choose between attempting to make homes in the inhospitable lands back from the St. Lawrence and emigration to the alien states to the south and west of them, were beginning to choose the latter. The slow process of internal expansion, accelerated by a fairly continuous flow of Americans and Old Countrymen, had occupied most of the agriculturally desirable parts of what is now the province of Ontario, and the children of the households in that region, in lieu of a Canadian West, were obliged to center their plans for fortune upon the West of the Republic. Montreal and New York exported the timber and wheat of the pioneer settlements and the returning vessels carried back to their home ports migrating Europeans who were also in search of land.

The upper lakes were the common highway of all these people. The Irishman who landed at Montreal traveled up the St. Lawrence, along the length of Lake Ontario, and by the Welland Canal (opened in 1829) reached the steamboats on Lake Erie; the German who disembarked at New York followed the well-established route of the Hudson River and Erie Canal to the same point; New Englanders, New Yorkers, and Canadians were their fellow passengers and, as they passed along by lake and river to the Straits of Macki-

24. W. P. Webb, *The Great Plains* (Boston, 1931).

nac and into Lake Michigan, representatives of the various groups left them at every port of call.

Michigan, hitherto neglected, was the first state to profit from this merging of the westbound streams of migrants. The early Yankee settlers had established a few tiers of counties across the bottom of the state and men from New York and New England joined with the children of these pioneers in an advance northward, township by township, into the interior. To spread from Ontario across the St. Clair River into the wooded valleys of the rivers that flow into Saginaw Bay was a natural continuation of the movement that had brought Canadians to the shores of their own Georgian Bay. French Canadians from Quebec learned of small settlements of trappers and Indian traders who spoke their language and were devoted to the same faith; thereafter each of these communities expanded by accretion. Occasionally Germans and Irishmen (often because they had no means to go farther) stopped at one of the numerous harbors on the rim of the peninsula and, starting as laborers, became farmers and permanent settlers. But the majority of the foreign-born continued across Lake Michigan to the eastern shore of Wisconsin where a northward movement, not unlike that under way in Michigan, was creeping up toward Milwaukee and Green Bay.[25]

When the railroad revolutionized transportation, it not only shortened both the distance and the duration of the trip to the West; it gave to the current of population expansion an even more pronounced unity than it had hitherto possessed.[26] Seventeenth-century explorers from Quebec had learned from the Indians of the trail that led from the head of Lake Erie to the head of Lake Michigan, and the "Chicago Road" which was constructed in the 1820's across the peninsula from Detroit was only an improvement of the red man's path. The surveyors who chose the course of the Michigan Central Railroad did not wander far from the primitive route and after 1852, when trains were running the entire distance, the passengers for the West gained several days by transferring from steamboat to

25. Joseph Schafer, *Four Wisconsin Counties: Prairie and Forest* (Madison, 1927), 64–68.

26. W. J. Wilgus, *The Railway Interrelations of the United States and Canada* (New Haven, 1937), 39, 40, 122.

railroad at Detroit. In the meantime the building of the New York Central had made unnecessary the tedious trip by canal. The lake journey from Buffalo to Detroit was the only gap in an all-rail route from New York to Chicago.

Passenger agents and investors, looking at the map, realized the advantages that would attend the construction of a line across Ontario connecting at each terminus with an American railroad. Instead of a water journey of from twenty-four to thirty-six hours on a lake on which navigation could be as dangerous as on the Atlantic, a trip of only nine hours was promised. Not local traffic within the province but the possibility of carrying the freight and passengers that accumulated at Buffalo and Chicago from the lines that radiated, fanlike, from either city was the inducement glowingly portrayed in the prospectus.[27] When completed in 1854 it bore the appropriate name of "Great Western Railway." Here, between 1851 and 1856, John A. Roebling built his great suspension bridge.[28]

A second link was finished in 1879, when the Canadian Grand Trunk Railway acquired control of several short Michigan lines and by building connecting sections secured entrance into Chicago from Port Huron, opposite its previous terminus at Sarnia. This line, combined with extensions from Montreal reaching across New England, provided another through system from the seaports on the Atlantic to the central continental junction point at Chicago.[29] With the increase in the volume of middle western agricultural exports, the great prize sought after by all companies engaged in transportation was a substantial share of this eastbound traffic; and in accordance with the general principle that migration and trade flow in the same channel (although usually in reverse directions) Chicago

27. Charles B. Stuart, *Report on the Great Western Railway, Canada West, to the President and Directors* (n.p., 1847), 2, 5, 7, 16, 19–22, 35.

28. *American Railroad Journal*, XXVII (New York, 1854), 105. W. J. Wilgus, *op. cit.*, 160.

29. William H. Breithaupt, "Outline of the History of the Grand Trunk Railway of Canada," *The Railway and Locomotive Historical Society Bulletin*, No. 23 (Boston, 1930), 37–74. See also G. P. deT. Glazebrook, *A History of Transportation in Canada* (Toronto, 1938), 313–318.

became the immediate destination of westward-moving North Americans and the distributing point for the population that was spreading through the Mississippi and Missouri valleys.

During the quarter of a century that followed the close of the Civil War in the United States the history of the economic development of North America may be written in terms of the railroads. They were not only carriers of commerce and people; they were land companies, endowed with millions of acres that had been granted as an encouragement to construction; and the location of these lands together with the policies adopted by the companies for their disposal determined the destination and, in some degree, the extent of the contemporary westward movement. Even the taking up of free homestead lands was influenced by the facilities offered by the transportation systems.

The area thus peopled by the railroads was the trans-Mississippi Middle West: Iowa, Minnesota, the Dakotas, Nebraska, and Kansas. The settlement of this region, between 1865 and 1890, was the great population phenomenon of the time. To every American east of the Mississippi it was "the West"; the Canadian, whether in New Brunswick or Ontario, had it in mind when he spoke of "the West"; and every foreigner who landed in New York or Quebec with the intention of proceeding to "the West" meant that one of these states or territories was his chosen destination. There was, it is true, a rival West—new provinces and territories beyond Lake Superior which the Canadian had in mind when he emphasized the pronoun in the expression "our West." Manitoba in particular had its enthusiastic advocates and for a short period in the early 'eighties, while the transcontinental Canadian Pacific Railway was being built, pioneers streamed out onto its prairies and built up mushroom towns with a recklessness that only the wildest "booms" in the States could parallel. But in spite of the remarkable character of the years from 1880 to 1882, the peopling of the Canadian part of the Red River Valley was only an offshoot from the far greater if less spectacular column of settlers who were filling in every unoccupied quarter section south of the forty-ninth parallel and east of the plains. They traveled over the same railroad lines to Chicago, continued in the company of many bound to Minnesota and the Dakotas through St.

Paul and on to Fargo, and did not finally part from their companions until the Canadian border was reached.

The pause that began in the late 'eighties and continued for well over a decade was another period of consolidation. Novel problems of crops, cultivation, and milling were the local accompaniments of a world-wide depression. "Hard times" was the term generally applied to the situation in which the pioneers found themselves: little money because trainloads of new neighbors were not daily disembarking upon the station platforms; no improvements and little construction because no one was building for the future; granaries glutted and prices low because every farm now had a surplus of grain to send to market. Irrespective of whether Winnipeg or Kansas City was the marketing point, the newly established farmers suffered from the same general conditions, but all were destined to profit from the same forces of recovery. The recent expansion in the world's gold production was reflected in a general rise of prices, beginning about 1895, and at once the rich prairie farms came into their own. Older agricultural regions of the continent could seldom compete with the fertile West in grain and livestock production, and if acres were not abandoned, they were frequently converted into mixed farms and dairy pasture. Freed from competitors, the Middle West had the grain market of the world for its own. Prices demanded for land gradually rose and finally reached a point that put it out of the reach of the "hired man" who had aspirations of ownership and beyond the means of the farmers' sons who were eager to set up farm homes of their own. A new *Aufmarschgebiet* which was merely the historical projection of the old area along the Atlantic had been created, and it was now ready to send out its sons and daughters and its acclimatized and trained immigrants to new conquests wherever opportunities might appear.

There was an immediate "West" for the Middle West, but it was an empire of ranches and mines, scattered upon the semiarid plains and among the mountains. Adventure in plenty was available for all; but it was not adventure and excitement that the young people of the Middle West wanted. A hundred and sixty acres of wheatland which he could cultivate by the methods that he already knew was the physical expression of the young farmer's ambition. There was no prospect of fulfilling this ambition in the old neighborhood; he had to look beyond, and his choice lay between a Southwest and a Northwest. Again the advertisers were in the field; agents swarmed in the rural districts describing the opportunities offered by the lands that they had for sale, and the special rates that every railroad gave to land seekers encouraged a wide response. The Southwest had many attractions in climate, government projects of irrigation, and modified homestead provisions. But it was the Northwest which embodied most of the features that had made the old West a promised land and in that direction the renewed current of migration flowed.

The Northwest was the Canadian West, which now at last came into the full sweep of the onward advance of population expansion.[30] Direct railroad connection with the other provinces in the East had been established and the transcontinental lines on the American side had built branches up to the boundary to tap the great supplies of wheat for which the eastern ports and the European markets still clamored. Foreigners and North Americans alike realized that again, and perhaps for the last time, the possibility of obtaining a farm merely by labor was at hand, and from 1902 to 1913 every spring witnessed a procession of trains crowded with new pioneers and every year recorded vast areas put under the plow. The international boundary meant as little to the American farmers from the Middle West as two decades before it had meant to the Ontario citizens who had moved into the Mississippi Valley. From the Atlantic to the Pacific the conquest of a wilderness of forest and prairie had been their common task. At last the western ocean was reached and the ranks of the army were demobilized and scattered.

Of the four columns that set out to cross the continent, that which followed the northern route retained an identity that is recognizable. The others mingled almost as soon as they had passed the Appalachians, to form the population of the Old Southwest—the states of Kentucky and Tennessee. This region was, in turn, the base of a further advance, sending out caravans of pioneers down to the Gulf coast, across the Mississippi to Texas and over the Ohio into the Old

30. A. S. Morton and C. Martin, *History of Prairie Settlement and "Dominion Lands" Policy* (Toronto, 1938).

Northwest, and finally into the valley of the Missouri. The stream of population which gradually wound its way along the Missouri was the most direct continuation of the pioneer movement over the mountains. However, it again tended to be lost as it spread over the plains, providing first trappers, and then cowboys and ranchmen, who were forced by incoming farmers farther and farther up into the American Northwest until they also were beyond the international line. Here, in Alberta, they enjoyed a brief period of ranching prosperity which at last met an inevitable end when the railroad and the farmer took possession of the prairie provinces.[31]

Ultimately, descendants of the men and women who had moved in every army of North American pioneers reached the British possessions to the north—some as trappers, cattlemen, or farmers in the foothills of the Rockies, others as miners, lumbermen, or fishermen along the shores of the Pacific. Meanwhile, industrialization and urbanization, both closely related to westward expansion and to the increased production which accompanied it, were setting up new currents of North American migration from one end of the continent to the other. Their interdependence, involving as it did both domestic and international migrations, requires detailed examination of causes, extent, and direction. Yet this can be made only after the continental westward movement is understood. There was unity within the westward movement and that unity makes clearer the pattern that lies beneath the confusing wanderings in which the Americans and Canadians were constantly engaged.

31. *Manitoba Free Press* (Winnipeg), Nov. 26, 1906. C. M. MacInnes, *In the Shadow of the Rockies* (London, 1930).

CHAPTER II

THE ESTABLISHMENT OF AN
ATLANTIC BASE
1604–1775

THE westward march of the people of the United States and Canada is such a romantic and colorful epic that it has dominated the discussion of the population history of both nations. But before they could get under way, like any other advancing army, the North Americans needed to create a base, and not until after 1815 had this preliminary work been entirely accomplished. For two centuries after the arrival of the first permanent colonists in Acadia in 1604, Europeans and their American descendants were engaged in occupying the plains and lowlands that sloped back from the Atlantic; at all promising harbors along the coast and at the mouths of rivers they established towns, surrounded them with farms, and began the slow but steady expansion of agricultural communities that gradually merged into one another.

The trend of these movements was inevitably from north to south or from south to north. The Atlantic was the first and for long the most convenient route of communication; the great rivers of English colonial expansion—the Merrimack, Connecticut, Hudson, Delaware, and Susquehanna in the north and the Shenandoah in the south— ran almost parallel to the sea. The confusing details of seventeenth- and eighteenth-century population history reveal the resultant processes in operation: New Englanders settling in every colony to the south, Virginians moving to Maryland, Marylanders crossing over into Pennsylvania, and finally Pennsylvanians, Marylanders, and Virginians moving south into the back regions of the Carolinas. This weaving together of human stuff was not limited to the thirteen continental provinces that became the United States. The West Indies occupied an essential position as a southern approach and center of dispersion; and to the north and east there existed another area which, by its position and the economic pursuits which it fostered, served as a way station on the route between the British Isles and the most populous parts of the colonies in America.

Between the remote outposts of New England (in the seventeenth century no farther from Boston than the mouth of the Merrimack) and the old fishing stations of Newfoundland stretched five hundred miles of coast line on which settlements of only the most precarious and scattered nature existed. Both France and Great Britain claimed the peninsula made up of the present-day Maine and Maritime Provinces that juts out into the Atlantic; and during the seventeenth century Englishmen fought against Frenchmen there, as did even the possessors of concessions which had emanated from the same Crown. The meager exchange of population that took place before 1700 between the two areas was incidental to this uncertainty and these struggles. Expeditions of freebooting New Englanders attempted to establish posts to the northeast of their home territory, and deserting French soldiers and company servants sought refuge in Boston.[1]

Entirely different was the situation with regard to Newfoundland. The fisheries were prosperous and every season hundreds of vessels from Europe visited its shores; contemporaries compared the island to a great ship anchored in the North Atlantic and this island was recognized as one stopping place on the immigrant route to America. For here the trading vessels from New England joined the fishermen from the Old World and, when they returned to Massachusetts and Rhode Island, they brought with them deserters from the British ships and servants who had tired of the dull routine of the fish-drying stations on the bleak Newfoundland coast. This transfer probably began almost as early as North American colonization, and by the closing decade of the seventeenth century had reached such proportions that fishing-company officials were constantly complaining to the colonial authorities of the desertion of skilled hands, and the Admiralty was concerned over the loss of able seamen whose services the navy might need at any time.[2] But the route was never effectively barred; it continued to serve throughout the colonial period, not being superseded until after 1815, when the timber ships

1. The confused history of this period is outlined in J. B. Brebner, *New England's Outpost, Acadia before the Conquest of Canada* (New York, 1927), 15–56, and the history of the region from 1710 to 1760 is taken up in greater detail.

2. Susan M. Kingsbury, *The Records of the Virginia Company of London,*

of New Brunswick, returning to St. John and St. Andrews, provided a more direct connection with ports to the south for immigrants whose ultimate destination was the United States.[3]

The southward drift of this migratory population is an indication of the close connection that the commerce of the English colonies had established with the more northerly and eastern regions of the continent. On land even more than on the sea the outlook was toward the north. This was particularly true in New England and New York. With the exception of a few scattered outposts up the river the seventeenth-century Dutch were clustered about the mouth of the Hudson. The neighboring Puritan pioneers had taken possession of the coast of Long Island Sound, Cape Cod, and the shores of Massachusetts Bay. It was as natural for the young generation of that time to look toward the north as for their successors of a later generation to center their futures in the west. New and fertile lands lay up the valleys of the Connecticut, the Merrimack, and the almost unknown rivers of the District of Maine. Many American colonists, above all those who sailed the sea as well as farmed the land, had already looked upon the shores of Acadia and had marked the wealth of timber and fish which might be exploited there. The star of empire led to the north.

But the path to empire was blocked by rivals and deadly enemies. Every frontier farm beyond Albany was a stockade; every adventurous youth who started a clearing in central New England had to keep on the alert for Indian war parties and French patrols. Cape Cod fishermen who wanted to become farmers and traders on the debatable land beyond the Kennebec were driven off by the French officials at Port Royal.[4] When war between England and France

I (Washington, 1906), 269. *Calendar of State Papers, Colonial Series, America and West Indies, 1669–74* (London, 1889), 257; *1667–80* (1896), 418, 491, 600; *1681–85* (1898), 105, 294, 708; *1697–98* (1905), 554. J.C.T.P., *1704–1708/09*, 103. R. G. Lounsbury, *The British Fishery at Newfoundland* (New Haven, 1934), *passim*.

3. M. L. Hansen, "The Second Colonization of New England," *The New England Quarterly*, II (1929), 539–560.

4. William D. Williamson, *The History of the State of Maine; from Its First Discovery, A.D. 1602, to the Separation, A.D. 1820, Inclusive*, I (Hallowell, 1832), 248, 249, 250.

broke out in 1689, French frontier policy undertook the offensive: now they were no longer content to keep out the advancing English-men; they would drive them back from positions already occupied. On all but one of the sectors their policy was successful. Acadia was too weak in people and resources to undertake any schemes of con-quest; and it was too remote from the seat of the French Empire and too exposed to naval attack to resist any determined onslaught. In 1690 Sir William Phips led a raiding expedition of Massachusetts farmers and fishermen against Port Royal and the Bay of Fundy settlements. The Acadians returned thereafter to their ravaged homes and held off conquest until they were overwhelmed in 1710 by an Anglo-American expedition originally designed to conquer Can-ada. By the Treaty of Utrecht in 1713 Acadia was finally trans-ferred from France to England.

The acquisition was an area rich in resources but poor in people. As in Canada, no active colonization had been carried on during the last quarter of the seventeenth century and in 1713 the Acadians numbered only about two thousand. Most of them were settled at the head of the Bay of Fundy on the rich alluvial lands that had been reclaimed by dikes from Chignecto Bay and the Basin of Minas; the original settlements were clustered about the fort and government buildings at Port Royal; and a few transients were at isolated fish-ing stations along the coast. If it were land that the empire needed, here was enough of it to accommodate tens of thousands of colonists without disturbing any of the already established inhabitants.[5]

Acadia was promptly rechristened Nova Scotia (the name given it in 1621 by James I), but with the new province in its hands the British government seemed to lose all desire to follow a vigorous pro-gram of development. The older British colonies still had a stronger "pull" for intending settlers. The native French were hostile, but time, it was believed, would mollify this feeling and no positive dan-ger was seen in their presence. No official plan of settlement was adopted, although various suggestions were made, among which the proposal that soldiers demobilized after the long era of wars be used

5. The description of Nova Scotia in 1720 by Major Paul Mascarene is printed in T. B. Akins (ed.), *Nova Scotia Archives,* I (Halifax, 1869), 39–49.

as a nucleus for British colonization received the most attention.[6]
Year after year passed and no decision was reached, while at the
capital (now called Annapolis) a royal governor ruled over a handful of merchants, the small garrison, and minor officials. A description of about the year 1748 complained that Nova Scotia "has
continued about 40 years to this time, a nominal British province
without any British settlement, only an insignificant preventative but
precarious fort and garrison."[7] In the meantime, the Acadians prospered and increased in number to about ten thousand without developing either any strong allegiance or antipathy to the British crown;
but the establishment by the French of the greatest fortification in
the world at Louisbourg on the neighboring Cape Breton Island
served notice that they, at least, considered the fate of the peninsula
far from determined.

Toward the close of the decade of the 1740's the British government felt that it could dally no longer with vague projects of colonization in this spot whose strategic position made it so vital to the
empire.[8] New England, which had captured Louisbourg in 1745
only to see it handed back in territorial bargaining at the peace
negotiations of 1748, was clamoring for effective occupation of the
Nova Scotian mainland at least, and past failures to stimulate voluntary settlement in this debatable land made it clear that assisted
colonization would be necessary. London decided to act. The plans
included a fortress to balance the French possession of Louisbourg
and some neighboring agricultural communities that would provide

6. The various projects for the settlement of Nova Scotia can be followed
in the *J.C.T.P.*, *1708/09–1714/15*, 434, 469, 582, 599, 603; *1714/15–1718*,
216, 231, 234, 235, 318, 322, 351; *1722/23–1728*, 90, 91, 99, 114; *1728/29–
1734*, 14, 26, 69, 104; *1741/42–1749*, 71, 165, 390.

7. William Douglass, *A Summary, Historical and Political, of the First
Planting, Progressive Improvements and the Present State of the British
Settlements in North America*, I (London, 1755), 330.

8. Two examples of the pamphlet propaganda of the time are: *The Importance of Cape Breton Considered in a Letter to a Member of Parliament
from an Inhabitant of New England* (London, 1746), and [Otis Little], *The
State of Trade in the Northern Colonies Considered with an Account of Their
Produce, and a Particular Description of Nova Scotia* (London, 1748). Brebner, *op. cit.*, 166–202, contains a detailed, analytical account of the new experiment in Nova Scotia.

grain and cattle for the garrison. To secure the first, the city and defenses at Halifax were constructed; and the second was attempted by offering bounties for agriculture on the rocky shores surrounding the harbor.

The site chosen for Halifax was symbolic of its purpose in the scheme of empire. It faced the open waters of the Atlantic, and in the commodious harbor merchant vessels trading between England and the colonies and fishing craft from New England might find shelter from storms or refuge from an enemy. From the naval base the royal fleet could readily provide protection for English commerce and offer a threat to the French connection with the St. Lawrence.[9] But the surroundings were not encouraging to an intending farmer. The prospects were barren and the soil rocky; by laborious effort these lands might be prepared for cultivation, but that was a task of years and while it was being accomplished only the bounty of the government could maintain the new colonists.

Accordingly, early in 1749 announcement was made in London of the inducements offered to persons who would volunteer to go to Nova Scotia as farmers or artisans: transportation, temporary victualing, and land. Former soldiers were particularly favored.[10] But since it was doubtful whether a sufficient number would come forward in England, agents on the Continent were authorized to publish the terms in Holland and Germany. The response was satisfactory in England and enthusiastic on the Continent. So many Germans and French Swiss indicated a willingness to go and so many of them started out for London at once without waiting for formal registration that the Board of Trade finally directed that further advertising should be suspended.[11]

The first expedition, that of 1749, marked the founding of the settlement, but the influx continued for some years. New England soon reacted to the stimulus that this enterprise gave to business.

9. "Copy of a Letter from One of the Settlers in Nova Scotia, Dated Chebucto Harbor, July 28, 1749," *The Gentleman's Magazine and Historical Chronicle,* XIX (1749), 408–410.

10. This proclamation is reprinted in the *Boston News-Letter,* May 4, 1749.

11. *J.C.T.P., 1741/42–1749,* 390, 391, 393, 411, 423, 472; *1749/50–1753,* 3, 51, 60, 62, 63, 65, 81, 88, 93, 115, 157, 183, 248, 261, 392.

The demand for building materials and supplies produced a lively trade to the north and the call for competent workers assured employment to all who came as passengers. New England soldiers who had served in the recent campaigns were given the same inducements that had been offered in the Old World.[12] During the first year approximately a thousand arrivals from the colonies to the south were noted and an official dispatch referred to them as "the best of settlers."[13]

As many attempts before and since have demonstrated, the European immigrant with no experience in the wilderness made at best an indifferent pioneer. The continental Europeans who were brought to Nova Scotia remained; there was little else they could do. But the detailed and heavily subsidized plans to foster agriculture in the vicinity of Halifax did not materialize in cultivated farms or garden plots. Finally, in 1753, a new township was laid out at a more promising location to the south of the capital. In this township (named Lunenburg) about fifteen hundred Germans and Swiss, transported from Halifax, were planted. But it was a costly venture. For nine years they were supported from the public stores before they could care for themselves; and at the close of that period desertions had appreciably reduced their numbers.[14] Undoubtedly the expense and confusion entailed in that experiment, contrasted with the aptitude of the New Englanders, persuaded the government to invite in more of the latter when next it undertook planned settlement.

The principal obstacle to the settlement of the peninsula was the presence not of Germans but of Frenchmen—the native Acadians who inhabited the most fertile meadows and who resisted by word and deed the entry of any interlopers. Small colonies sent out from the older Acadian settlements had gradually occupied all desirable spots on the Bay of Fundy and continuation of this process would inevitably hinder future British expansion in that direction. Many

12. *The Gentleman's Magazine and Historical Chronicle,* XIX (1749), 571–572. *The London Magazine or Gentlemen's Monthly Intelligencer,* XIX (May, 1750), 196–197. *Boston News-Letter,* June 29, July 6, Aug. 17, 1749.
13. *J.C.T.P., 1749/50–1753,* 4, 116.
14. "Description and State of the New Settlements in Nova Scotia in 1761, by the Chief Surveyor," *P.A.C.R., 1904,* 289–300.

of the foreign settlers who had been brought in and colonized at public expense were deserting to the Acadian villages where they were welcomed so warmly that others were encouraged to follow.[15] Another struggle between the two rival powers was impending. The local authorities believed that the continued presence of the alien group would be fatal when war did break out because it was apparent already that the French of Canada and Cape Breton would make it impossible for them to remain neutral. They listened to the voices of those advisers who said that expulsion was the only remedy: get rid of them all—men, women, and children—and substitute for the traitors a loyal and industrious population who were acquainted with the agriculture of the New World and equipped to subdue the wilderness.[16]

In 1755, alarmed by news of Braddock's crushing defeat in the Ohio country, the governor of Nova Scotia, Charles Lawrence, reached a decision. Several prominent New Englanders to whose counsel he lent his ear urged the most drastic of action and it was to a Massachusetts officer, Colonel John Winslow, that the unpleasant task of removing the Acadians was assigned.[17] September was the month chosen for the deportation. The residents were summoned from the farms and herded together in the village churches; their fate was declared to them and then they were transferred to the waiting ships. Crops that had been harvested were destroyed, the livestock confiscated, and all but a few buildings standing on remote farms were burned. Such was the first step in the most violent popu-

15. *P.A.C.R., 1894,* 87, 194, 196, 197, 199.

16. The advisability of expulsion was discussed as early as 1745. Governor Shirley of Massachusetts favored the removal of only those who were considered obnoxious; Captain Charles Knowles, the governor of Louisbourg, desired complete eradication. Brebner, *op. cit.,* 122–133. Charles H. Lincoln (ed.), *Correspondence of William Shirley,* I (New York, 1912), xxvi, 336, 354, 370, 371.

17. The decision to expel the Acadians was made by Lawrence and five members of his council, three of whom were New Englanders, and all of whom had been actively concerned for ten years in New England's expansive policy. Brebner, *op. cit.,* 203–233. For a contrasted account of this long-disputed matter, see E. Lauvrière, *La Tragédie d'un peuple* (2d ed., 2v., Paris, 1926).

lation revolution in the history of the New World—the uprooting of a well-established people.[18]

Forced though it was, the expulsion was a form of migration. Of the thousands who were expelled from their homes, perhaps two thousand avoided seizure or escaped from the soldiers; the rest, about six thousand, were packed into transports and landed, some in each colony, from Massachusetts to Georgia. Transportation was not enough; the French blood must be diffused. To each colony was assigned a "quota," and in turn some of the colonies apportioned their contingent of "French neutrals" among counties and towns in the hope that in the even spread any perils inherent in their presence might be dissipated.[19] During the next generation the Acadians showed extraordinary determination in retaining their separate identity. After the most varied vicissitudes in North America from St. Pierre and Miquelon to the West Indies during the 'sixties, substantial groups reëstablished themselves in Nova Scotia, Canada, France, and Louisiana. A considerable number, however, could not get away from the colonies to which they had been sent, and were lost in the general population—immigrants whose "Americanization" was as rapid and significant as that of any other alien group.[20]

For three years the lands lay waste; the waters of the Bay broke through the uncared-for dikes and flooded the luxuriant meadows.

18. The journal of Colonel Winslow is printed in the *Collections of the Nova Scotia Historical Society,* III and IV (Halifax, 1883 and 1885).

19. An extensive collection of documents relating to the expulsion and dispersion of the Acadians is printed in Placide Gaudet, "Acadian Genealogy and Notes," *P.A.C.R., 1905,* II, Appendix A: Bibliography, 357–361. See also Ernest Martin, *Les Exilés acadiens en France au XVIIIe siècle et leur établissement en Poitou* and *L'Evangéline de Longfellow et la suite merveilleuse d'un poème* (both Paris, 1936); and S. T. McCloy, "French Charities to the Acadians, 1755–1799," *Louisiana Historical Quarterly,* XXI (July, 1938), 656–668.

20. Some estimate of the French element in the colonial population is made in M. L. Hansen, "The Minor Stocks in the American Population of 1790," *Report of the American Historical Association, 1931,* I, Proceedings (Washington, 1932), 380–390. For the Acadians see 387, 389. See also R. A. Hudnut and Hayes Baker-Crothers, "Acadian Transients in South Carolina," *American Historical Review,* XLIII (April, 1938), 500–513; G. S. Brookes, *Friend Anthony Benezet* (Philadelphia, 1937); and M. B. Hamer, "The Fate of the Exiled Acadians in South Carolina," *Journal of Southern His-*

The general war and the guerrilla raids in Nova Scotia were never absent from the minds of administrators and people, and so long as the French were secure behind the moats of Louisbourg all schemes of occupying the Acadian lands had to be postponed. But in 1758 the French stronghold again fell before the assault of the British Navy and New England militiamen and this time everyone knew that, whatever the outcome of the war, diplomats would not dare to take it out of the hand of the victors. Conditions now seemed favorable for the settlers to come.

Governor Lawrence of Nova Scotia was prepared to act. On October 12, 1758, he issued a proclamation inviting the loyal inhabitants of the neighboring colonies to form associations that would be encouraged with liberal grants of land and assistance during the first trying months of pioneering.[21] To his surprise the response was not great. New Englanders wanted to be assured of something besides land: What would be the nature of the government? Would there be a popular assembly? What assurance would be extended that the local institutions which meant so much to them in church and community life would not be tampered with?

The governor was quick to respond. A second proclamation came from his hand on January 11, 1759. In this document the constitution of Nova Scotia was explained, the franchise qualifications described, and a guarantee of civil and religious liberties was extended.[22] With this clarification the hoped-for interest on the part of residents of the more southern colonies was at once revealed. But active response was slow. War was still in progress; facilities for a mass movement by individuals were lacking, and the colonizing asso-

tory, IV (May, 1938), 199–208. For the reëstablishment of some Acadians in Nova Scotia and the emigration of others, see J. B. Brebner, *The Neutral Yankees of Nova Scotia* (New York, 1937), 44–49, 102–109. For their settlement in Louisiana see E. Martin's volumes cited above.

21. *Boston News-Letter*, Nov. 2, 1758. The migration from New England and the life of the province to the end of the American Revolution are discussed in detail in Brebner, *Neutral Yankees,* cited.

22. The second proclamation, which answers some of the questions that had arisen concerning Nova Scotia, appears in the *Boston News-Letter,* Feb. 15, 1759, and is also printed in W. O. Raymond, "Col. Alexander McNutt and the Pre-Loyalist Settlements of Nova Scotia," *R.S.C., 1911* (Ottawa), Sec. ii, 23–115, Appendixes.

ciations which the governor hoped would overcome this handicap took time to organize, and even then lacked the capital and equipment with which they might swiftly have accomplished their purposes.

Judged by the standards of the time, the movement that followed was a migration of unusual proportions. The field of settlement was widened beyond the rather restricted limits of the deserted Acadian acres. Every land association that was formed was invited to send a committee to Halifax where they would be provided with guides to conduct them on exploring expeditions to whatever part of the province they desired to view, and during 1759 and 1760 several such delegations were engaged in spying out the land, keeping in mind the future possibilities of any particular location as well as its present advantages.[23] In general, the relatively barren southern shore of the peninsula, facing the gales of the Atlantic, was neglected, preference being given to the more sheltered coast line, well studded with harbors, and the sunny, fertile farm lands that bordered on the Bay of Fundy. Only the groups that had fishing and lumbering opportunities in mind planted themselves beside the open Atlantic at convenient harbors along the South and Cape Sable shores.

The lure of highly advertised lands was not the only factor that set the northbound trek in motion. Certain areas in the older provinces were like crowded beehives with occupants ready to swarm, and the announcement of the new opportunities coincided with an economic pressure that fell heavily upon the inhabitants of those places. Emigrants set out from all the colonies north of Maryland, but the overwhelming majority came from all parts of New England, notably from eastern Massachusetts, eastern Connecticut, Rhode Island, and the islands off the coast. The townships of this long-settled and closely held area were congested with people, men with young families who for years had been eager to strike out into the wilderness, but who had been deterred by the unsettled status of a

23. The journal of Henry Evans, a land explorer for a Massachusetts association, is printed in W. A. Calnek, *History of the County of Annapolis Including Old Port Royal and Acadia* (Toronto, 1897), 148–151. See also *The New London Summary*, Feb. 16, 1759; Oct. 24, Nov. 28, 1760; Feb. 20, March 20, 1761.

frontier where pioneers were too often the victims in the bitter contest between France and Great Britain and between their colonies.[24]

Although this crowded area was part of three distinct colonial jurisdictions, the sea gave it a unity otherwise lacking. The Atlantic was a great highway and enterprising men sailed its waters in trading from place to place along the coast and in the more extensive journeys with flour and fish to the West Indies and the shores of Europe and Africa. But war interrupted the trade and French privateers seized the vessels that ventured beyond the protection of the British Navy. It was dangerous for the fishermen of Cape Cod to sail for the more distant banks; Nantucket whalers did not dare start on long expeditions; and legal exports to the West Indies practically came to an end.[25] The farmers who depended upon the market that fishermen and traders provided suffered financial reverses as acute as those that depressed the towns. The newspapers of 1757 and 1758 bear evidence of the wartime depression in the columns of advertising of bankruptcy proceedings;[26] and contemporary observers comment on the decaying state of trade, the oppressive burden of taxes incurred by the expense of keeping thousands of men under arms, and the great deflation in the value of lands. War brought its usual heritage of debts, of farms and shops lost by mortgage, and of men discouraged by the experiences through which they were passing.[27]

24. The importance of the problems concerning population and settlement in the colonies is indicated by a report made by the Lords of Trade, June 8, 1763, which is printed in Adam Shortt and Arthur G. Doughty (eds.), *Documents Relating to the Constitutional History of Canada, 1759–1791* (new and revised ed., 2v., Ottawa, 1918), I, 132–147. See also Ian F. MacKinnon, *Settlements and Churches in Nova Scotia 1749–1776* (Montreal, 1930), 39, 42. For the effects of land monopoly in the older colonies see R. H. Akagi, *The Town Proprietors of the New England Colonies* (Philadelphia, 1924).

25. The difficulties under which the Quaker fishermen of Nantucket attempted to carry on their trade and which led to their emigration to Nova Scotia are described in Arthur G. Dorland, *A History of the Society of Friends (Quakers) in Canada* (Toronto, 1927), 30, 31.

26. See, for example, the issues of the *Boston News-Letter,* Dec., 1757, to April, 1758.

27. Andrew Burnaby, *Travels through the Middle Settlements in North America in the Years 1759 and 1760* (3d ed., London, 1798), 99, 111, 112. Franklin B. Dexter (ed.), *Extracts from the Itineraries and Other Miscellanies of Ezra Stiles* (New Haven, 1916), 50, 81.

The empty French farmsteads about the Basin of Minas naturally attracted the first venturers to Nova Scotia. Perhaps the reports of the New England militiamen who had herded out the unfortunate Acadians had circulated among the would-be emigrants. In any case, companies of settlers were readily formed in Rhode Island and eastern Connecticut and plans for moving in the fall of 1759 were drawn up. But a threatened Indian war, in which the Frenchmen skulking about on the isthmus between the Bay of Fundy and the Gulf of St. Lawrence were suspected of having a part, postponed all activity until after the fall of Quebec in September. This victory, together with the surrender of the scattered Acadians who came into the military forts and gave themselves up as prisoners of war, promised a reasonable assurance of peace. But it was then too late in the season to undertake any ventures.[28]

In the spring of 1760 the northward movement got under way. From Salem, Boston, Plymouth, Providence, and New London ships sailed for the new lands carrying the organized bands. In some cases passengers were so numerous that a fleet of vessels was necessary. The most famous of all was that made up of six transports which departed from New London in June bound for the settlement at Horton.[29] With the professional aid of the captive Acadians the dikes were repaired and the fields reclaimed for cultivation. The townships of Cornwallis, Horton, and Falmouth were begun, new settlers came to Annapolis and Granville, Liverpool was founded, other sites were investigated on the South and Cape Sable shores, and all was ready for an acceleration of the movement in the following spring.[30]

During 1761 four new Minas townships began: the Rhode Islanders at Newport, and the Ulstermen, drawn partly from Massachu-

28. *P.A.C.R., 1894,* 217. Ray G. Huling, "The Rhode Island Emigration to Nova Scotia," *The Narragansett Historical Register,* VII (Providence, 1889), 89–135.

29. W. A. Calnek, *op. cit.,* 150. Arthur W. H. Eaton, *The History of Kings County, Nova Scotia* (Salem, Mass., 1910), 67. *The New York Mercury,* June 2, 30, Nov. 10, 1760.

30. *Boston News-Letter,* June 26, 1760. Arthur W. H. Eaton, *op. cit.,* 67. Benjamin Rand, "Glimpses of the Past: The New England Emigration," *The Saint Croix Courier,* Sept. 15, 22, 1892.

setts and New Hampshire and partly from Ireland, who opened up Truro, Onslow, and Londonderry at the eastern end of the basin.[31] These families and their predecessors of the previous year received assistance in varying degree, an expense of which the Board of Trade in London did not approve. But their prohibition did not arrive early enough to influence provincial policy in the year 1761 and not until 1762 did it go even partially into effect.[32] Meanwhile, individuals and families continued to join relatives and friends who had preceded them.[33] With the establishment of these townships, the main outlines of the settlement about the Minas Basin were drawn. To the northwest at the head of the Bay there were three embryonic townships, but much of the land in that region was reserved for other projects—an organized emigration from Ireland and a proposed colony to be made up of the soldiers who would be disbanded when the war was over.[34]

An attempt was made to develop the vicinity of the old provincial capital and two townships, Annapolis and Granville, were founded. But the area did not stand in high favor with the prospectors for new lands, and the presence of government reserves raised questions as to the possibility of expansion.[35] Higher hopes were attached to the series of townships projected at harbors of the Cape Sable and South shores whose combination of river meadows, thick forest, and proximity to the fisheries might ultimately, it was believed, supplant Cape Cod and Nantucket in the affections of emigrants from those places, many of whom came with families and equipment in their own ships. These newcomers planned to engage in farming and lumbering as well as fishing, in order to be less dependent upon the uncertain fortunes of the sea.[36]

31. Edward L. Parker, *The History of Londonderry, Comprising the Towns of Derry and Londonderry, N.H.* (Boston, 1851), 98, 200, 201. Benjamin Rand, "New England Settlements in Acadia," *Annual Report of the American Historical Association for the Year 1890*, 42.

32. *P.A.C.R., 1894*, 228.

33. *Boston News-Letter*, Jan. 8, 15, March 19, May 7, 21, 1761; March 25, 1762.

34. *P.A.C.R., 1904*, 296, 297.

35. Thomas C. Haliburton, *An Historical and Statistical Account of Nova Scotia*, II (Halifax, 1829), 154.

36. Edwin Crowell, *A History of Barrington Township and Vicinity,*

Although the majority of the emigrants settled in the present-day Nova Scotia, the foundation of the future province of New Brunswick was also laid. The wilderness north of the Bay of Fundy was in 1760 governed from Halifax and the officials were therefore authorized to include parts of this territory in their grants. But at first the region had a manifest disadvantage. Any settlement located on the coast would back directly up against the primeval forest peopled by Indians who would not for some time realize that they were now dependent on the English and must abandon their hostile attitude. For traders and trappers the region had a powerful appeal, and the first place that was occupied (Portland Point at the mouth of the St. John River) was largely a post for the Indian trade. But the hinterland that opened up along the valley of the river was possessed of so many advantages in timber and soil that the traders were soon followed by farmers, and in the years that followed 1760 there was a substantial infiltration of settlers from the lower colonies who located on the banks of the St. John and in the valley of the neighboring St. Croix.[37]

The obvious advantages to be gained from colonizing the Acadian farm lands in Nova Scotia naturally attracted a cluster of official and private speculators who gathered round the dispensers of land in London and Halifax to snatch what profits they could. The earliest and most flamboyant of them was Colonel Alexander McNutt, a Virginian gentleman of Ulster descent, who from 1760 to 1765 bewildered most onlookers by the contrast between the grandiose designs he sketched and the meager results he attained.[38] In 1765 he escorted to Nova Scotia a group of promoters from the Middle Colonies who applied for some 8,000,000 acres and secured about

Shelburne County, Nova Scotia, 1604–1870 (Yarmouth, N.S., n.d.), 85, 86, 104, 106, 109, 110, 115. George S. Brown, *Yarmouth, Nova Scotia. A Sequel to Campbell's History* (Boston, 1888), 127. On pages 159–161 is a list of settlers giving the year of arrival and place from which they came. For the other coastal townships, see Brebner, *Neutral Yankees,* 52–56, 112–113.

37. William F. Ganong, "A Monograph on the Origins of Settlements in the Province of New Brunswick," *R.S.C., 1905,* Sec. ii, 3–185, especially 42–52: "The English Period (1760–1783)." *The New London Summary,* Sept. 26, 1760.

38. W. O. Raymond, *op. cit.* Brebner, *Neutral Yankees,* 37–41, 96–100. *The New York Mercury,* Nov. 2, 1761.

2,500,000 acres, including a township at Pictou in which Benjamin Franklin had an interest and which was known for some years as the Philadelphia Plantation.[39] McNutt had hoped to organize a great migration from the north of Ireland, but had been checked when the Privy Council forbade such a movement for fear of depopulation.[40] Now he and his associates planned to divert northeastward the men and women of the Middle Colonies who were on the move in search of cheap lands. These projects failed, partly for reasons of cost, but largely because these restless people had their eyes fixed upon the trans-Appalachian regions which they hoped to enter in spite of London's prohibition and in spite of the remarkable Indian resistance which Pontiac had organized all along the frontiers. Most of the millions of Nova Scotian acres granted away in the land boom of 1765 reverted to the Crown for nonfulfillment of settlement conditions.

Yet in spite of the speculators a great outward movement from New England was occupying Nova Scotia more thoroughly than the Acadians had done. Every family narrative and every description of institutional development—churches and schools—indicates how completely the new Nova Scotia was the child of New England. Ministers and schoolmasters came along with the farmers and their imprint upon the impressionable society was so deep that the even larger inflow of bitter and determined Loyalists two decades later could not efface it. To many Nova Scotians for several decades New England was considered "home."[41]

The inrush of settlers had slowed down temporarily in 1763. Governor Lawrence had died in 1760 and there were many questions asked regarding the land transactions in which he had been involved which led to a reluctance in granting more townships.[42] Although Lieutenant-Governor Jonathan Belcher issued a proclamation that

39. William O. Sawtelle, "Acadia: The Pre-Loyalist Migration and the Philadelphia Plantation," *The Pennsylvania Magazine of History and Biography,* LI (1927), 244–285.

40. *P.A.C.R., 1894,* 232.

41. Brebner, *Neutral Yankees,* chapter vii, "A New New England."

42. *P.A.C.R., 1894,* 222, 225. Ian F. MacKinnon, *op. cit.,* 26, 34, 35, 46. Margaret Ells, "Clearing the Decks for the Loyalists," *Annual Report of the Canadian Historical Association,* 1933 (Ottawa, 1933), 45.

winter making valid the land titles granted by Lawrence and inviting more settlers,[43] an influential factor in bringing about the decline
was the actual state of the settlements. They had suffered hardships
even more severe than those that were usually the lot of pioneers.
Late planting, summer droughts, and early frosts ruined the crops
of grain in the fall of 1761 and some communities were forced to call
upon the government for supplies in order to survive the winter.
The following season witnessed little improvement. Again drought
and vermin prevented the expected harvest and brought about a
second winter of suffering. The towns in which fishing was the principal activity were also forced down to the poverty level because
their vessels were few and equipment meager.[44]

Improved harvests and increasing mastery of the ways of living
which Nova Scotia demanded revived migration after 1763 and provided the setting for the land boom of 1765.[45] Indeed, a remon-
strance from the inhabitants of Halifax to the Board of Trade complained that there was being unloaded upon them "all the scum of
the colonies," useless and burdensome persons who were taken from
jails, workhouses, and hospitals and given free passage from the
older colonies who wanted to be relieved of them.[46] Yet the new influx
was short-lived, for in 1768 the Treaty of Fort Stanwix, concluded
with the Indians, opened up a part of the fabulous Ohio country to
settlement and a long-dammed-up flood of land seekers burst through
the mountains. Nova Scotia at once felt the effects, for there began
the secondary migration that always passes on from any area congested by the presence of prospective settlers who cannot decide
where to settle and the crowds of adventurers who have been drawn
along in the wake of the pioneers. To them only one course was available. They could not move on, so they moved back, and they set in
motion a reverse current that gained force when in the same year a
large part of the military garrison was transferred from Halifax to
overawe the riotous population of Boston. Merchants, laborers, and

43. *The New London Summary,* Dec. 26, 1760.
44. "State and Condition of the Province of Nova Scotia together with
Some Observations etc. 29th October 1763," *Report of Board of Trustees of
the Public Archives of Nova Scotia, 1933* (Halifax, 1934), 21–26.
45. Margaret Ells, *op. cit.,* 51.
46. *P.A.C.R., 1894,* 270.

military hangers-on also departed for southern ports when the troops had gone; and the speculation in western lands that had gripped Philadelphia and New York spread the repute of the "Ohio country" so widely that even from Nova Scotia a few restless spirits set out for the distant Eldorado.[47]

The extent of the New England colonization of Nova Scotia cannot be exactly determined, partly because of the presence of Acadians, Germans, Swiss, and groups of migrants from the British Isles, and partly because the many returns of population after 1759 are both incomplete and contradictory. The figures for 1775, when critically examined, probably convey the best idea, for the natural increase since 1760 and the emigration after 1768 would somewhat offset each other. These figures suggest a total population (excluding Indians) of about eighteen thousand, of whom at least two-thirds and possibly three-quarters were New Englanders.[48] There were in addition a few hundred Acadian, New England, and Middle Colonies inhabitants of the Island of St. John (now Prince Edward Island) and other non-Nova Scotian islands in the Gulf of St. Lawrence, whose presence reflected both land hunger and certain special kinds of exploitative and commercial activities in those regions.[49]

The population history of Nova Scotia during the two decades preceding the American Revolution is incomplete without some consideration of the wanderings of the Acadians. For the majority the expulsion of 1755 marked merely the beginning of travels. Within a few months some were straggling back and during the succeeding years others followed until in 1762 they were so numerous that when the sudden attack of the French fleet upon Newfoundland aroused the fear that Halifax would be the next objective, their presence

47. A list of arrivals at the port of Boston from 1763 to 1769 is to be found in *Boston: Record Commissioner's Report*, XXIX (Boston, 1900), 245–318; for the emigration from Nova Scotia see J. Robinson and Thomas Rispin, *A Journey through Nova Scotia Containing a Particular Account of the Country and Its Inhabitants* (York, 1774), 14; Brebner, *Neutral Yankees*, 94, 118, 164–166; Ian F. MacKinnon, *op. cit.*, 56, 72.

48. For a collection and criticism of the available population returns, see Brebner, *Neutral Yankees*, 95n; also chapters iii and v, *passim*.

49. "Report of the Present State and Condition of His Majesty's Province of Nova Scotia, 1773," *Report of Board of Trustees of the Public Archives of Nova Scotia*, 1933, 28–34.

caused such a panic among the officials that a second expulsion was determined on.[50] In August, 1762, three transports bearing approximately a thousand of these "prisoners" sailed for Boston. But Massachusetts had not forgotten the inconvenience and expense that the first exiles had caused. The General Court directed the governor to prohibit the landing of this second contingent, and within a month they were back in Halifax where the fear of a French invasion had subsided and with it some of the anti-Acadian sentiment.[51]

Yet the problem of the Acadians was by no means solved. Not until the autumn of 1764 were instructions received from London which allowed them to remain in Nova Scotia as settlers, and then only upon taking the oath of allegiance which they had stubbornly resisted for over fifty years. Their own lands were lost to them and now they were not to be allowed to establish compact settlements. In these circumstances, substantial groups of them in Nova Scotia and the older colonies emigrated to French territory in the West Indies and St. Pierre and Miquelon, or made their way to join the French-speaking subjects of Spain in Louisiana or of Great Britain in Canada. One large group in France itself, after discovering that as North American pioneers they had developed traits which made them intractable material for European landlords and even for a well-meant physiocratic experiment in Poitou, finally secured permission to join their predecessors in Louisiana. For a number of these sorely tried people, however, Nova Scotia was a homeland which they could not bear to abandon. These gradually learned that the King of France had admitted that the King of Great Britain had a right to dispose of them. In 1767 the news spread that the French government had forcibly reduced the population of St. Pierre and Miquelon to forty families and that two hundred Acadians there had decided to become Nova Scotians. In 1768 a special township was set up for solid Acadian settlement on not very desirable lands around St. Mary's Bay at the southwestern corner of the Nova Scotian peninsula. The tide had at last turned for the Nova Scotian Acadians and now the land began to draw some of

50. *P.A.C.R., 1894*, 213, 229, 234, 236, 251.

51. J. S. Martell, "The Second Expulsion of the Acadians," *The Dalhousie Review*, XIII (Halifax, 1933), 359–371.

them home from their refuges in North America and in France. The Nova Scotian authorities could secure very little exact information as to their numbers, particularly in the Cape Breton and Gulf of St. Lawrence fisheries and along the forest fringes north of the Bay of Fundy, but they probably amounted to about fifteen hundred persons in 1775.[52]

But these restless travels, however picturesque they were, could not compare in importance with the influx of the New Englanders who came to occupy the lands from which the Acadians had been expelled. The full significance of this first important emigration from the territory now the United States to the territory now Canada can be appreciated only in realization of the fact that it was the easternmost flank of a general colonial advance to the northward. The decision of a family to settle in Nova Scotia was not based upon the absence of any other choice. The same military events that had removed the danger of the French from Nova Scotia had also brought security to the frontiers of Maine; and many of the emigrants to the shores of the Bay of Fundy left their homes on Cape Cod or in Rhode Island just when their neighbors set sail for the broad estuaries that mark the mouths of the Kennebec, Androscoggin, and other rivers in Maine.[53] In fact, the real agricultural colonization of that part of Maine which lies north and east of Portland began during the early 1760's; and at the same time the young men of central Connecticut and Massachusetts swarmed up the valley of the Connecticut River into the area claimed by both New Hampshire and New York, later to be known as Vermont.[54]

Still farther to the west, beside the great north-and-south high-

52. Brebner, *Neutral Yankees*, 102–109. Martin, *Les Exilés acadiens*, cited. *P.A.C.R., 1894*, 253, 254, 256, 259, 260, 262, 278, 281, 282, 283, 286. *London Chronicle*, Dec. 2–4, 1762, 536; May 21–24, 1763, 494; Feb. 28—March 2, 1765, 214; March 30—April 2, 1765, 318; Feb. 11–13, 1766, 150; May 17–20, 1766, 478.

53. William D. Williamson, *op. cit.*, II, 346. The geographical origin of the population is discussed by B. Lake Noyes in *Sprague's Journal of Maine History*, VI (1918), 28, 29.

54. Samuel Williams, *The Natural and Civil History of Vermont*, II (2d ed., Burlington, Vt., 1809), 14. Zadoch Thompson, *History of Vermont* (Burlington, Vt., 1853), Part II, 13, 16, 62, 85, 87, 88, 110, 129, 135, 144, 172.

way that nature had provided in Lake Champlain, the fall of Montreal in 1760 also opened for settlement lands that many wilderness scouts had looked upon with favor. Here the northward expansion of the English had met the southward expansion of the French. The Canadian habitants hesitated to leave the banks of a river and the process of settlement that had peopled both sides of the St. Lawrence from Quebec to Montreal had started to move up the Richelieu toward Lake Champlain. The authorities at Quebec had disregarded the undetermined status of the lands bordering the lake and had granted seigniories to successful colonizers who awaited only the coming of peace to bring in scores of eager settlers. Meanwhile the New Yorkers in the Hudson and Mohawk valleys, blocked in any movement toward the western and central regions of their province by the presence of the Iroquois confederation and the conciliatory attitude that the imperial officers adopted toward them, were being forced into the same debatable ground.

The conquest and cession of Canada decided the fate of this desirable area. As soon as the capitulation of Montreal on September 8, 1760, was known, the New Yorkers took possession of all vantage grounds and began a steady march on a wide front that was ultimately to bring the point of a wedge of American settlement almost to the St. Lawrence. This prompt squatter action discouraged any compromise which the British government might have made with the claimants to the French grants;[55] and it gave a new direction to the course of French expansion, shunting it eastward from Quebec on the south bank of the river and up the tributaries that pointed toward Maine.

The transfer of jurisdiction over Canada had little immediate effect upon its population. The habitant accepted the change with little concern, being satisfied with the guarantees regarding language and religion that the new regime offered. The officials of the defeated empire went back to France and several hundred merchants and professional men from the towns joined them.[56] Many problems faced the new government in Canada and in most of them population

55. Ruth L. Higgins, *Expansion in New York with Especial Reference to the Eighteenth Century*, 87, 88.

56. Emile Salone, *La Colonisation de la Nouvelle-France* (3d ed., Paris, n.d.), 443. *London Chronicle*, Jan. 31—Feb. 2, 1765, 120.

was involved. A rebellious spirit among the Indians in the West could be appeased only by checking the inrush of colonial settlers that now threatened; and the fear that the French Canadians, although now quiet, would plot to overthrow the alien rule could be allayed only by introducing so many subjects of whose loyalty there would be no question that the French would become a minority. The desire to achieve these two ends brought forth the historic Proclamation of 1763 prohibiting settlement west of a line following the crest of the Alleghenies.[57]

It was hoped that those who were denied opportunity in the West might be induced by substantial rewards to go to the Floridas and to other newly acquired regions. Colonization in Canada was encouraged by the proclamation's offer of liberal grants of land to soldiers and militiamen who were being demobilized from the armies; and the instructions that were issued to Governor Murray on December 7, 1763, authorized him to grant lands to civilians "in proportion to their ability to cultivate."[58] It was not until the spring of 1765, however, that Governor Murray himself issued a proclamation calling attention to the lands available for civilians and, in order to reach the Americans who, it was hoped, would respond, provision was made for its publication in the newspapers of New York, Philadelphia, Boston, and New London.[59]

Yet actually the time had not come for a migration of this nature. Not lack of encouragement but the absence of necessity stood in the way. There was no need to cross the two hundred miles of wilderness that intervened between the frontier of the older colonial settlements and the new Canadian townships to find lands on which to establish a home. The wilderness would be peopled first, and then, in due course, the tide of pioneers would reach the valley of the St. Lawrence. Only a few Americans, and these chiefly merchants and fur traders, moved to Canada. The increase in the number of non-French was slow. In 1766 they amounted to only six hundred and in

57. Shortt and Doughty, *op. cit.*, I, 163–168.

58. *Ibid.*, 181–205.

59. Alfred L. Burt, *The Old Province of Quebec* (Minneapolis, 1933), 93. This proclamation, which in rather unofficial language sought to dispel the idea that Canada was a barren land of perpetual snows, may be found in *The New York Mercury*, April 29, 1765.

1774 they were estimated at "about two or three thousand," and it is impossible to distinguish between those who were natives of Great Britain and those who came from the older colonies. The majority were undoubtedly merchants, traders, and innkeepers. The agricultural invasion had not yet commenced.[60]

The decade from 1763 to 1773 was a very active period in the thirteen English colonies. Dissension over stamp taxes and tea bore testimony to increasing economic tension in the mercantilistic empire, but the fluctuations born from tension and agitation in the colonies gave a false impression of weakness. A large immigration of propertied English farmers helped to fill in the remaining unoccupied areas near the coast, and, when they brought means sufficient to pay for improved farms, the American colonials whom they displaced struck out for the frontier lands. Many Irish and German redemptioners also arrived, young men who, when they had served their time, would also begin wilderness pioneering. By 1774 the Atlantic population base was almost established and settlement was proceeding from the older area toward the future Canada following four lines: along the coast of Maine to the forests beyond the St. Croix; up the valley of the Connecticut to the remote parts of the Province of Quebec; along Lake Champlain, directed toward the St. Lawrence Valley and the avenue it provided to Lake Ontario; and westward into the country of the Iroquois and the peninsula beyond the Niagara River. The events of the Revolutionary years did not deliver a final check to these movements, but they did give them a new and unexpected twist in character which for the next half century profoundly affected the population relations between the new republic and the provinces that remained faithful to the British crown.

60. Shortt and Doughty, *op. cit.*, I, 257, 457. For the difficulties attending agricultural settlement at this time see Ivanhoe Caron, *La Colonisation de la Province de Québec* (Quebec, 1923), 143–150.

CHAPTER III

THE MIGRATION OF THE LOYALISTS
1775–1790

THE war of the Revolution did not interrupt for long the rovings of the restless American population. During the first three years of the struggle while most of the battles occurred on northern soil, there was a steady migration from the southern and central colonies over the mountains to Kentucky;[1] but after 1778 when the seat of the war was transferred to the South, many of the northern regiments were demobilized and the young men returned to their homes to face the question of the future.

The northward and eastward migrations were resumed, but the outlook had materially changed. The majority of the Nova Scotian settlers, who were friendly to the revolutionary cause, after discovering that their remoteness and Congress' naval weakness prevented their incorporation in it, had followed the example set a generation earlier by the Acadians whom they had supplanted and had asked to be regarded as neutrals. The most ardent revolutionaries among them and others who were in bad odor with the loyal administration at Halifax departed for New England, where a more congenial atmosphere could be found. There were also less rabid partisans of the cause who felt so strongly the family and social ties that bound them to their old homes and neighbors that they, perhaps regretfully, traveled back to the land of their birth. Thereafter, for a time, Nova Scotia and New England became enemy countries almost as remote from each other as they had been in the days of the French regime.[2]

In northern New England, however, land-seeking youth could dis-

1. R. G. Thwaites and L. P. Kellogg, *The Revolution on the Upper Ohio, 1775–1777* (Madison, Wis., 1908), 2, 3, 10, 16.

2. J. B. Brebner, *Neutral Yankees,* 291–353, and references cited therein. J. Hannay, "The Maugerville Settlement, 1763–1824," *N.B.H.S.* (St. John), I, 63–88, especially 76, 77. W. O. Raymond, *History of the River St. John* (St. John, 1905), 426–504. E. M. Saunders, *History of the Baptists of the Maritime Provinces* (Halifax, 1902), 103.

cover many opportunities. Except for the region from the Penobscot to the St. John which the British conquered and held, here war had come early and disappeared soon. Here men had been stirred by one of the most spectacular exploits of the contest. Benedict Arnold's campaign of 1775–1776 up the Kennebec River in Maine and across the wilderness to Quebec had failed to conquer that stronghold or to cause a rising among the French, but it had been a revelation of power that impressed the Indian tribes almost all along the border and mollified the hostility which they had hitherto exhibited to intruding settlers.[3] The Battle of Saratoga, in which the militiamen from the Green Mountains had joined with Continental Army troops to check Burgoyne and his German mercenaries and Indian allies, had a similar pacifying effect throughout the entire upper Connecticut River Valley. From 1779 to 1783 tier upon tier of townships was erected there and settlements multiplied rapidly.[4] Every year brought the fringe of the pioneer's frontier closer to the international frontier that the peace negotiations at Paris had delineated. Within a decade the two were destined to meet.

Changes even more profound in their nature transformed another area which pointed directly toward the fertile lands north of Lake Erie. When the Iroquois confederacy decided to assist the British by harassing the scattered colonial communities along the Pennsylvania frontier, they sealed their own doom and opened an avenue that was to become the greatest of all routes of continental migration. In 1779 most of the military interests of the revolutionary movement centered in the expedition of General Sullivan, which moved northward from Pennsylvania bent not merely on the defeat but on the destruction of the enemy warriors. The results satisfied even the most vindictive among the invaders. Burned villages, ruined fields, and Indian women and children scattered throughout the woods marked the course; and when the destruction was complete, the enterprise turned into an expedition of land seekers who noted fertility and resources and vowed to return when the exigencies of

3. William D. Williamson, *The History of the State of Maine; from Its First Discovery, A.D. 1602, to the Separation, A.D. 1820, Inclusive*, II, 450, 506.

4. Zadoch Thompson, *History of Vermont*, Part II, 5, 27, 54, 70, 75, 123, 180.

the war had passed.[5] Many of them did, and during the twenty years after 1783 the lake region of New York and the valleys of the Mohawk and Genesee filled up rapidly with energetic pioneers, who formed a vigorous and prolific base for a later advance to the west and north.[6]

But it was not in these developments that the repercussions of the Revolution upon North American population were immediately felt. The breakdown of imperial administration turned many officeholders out of stations high and low; the interruption of trade ruined the business and prospects of many importers and exporters who were agents of English firms. The response of these individuals to the prevailing disorders was naturally one of opposition to the Revolution and, since many of them were English by birth, a return "home" was the logical course for a goodly number to follow. In London they were joined by later comers who not only sought safety far from their persecutors but also hoped to find a practical sympathy extended by the government.[7] A few of the more fortunate among them received pensions or positions, but for the majority the war period was a weary and tiresome wait that brought little financial recompense and many expenses. One of the best known among them warned a friend that those who came without any means of support would "find to their cost the hand of charity very cold."[8] A letter written at the close of the war declared that London swarmed "with Americans grumbling and discontented."[9] For many of them the

5. Alexander C. Flick, "New Sources on the Sullivan-Clinton Campaign in 1779," *Quarterly Journal of the New York State Historical Association,* X (Albany, 1929), 185–224, 265–317.

6. O. Turner, *History of the Pioneer Settlement of Phelps and Gorham's Purchase, and Morris' Reserve* (Rochester, 1851), 130, 134.

7. W. H. Siebert, *The Flight of American Loyalists to the British Isles* (Columbus, 1911). W. H. Siebert, "The Colony of Massachusetts Loyalists at Bristol, England," *Proceedings of the Massachusetts Historical Society,* LXV (Boston, 1912), 409–414.

8. Samuel Curwen, *Journal and Letters, 1775–1784* (New York, 1842), 59. References regarding assistance given by the British government may be found on pages 103, 280, 357, 364, 367, 368, 378, 411.

9. Colonel J. H. Cruger to Edward Winslow, London, March 13, 1784; W. O. Raymond (ed.), *Winslow Papers A.D. 1776–1826* (St. John, N.B., 1901), 174.

truth of the matter revealed itself to be that they had become far too truly Americans to find life in England congenial or even tolerable.[10]

Other men who chose to remain faithful to the royal cause followed a more active course and one that promised an adequate reward when the rebellion should be crushed. No provision existed by which American Loyalists could enlist in the British Army, but one after another several regiments made up of volunteers and officered by their own leaders were organized and mustered into the military forces. The services of these soldiers who were acquainted with the country and its resources were particularly effective in spying expeditions and foraging raids; but in conducting such enterprises they became the especial object of patriot bitterness, and when the war was over the majority understood that a return to their former homes would mean a tar-and-feathering or imprisonment.[11] Some hoped to continue in the military profession, but in 1783 the demobilization of the British armies was proceeding rapidly and there was already a larger number of officers commissioned than the peacetime plans called for.[12] Emigration and a new start elsewhere were the inevitable fate of these fighting Loyalists.

A third class of Loyalists was made up of the large group that had no military talents nor taste for a life in camp or on the march. They, and usually their families, sought the protection of the royal army. During the first year Boston was the city of refuge and when in March, 1776, General Howe decided upon evacuation, the civilian adherents sailed away with him to Halifax.[13] But Halifax was too small a place to accommodate many, and some enrolled in a regiment that was recruited and sent to the scene of conflict; a very few others scattered among the Nova Scotia settlements and, for a time, received a grant of provisions from government stores. The eastern province seemed the natural rendezvous for exiles from New England, but there was little prospect for their support there and the scheme of erecting a Loyalist colony on the north bank of the Penob-

10. Chipman to Winslow, London, June, 1784; Marston to Winslow, London, March 17, 1790; *ibid.*, 209, 377.

11. W. O. Raymond, "Loyalists in Arms," *N.B.H.S.*, V, 189–223.

12. Colonel Benjamin Thompson to Edward Winslow, London, July 8, 1783; W. O. Raymond (ed.), *Winslow Papers A.D. 1776–1826*, 104.

13. *P.A.C.R., 1894*, 349.

scot (which some geographers claimed was the eastern boundary of Maine) brought many to the vicinity in 1779, where they remained as long as the British maintained a fort for their protection.[14]

The British campaign of 1776 was directed against New York, and the occupation of the city by the army of General Gage in September provided a new gathering place for the refugees. Not until November, 1783, did the troops, in accordance with the treaty of peace, sail away, and until that time New York gradually drew within its lines Loyalist exiles from all the colonies. No charity was necessary. The city was filled with soldiers and the navy was stationed in the harbor; government money circulated freely and business was lively. Gentlemen and their ladies may have found living somewhat difficult, but artisans and laborers (and there were many such among the refugees) enjoyed steady employment and good wages.[15] When the success of the revolutionary movement became assured in 1782, the number of temporary residents increased and real refugee camps were established on Long Island, Staten Island, and the adjacent shores of New Jersey.[16]

The close of the war revealed one other group of Loyalists for whom provision would have to be made. Many of the conservative Dutch, Scots, and Germans of the valleys of the upper Hudson and the Mohawk had refused to join in the revolt; and when General Burgoyne in 1777 started south from Canada with the army which was expected to put an end to the uprising, they flocked to his standard and contributed supplies and information.[17] The disastrous failure at Saratoga did not make them prisoners of war, but it did leave

14. J. B. Brebner, *Neutral Yankees*, 326–330, 339. W. H. Siebert, "The Exodus of the Loyalists from Penobscot and the Loyalist Settlements at Passamaquoddy," *N.B.H.S.*, IX, 485–529. *Great Britain, Historical Manuscripts Commission, Report on American Manuscripts in the Royal Institution of Great Britain*, I (London, 1904), 284.

15. The wages of unskilled laborers in the city were reported as being almost five times the rate prevailing before the war. Oscar T. Barck, *New York City during the War for Independence* (New York, 1931), 141.

16. *Great Britain, Historical Manuscripts Commission, Report on American Manuscripts in the Royal Institution of Great Britain*, IV (Hereford, 1909), 28, 480, 481. *N.B.H.S.*, V, 273.

17. William Canniff, *History of the Settlement of Upper Canada (Ontario) with Special Reference to the Bay of Quinté* (Toronto, 1869), 59, 67.

them most obnoxious to their neighbors, so unpopular that flight was the wisest policy. Oswego and Niagara remained in British hands and about these posts many of them clustered, performing some services and drawing supplies from the commissary.[18]

These frontier stations, however, did not offer the security that the fleeing Loyalist and his family wanted. A few score miles to the north royal authority was still preëminent and British garrisons held every strategic point on the St. Lawrence and its approaches. Montreal and Quebec were symbols of something permanent and to reach the safety of their environs became the goal of many of the troubled residents of upper New York and western New England. They came at first as families and unorganized groups. Many of the able-bodied men among them were mustered into the companies of rangers and scouts which very often sallied out on surprise raids into enemy territory to rescue friends and relatives who could not find their way to British territory alone.[19] The number of these refugees increased rapidly and Governor Haldimand was faced with the problem of finding for them a place of safety that would not hinder military operations.

To allow them to congregate in Quebec or Montreal was unwise since both places were congested with troops. It was dangerous to permit them to remain near the outposts on the Richelieu River where they usually entered the province because in case of invasion the valley was bound to be the route of any army advancing northward from the Hudson and Lake Champlain. After considering various sites the governor finally chose the seigniory of Sorel, an undeveloped tract at the junction of the Richelieu and St. Lawrence. It was easy of approach from all directions and it could be readily provided with supplies.[20] Here a large part of the refugees were assembled during the summer of 1778 and barracks were erected for winter use. In the course of the five years that followed,

18. William Kirby, *Annals of Niagara* (Welland, Ont., 1896), 54, 62. W. H. Siebert, "The Dispersion of American Tories," *Mississippi Valley Historical Review,* I (1914), 185–197.

19. *P.A.C.R., 1887,* 370; *1888,* 732. W. H. Siebert, "The American Loyalists in the Eastern Seigniories and Townships of the Province of Quebec," *R.S.C., 1913,* Sec. ii, 3–41.

20. A. L. Burt, *The Old Province of Quebec,* 279, 280.

Sorel was the scene of much activity: arrivals and departures, re-unions and separations. The sick and most needy, together with un-attached women and children, were sent to the town of Machiche (Yamachiche), where food and clothing were dispensed with greater liberality.[21]

Many hopes and fears occupied the attention of the refugees in London, Nova Scotia, New York, and Canada as the conflict neared its end. Little could be expected from the rebellious colonies if they became independent and if the disposition of the Loyalist problem were left entirely to them. But certainly the British diplomats who were negotiating the treaty would not desert them; surely they would insist that reparation be made for property seized and indig-nities suffered. Yet the diplomats did almost desert them after a long but fruitless effort, and the Treaty of Paris did not go beyond a mild statement that Congress agreed to recommend to the states that they put no obstacle to the restoration of confiscated property, and an article providing that an exile might reside for a year in the United States if necessary to facilitate the collection of his claims.[22]

When this agreement became known, hopes were shifted to Lon-don in the expectation that the failure of the diplomats would lead Parliament to make a prompt and generous appropriation for the assistance of those who had remained faithful through an eight-year struggle and had finally lost all but life. The British ministry, how-ever, was little more alert to their plight as revealed to them through petitions for aid than the diplomats had been. The only legislation was an act creating a board of commissioners to whom all claimants might submit their cases and evidence.[23] Its procedure was slow and

21. *P.A.C.R.*, *1887*, 338, 369, 381; *1888*, 732, 734, 742. W. H. Siebert, "Temporary Settlement of Loyalists at Machiche, P. Q.," *R.S.C.*, *1914*, Sec. ii, 407–414.

22. Samuel F. Bemis, *The Diplomacy of the American Revolution* (New York, 1935), 231–233, 237–238.

23. The legislation of Parliament concerning the Loyalists is summarized in Thomas Jones, *History of New York during the Revolutionary War*, II (New York, 1879), 645–663. Some of the Loyalist petitions were published in the *London Chronicle*, March 7–9, 1782, 233; March 12–14, 1782, 253; June 14–17, 1783, 572, 573. The proceedings of the commissioners in British North America have been printed in Ontario Bureau of Archives, *Second Report* (2v., Toronto, 1905).

its investigations were searching; so searching, in fact, that it was popularly described as the "Inquisition."[24] At best, the successful petitioner would have to wait months, perhaps years, before a decision and some money recompense could be obtained.

In the meantime, the British military authorities in New York and the colonial administrations in Quebec and Nova Scotia were face to face with a situation that was taking on an emergency aspect. The former could not sail away leaving their civilian comrades with no employment, no supplies, and no homes; the latter could not support the refugees as perpetual guests. While London was getting its cumbrous machinery into motion, the authorities in America rapidly combined their resources for an emergency policy whose result was the migration of the Loyalists from the new United States into the British provinces still remaining on the North American continent.

This migration was far from being a haphazard inrush of individuals who allowed chance to determine their fate, although fear for the future was the principal stimulus. Contemporary dispatches from New York reveal that the Loyalists felt their own position amid the victorious colonists to be highly dangerous; already legislation had been passed against the British supporters in various states and property had been alienated from them. The only logical procedure, therefore, was that of removal to territory where loyalty to the British crown was an asset rather than a liability and a stigma. To that end, not only those already resident within the New York lines proposed to depart, but the Loyalists in surrounding states also made their way to that refuge and from there embarked with their like to Nova Scotia.[25]

In working out their plans, the supervising authorities were dominated by two circumstances: the concentration of the Loyalists at the Port of New York, along the frontiers of New York State, and in eastern Maine; and the availability of lands within already established loyal colonies. The net result, therefore, was that the involuntary Loyalist migrations followed and broadened North American

24. William Canniff, *op. cit.*, 61.
25. *London Chronicle*, Aug. 22–24, 1782, 190; May 15–17, 1783, 471; May 17–20, 1783, 480; June 5–7, 1783, 543, 544; June 7–10, 1783, 552; June 12–14, 1783, 568; July 3–5, 1783, 21; Aug. 12–14, 1783, 154; Oct. 2–4, 1783, 336; Nov. 13–15, 1783, 447.

routes which had been established by voluntary land seekers long before their day. Pre-Loyalists or Loyalists, they were all North Americans bent upon doing the best they could for themselves on the continent which they were making their own.

Land was the only asset that Nova Scotia (then including New Brunswick) and Quebec (then including Ontario) possessed in abundance. But land without people was profitless, whereas a skillful handling of the Loyalist problem should yield large benefits. As early as 1781 General Clarke, acting governor of Quebec, had realized the advantages to be gained, and had started the survey of a range of townships in anticipation of the close of the war.[26] But it was to Nova Scotia that the flood of people was at first directed because it was most accessible to those whose departure was most in the nature of a flight.

The Loyalist community at New York enjoyed in its departure the coöperation of the British Navy and the military authorities. The martial air that pervaded the city undoubtedly facilitated the organization of "loyalist companies" each of which was under the direction of a "captain."[27] Some of these companies traveled as units, one company to a vessel, in the "spring fleet" of 1783 (made up of about twenty ships) and in the "fall fleet" of the same year. Some, however, had gone as early as the fall of 1782 in government transports and others came later, paying their own expenses, on regular trading vessels.[28] "Nova Scotia is the rage" and "Everybody, all the world, moves on to Nova Scotia" were the reports that came from the city while the movement was at its height.[29]

The military authorities, in addition to providing transportation, also undertook to furnish provisions: full rations for the first year, two-thirds the second year, and one-third for the last. With this their responsibility ended and the duties of the Nova Scotia government began. For several years that province had been losing population to the south and west and there was still to be found much unsettled land; the policy in mind was logical—to fill in the agricul-

26. William Canniff, op. cit., 156.   27. N.B.H.S., VIII, 255.

28. H. P. Johnston, "Evacuation of New York by the British, 1783," Harper's New Monthly Magazine, LXVII (New York, 1883), 909–923. Oscar T. Barck, op. cit., 207–230.

29. W. O. Raymond (ed.), Winslow Papers A.D. 1776–1826, 11, 124.

tural areas left unpeopled between the New England townships that had been planted two decades before and to establish villages from which fishing and whaling might be carried on to advantage. "Nova Scotia shall be made the envy of all the American states" was the challenging statement of this program.[30]

But giving away land was not the simple transaction that its generous nature implied. At various times in the past, extensive grants of territory had been made to individuals and groups; all of them had been contingent upon the introduction of a number of settlers and in many cases the conditions had not been fulfilled. This encumbrance could be done away with by having the grant revoked but the legal proceedings necessarily involved some delay.[31] In the meantime the new arrivals, crowded together in camps, became impatient; many did not like the strict supervision that was exercised over them. All were forced to perform a certain amount of labor and it was difficult to persuade some of them who had lived on public bounty to engage in this work. Officials complained that they became "indolent" and "mutinous" and when at last the distribution of lots began, many of them demanded that they be allowed to make their own choice. One of the officials lamented that the "cursed republican, town-meeting spirit has been the ruin of us already," and he dreaded to see its spread among the people whose future he was determining.[32]

The earlier colonization had left two principal regions on the peninsula of Nova Scotia somewhat undeveloped. One was halfway down the Fundy shore between the Basin of Minas and the townships laid out in the 1760's near Cape Sable. The other was on the Atlantic coast just east of Cape Sable. By establishing vigorous communities at these points, it was hoped that the peninsula would be practically fringed with vigorous townships which, in the course of natural expansion into the interior, would people all the available area in two or three generations.

30. *Ibid.*, 170.

31. Margaret Ells, "Clearing the Decks for the Loyalists," *Annual Report of the Canadian Historical Association*, 1933, 53–59.

32. The diary of Benjamin Marston, who was engaged in laying out the town of Shelburne, illustrates these difficulties. Extracts are published in W. O. Raymond (ed.), "The Founding of Shelburne. Benjamin Marston at Halifax, Shelburne and Miramichi," *N.B.H.S.*, VIII, 204–277.

It is true that the first site for more than a century had been the seat of government—French and English. But Port Royal and its successor, Annapolis, had never been more than a village housing a few officials, soldiers, and traders, and its surroundings were sparsely settled. The townships of Annapolis and Granville had received a few hundred New Englanders in 1761, but east and west of them tens of thousands of acres were still available. To the Annapolis Basin, therefore, several shiploads of Loyalists were sent and their establishment was facilitated because many of them possessed funds sufficient for the purchase of farms. The willingness of the "old planter" to dispose of his property and move elsewhere to unimproved locations fitted admirably into the situation and the shift in population that resulted from the sale and purchase made it unnecessary for many of the Loyalists to attempt the strenuous business of pioneering which, however courageous their spirit, was a task that few could carry through with unqualified success.[33]

Far different was the experience on the Atlantic side. Here the harbor of Port Roseway, long known to traders up and down the coast, was chosen as the rendezvous for the arriving exiles and the city of Shelburne was projected as a future commercial metropolis. The first two years of its history lived up to every hope of coming prosperity that had been expressed. By the autumn of 1784 upwards of ten thousand ambitious people had gathered in the new town and for a few months it enjoyed the distinction of having the largest population of any city in British North America and ranking next to Philadelphia, Boston, and New York in the list of the cities on the continent, north of Mexico.[34]

But the distinction was of short standing, and Shelburne was, in fact, nothing but a great concentration camp that suffered from all the disorders and discomforts of such a community. A considerable number of free Negroes had come as refugees from New York and

33. W. A. Calnek, *History of the County of Annapolis*, 168, 169, 170, 211, 229, 243, 257. [S. Hollingsworth], *The Present State of Nova Scotia with a Brief Account of Canada and the British Islands on the Coast of North America* (2d ed., Edinburgh, 1787), 124.

34. *N.B.H.S.*, VIII, 207. However, most of the contemporary estimates of the population of Shelburne were greatly exaggerated. See the note in *P.A. C.R., 1894*, 409.

these formed a town of six hundred families bordering Shelburne; other laborers found it unpleasant to work in their company. A race riot followed and ultimately, after an experiment in trying to make settlers out of them, the authorities shipped many of the Negroes off to the colony of Sierra Leone in Africa.[35] The cod fishing did not prosper because the harbor was sometimes blocked by ice and the fishermen did not possess the technical skill that their competitors in Massachusetts had acquired in a century of experience.[36] Many individuals dreaded the isolation of wilderness life and, deserting their grants without an attempt at improvement, went away to Halifax to find whatever employment offered. Some discovered that homesickness was a stronger force than political discontent and returned to the United States.[37]

The majority gradually dispersed onto the allotted farms and took up the serious routine of pioneering. Special arrangements had been made for settling disbanded military companies and regiments as units and several soldier townships appeared. Some smaller groups were settled to the north and east of Halifax.[38] In ten years Shelburne dwindled to a town of a few hundred, but it had served its purpose and Nova Scotia as a whole had acquired an addition to its population of almost twenty thousand souls—the second great immigration from the south in its history.[39]

35. A. G. Archibald, "Story of Deportation of Negroes from Nova Scotia to Sierra Leone," *Collections of the Nova Scotia Historical Society*, VII, 129–154. *London Chronicle*, May 25–27, 1784, 509; Dec. 4–7, 1784, 546. Margaret Ells, "Settling the Loyalists in Nova Scotia," *Annual Report of the Canadian Historical Association*, 1934, 106, 107.

36. *N.B.H.S.*, VIII, 269.

37. Thomas C. Haliburton, *An Historical and Statistical Account of Nova Scotia*, II, 193.

38. *N.B.H.S.*, VIII, 256. The distribution of the Loyalist grants is described in detail by M. Gilroy in *Loyalists and Land Settlement in Nova Scotia* (Halifax, 1937).

39. A muster of the Loyalists (military and civilian) in Nova Scotia in the summer of 1784 revealed a total of 28,347. "Report on Nova Scotia by Col. Robert Morse, R.E., 1784," *P.A.C.R., 1884*, xxvii–lix. Subtracting the number in the settlements that were included in the new province of New Brunswick (see note 43) leaves 16,444. Upon the basis of a careful and exhaustive analysis of muster rolls and actual land-grant records up to 1800, Margaret

This figure would have been larger had not the old province of Nova Scotia been divided in 1784 by the setting up of the part north of the Bay of Fundy as the province of New Brunswick and of Cape Breton as still another separate province. With the choice of the St. Croix River as the eastern boundary of the United States at the peace of 1783, it became desirable to plant a population that could be trusted along that border and the high repute in which the lands of the St. Croix and St. John valleys were held encouraged the policy. Settlers from Maine had already located on the islands in Passamaquoddy Bay and during 1783 and 1784 the east bank of the St. Croix filled up rapidly with practical pioneers who understood the advantages in agriculture, lumbering, and fishing that the location offered.[40]

It was to the new town of St. John at the mouth of the St. John River that the largest wave of Loyalist emigration was directed. Thirty miles up from the bay the river valley widened into broad meadows that equaled in fertility the most favored spots in New England. There were already perhaps as many as three thousand settlers in the area, numbers of whom sold their "improvements" to the newcomers and scattered to more remote regions, some of them to the United States.[41] The settlers who now established homes in the new province were remarkable for their variety. A large proportion of the arrivals were military men from the Loyalist corps and from two disbanded Scottish regiments that chose to remain in the New World when the war was over. Three blocks of land were assigned to the Negroes who had followed their masters into exile when the Revolution began. There were also some Americans who were hardly entitled to be called Loyalists; in fact, they were nothing but immigrants who thought it an act of foresight to move into an area that was destined to enjoy so vigorous a growth. Many of the refugees at Shelburne and Annapolis chose New Brunswick as their final

---

Ells, in her article "Settling the Loyalists" (cited), 105–109, gives the number of Loyalists settled permanently in Nova Scotia as 19,362. See also M. Gilroy, *op. cit.*

40. *N.B.H.S.*, IX, 502–519.

41. W. O. Raymond (ed.), *Winslow Papers A.D. 1776–1826*, 338. Brebner, *Neutral Yankees*, 116–117.

destination.[42] All told, New Brunswick may have received as many as fourteen thousand Loyalists, even if it did not retain that many. About six hundred went to Prince Edward (formerly St. John) Island and about four hundred to Cape Breton.[43]

But a great deal of population readjustment was necessary before the settlers in New Brunswick were satisfied. The majority of the Negroes drifted into the towns. Many of the Loyalists abandoned their allotments and bought lands in the older townships. Some traveled down to the coast and located in the numerous islands. A number of families gave up their grants and trekked northward through the wilderness to the valley of the Miramichi River, which flows into the Gulf of St. Lawrence. The appearance of these thousands of new inhabitants in the province of New Brunswick tended to accentuate the segregation of the Acadians on the upper St. John near the border of the United States, where they built up the district of Madawaska, a frontier settlement that later was to send the first French emigrants across the line into New England.[44]

The Loyalist migration was the last eastward thrust of population along the Atlantic coast line. It completed the process of planting a fertile people in each of the valleys opening out to the sea. During the next generation these centers gradually grew together and at the same time a steady advance into the interior began. It is a mistake to think that the American Revolution brought about the occupation of the northeastern region. Actually its preliminaries and its course interrupted or hampered it for about fifteen years. What the Revolution did was to exercise a selective process upon a logical movement of North American population and thereby cast a unique, romantic color over the Loyalists which has too often eclipsed the

42. W. F. Ganong, "A Monograph on the Origins of Settlements in the Province of New Brunswick," *R.S.C., 1904,* Sec. ii, 3–185, especially 52–73: "The Loyalist and Native Expansion Period (1783–1812)."

43. The settlement of these regions has not yet been exactly investigated, and the estimates given here have been supplied by Professor D. C. Harvey, author of *The Colonization of Canada* (Toronto, 1936). Colonel Morse's muster of 1784 (see note 39) reported 9,260 on the St. John River, 1,787 at Passamaquoddy, and 856 at Cumberland and other small settlements—a total of 11,903. See also W. H. Siebert and F. E. Gillam, "The Loyalists in Prince Edward Island," *R.S.C., 1910,* Sec. ii, 109–117.

44. *R.S.C., 1904,* Sec. ii, 59–62.

underlying character of the migration in which they took an involuntary part.

The authorities at Quebec and Montreal were faced with a situation no less pressing but even more complicated than that which worried the officials at Halifax. There were many refugees from northern New York and New England who had fled north by various routes to be temporarily settled along the St. Lawrence; they had followed the military roads that led to Ogdensburg, or the natural highways of Lake Champlain and the Richelieu River, or the Hudson River into the Mohawk and to Fort Stanwix, and thence by waterways and portages to Oswego.[45] Settlers were welcome but the choice of a location to which they should be directed involved such delicate problems as their relationship to the French population and their position with respect to the unguarded American frontier. Because of these considerations one of the areas which normally would have received many of the refugees who had gathered in its vicinity was passed over and a region more remote, less accessible, and more primitive in its life was chosen.

St. John's on the Richelieu, where so many of the Loyalists from New England and New York had found refuge, offered one route of expansion to the east and another to the west. The former led to the uninhabited area which stretched between the French seigniories on the St. Lawrence and the international boundary, the territory later known as the "Eastern Townships." The latter was the way to the triangle which lay between the river and the boundary to the west—lands which had been granted as seigniories but which were, as yet, unpeopled. These two regions, the administrators decided, should, for the present, remain uninhabited, because there was no natural boundary separating the province of Quebec from the States and the population north and south of the as yet undetermined line would probably form one community in trade and, perhaps, in politics.[46]

The prospective Loyalist settlers did not acquiesce gracefully in this decision, which seemed to them arbitrary and unreasonable. Like their brethren in Nova Scotia, they held indignation meetings. The

45. H. H. Van Wart, "The Loyalist Settlement of Adolphustown," *The Loyalist Gazette*, II (Aug., 1932), 2.
46. *R.S.C., 1913*, Sec. ii, 31–38.

northeastern shores of Lake Champlain bordered upon the area, and the inlet known as Missisquoi Bay was a promising site offering fertile soil and excellent communications with the outside world. But Governor Haldimand was resolute in his earlier decision not to "give an acre to gratify individuals at the expense of the public good,"[47] and he fortified this decision by refusing to extend any supplies to the Loyalists who persisted in remaining in that quarter.[48] Some of them bought up a claim to the lands that was derived from a dubious Indian treaty and started to make clearings. But the governor's threat to burn down their houses when constructed put an end to this activity and although a few pioneers did defy the authorities, the real settlement of the region did not begin until a new policy of colonization was adopted after 1791.[49]

Although he did not prohibit it, Haldimand discouraged the Loyalists from becoming tenants upon the old seigniories. Some of the refugees, weary of waiting for the government to announce a policy, accepted lands from private owners on the customary Canadian terms, and a general exception was made in the case of Sorel. So many official activities, military as well as civil, had centered about the place that in 1782 the government bought the estate, and in 1783 when the war operations came to an end, the lands were divided into small allotments and distributed among the residents already on the ground. But they were not happy over these arrangements and a decade later complaints regarding the feudal terms of tenure were still coming in to the authorities.[50] Thus two areas—the Eastern Townships and the old seigniories (which were far from being completely settled)—having been eliminated, Haldimand was obliged to look farther afield to discover lands on which to establish his scattered subjects, who, after seven years or more of uncertainty, were now bent on determining their future once and for all.

47. *P.A.C.R., 1886,* 414.
48. *Ibid.,* 418. C. C. Jones, "The U.E.L. Settlement at Missisquoi Bay." *The Loyalist Gazette,* III, 5.
49. *P.A.C.R., 1888,* 711, 844. A. L. Burt, *op. cit.,* 367. T. C. Lampee, "The Missisquoi Loyalists," *Proceedings of the Vermont Historical Society,* VI (2), 81–138.
50. *P.A.C.R., 1888,* 710, 845; *1891,* 118.

A beginning had been made at Niagara. The fort was on the east bank of the river, one of the posts that by the treaty was destined to be handed over to the United States, but on the Canadian side a permanent agricultural settlement had been established in 1780 in order to provide supplies for the garrison and to turn consumers into producers. At the close of 1782 the community numbered no more than eighty-four, but with the disbanding of Butler's Rangers, who had made Niagara their headquarters, a large addition was received. By the summer of 1785 the population had reached a total of 770. But Niagara was remote from the main body of refugees and the real significance of this pioneer beginning does not reveal itself until a decade later. One other development on the Niagara frontier facilitated the later influx of immigrants. The warriors of the Iroquois confederacy had fought valiantly for the British cause, which, since it involved the protection of their lands, was their cause. Now they were dispossessed and as much refugee Loyalists as many of those who were receiving lands and provisions. Haldimand was resolved to slight none of the participants in the war and a tract of land on the Grand River was set aside for the remnants of the New York tribes that had taken refuge within the bounds of the province. By this conciliatory policy the officials won the friendship of the Indians; and thus, at a time when pioneering in the United States meant constant vigilance against the red man, the Canadian settler was not distressed by this problem or distracted from the everyday business of establishing a home.[51]

Many of the Loyalists who were quartered along the St. Lawrence looked toward the east. The vogue of Nova Scotia so prevalent in New York also had its adherents in Canada, but the government of the Atlantic province was already so flooded with helpless newcomers that no special inducements were offered to anyone coming from the west. Cape Breton, which had just been set up as an autonomous province, seemed like a locality with a bright future and in the fall of 1784 three vessels carrying 124 passengers sailed from Quebec bound for the island. A more extensive project for settlement there did not materialize.[52] But Governor Haldimand did turn his most serious attention to the peninsula of Gaspé, which marks the southern entrance to the estuary of the St. Lawrence. In 1783 a thorough investigation of its possibilities was conducted by one of the governor's agents and between June and November, 1784, over four hundred persons were sent on from Sorel and Quebec. They were, however, far from contented with the conditions that they found or satisfied with the prospects that the future offered.[53]

These migrations to the east did not reduce materially the number of persons whose fate had to be determined by the governor of Quebec and the loss had been more than balanced by the arrivals by sea of several hundreds of Loyalists from the city of New York.[54] A certain Michael Grass, who had occupied a humble position as a harness maker in that city, was the leader of this expedition and with his appearance upon the scene there arose an insistent demand for the immediate choice of locations. Grass, who in the course of earlier military experiences had learned something about the country, was convinced that no site was more desirable than the area immediately north of the east end of Lake Ontario known as Cataraqui. Governor Haldimand had also, somewhat reluctantly, come to the conclusion that somewhere in this vicinity the bulk of the people would have to be placed.[55]

French settlement had advanced along the north bank of the St. Lawrence only as far west as Lake St. Francis, a widening of the river about fifty miles above Montreal. Westward from this point, continuing along the river and swinging around the north shore of Lake Ontario, a succession of townships was surveyed; and to these lands which were still the deepest wilderness the refugees that were quartered at a dozen different places and the troops stationed at various posts were directed. The process of settlement was, however, strictly supervised and as a first step all were ordered to rendezvous

52. *P.A.C.R., 1886,* 450, 452, 453; *1888,* 707, 732, 738, 753, 754; *1895,* 4, 13.

53. *Ibid., 1888,* 30, 752, 839; *1889,* 108. W. H. Siebert, "Loyalist Settlements on the Gaspé Peninsula," *R.S.C., 1914,* Sec. ii, 399–405.

54. H. H. Van Wart, *op. cit.*

55. A. L. Burt, *op. cit.,* 369.

at certain places where the soldiers were joined by their families and the civilians were organized into loose settlement companies.[56]

The settlements were arranged in two series. From Lake St. Francis to Lake Ontario were eight known as "royal townships"; beyond were five (later increased in number by subdivision) described popularly as "Cataraqui." It was assumed that those who had been comrades in arms or in exile would be more congenial comrades in hardships, and the general policy was to locate disbanded troops of the same corps or regiment, or refugee civilians from the same camp, in the vicinity of one another. As a result, at first, many of the townships possessed a decided individuality—Hessians in one community, Mohawk Dutch in another; Hudson River farmers in one place and veterans of Jessup's Corps as their neighbors. Much of this individuality was lost, however, by the shifting of population that followed the initial occupation.[57]

Not all the Loyalists were eager to engage in the venture. They questioned the terms on which the lands were granted, fearing a system little different from the Canadian feudalism of the seigniories; they complained that the lack of cattle would make pioneering much more difficult. Cataraqui in particular seemed remote, being accessible only by a tedious trip on the rapid-strewn river and the lake. This disadvantage was the more annoying to those who had centered their desires in the Eastern Townships, and only the continued refusal of the officials to reconsider the decision persuaded them to set out for the destinations to which they had been assigned.[58]

It was, in fact, a very serious and, to many of them, a rather terrifying enterprise upon which they were embarked. Frontier pioneering was an experience with which not all of them were acquainted, and only the government assistance and the encouraging presence of government agents made it seem at all feasible. During the summer of 1784 several military groups which, because of their organization, were ready to begin the adventure, were located, and in the

56. William Canniff, *op. cit.*, 62, 63.

57. R. W. Cumberland, *The United Empire Loyalist Settlements between Kingston and Adolphustown (Bulletin of the Departments of History and Political and Economic Science in Queen's University, Kingston, Ontario,* No. 45, May, 1923).

58. *P.A.C.R., 1888,* 710, 713, 714, 725.

following years, one after another, the townships were taken over by the Loyalist families.

Lands, supplies, and equipment were dispensed with a generous hand. The officials were not governed by any definite instructions as to what the extent of each grant should be. The standard was very similar to that which had been established in the proclamations of 1763 and 1765. Military veterans were rewarded on a sliding scale which ranged from five thousand acres for a field officer down to two hundred acres for a private; and among civilians every adult male and every widow usually received two hundred acres. But to this generalization there are exceptions. Grants larger than five thousand acres are recorded and some of the civilians who came later had to be content with fifty or one hundred acres.[59] Evidence of the right that any individual received was provided by a "location ticket" which would finally be exchanged for a deed. The bounty of the government did not end with this. In these other matters there was again a variation according to the needs of the settlers or the peculiar circumstances of the environment. Rations and clothes were distributed over a period of months, sometimes years. In general, after 1786 the settlers received no provisions. In some communities every family received building materials and every group of five families was provided with a set of tools, a musket, and forty-eight rounds of ammunition.[60]

Unfortunately, the "location ticket" was transferable. The holder need only sign his name upon the back and all the rights to the land indicated thereon passed to the new possessor. Speculators and their agents were present in the camps buying up the tickets of those who were discouraged or of others who were in such pressing need of money that the future had to be sacrificed to the present. Storekeepers did a thriving business in exchanging goods for certificates —sometimes as little as a calico dress in return for one ticket—and later selling the rights at two to four dollars an acre to immigrants and investors who passed through the country. By such purchases large areas came into the hands of men who were not interested in immediate development and these spaces lay unoccupied, sometimes

59. Ontario Bureau of Archives, *Second Report*, I, 12, 13.
60. William Canniff, *op. cit.*, 184, 185, 200, 220.

for decades, in the midst of the thriving settlements that later marked the townships of the Loyalist tract.[61]

There was one more center that brought together isolated traders and settlers who could not forswear allegiance to the crown of Great Britain. The post of Detroit remained in British hands during the war and although the treaty of 1783 had determined its fate as being on the soil of the United States, the final transfer did not take place until 1796. Some disbanded soldiers had already been established at Amherstburg on the Canadian side of the river and their number was increased at the time of the transfer by the exodus from Detroit of British people who had hoped in vain that the temporary retention would become permanent. A few of the more adventurous among them pushed on into the interior of the Canadian peninsula and on the banks of the Thames River made the pioneer clearings in what was to become the agricultural center of the future province of Ontario.[62]

The bands of Loyalists moving to the north may have met occasional individuals who were passing to the south for reasons similar to theirs: dissatisfaction with the outcome of the struggle in which they had been engaged. The latter numbered only hundreds instead of tens of thousands but they, also, thought it wise to seek a refuge on the other side of the boundary, and like the Loyalists they had a claim on the generosity of the government to which they entrusted their future. As early as 1780 Congress provided many of these refugees with rations and the states of Massachusetts and New York offered lands to such as desired a permanent location. In May, 1785, three townships adjacent to Lake Erie were set off as a Canadian refugee tract; but owing to the exposed position and the fact that Congress had no jurisdiction over that land, the location was later changed to the region near the mouth of the Great Miama River. The majority, however, pressed their claims upon the Federal government, meeting with no satisfactory success until 1798, when provision was made for compensating the refugees, their widows,

61. T. W. H. Leavitt, *History of Leeds and Grenville, Ontario, from 1749 to 1879* (Brockville, Ont., 1879), 17. William Canniff, *op. cit.*, 169–171.

62. Silas Farmer, *History of Detroit and Wayne County and Early Michigan*, I (3d ed., Detroit, 1890), 335. Hugh Cowan, *Canadian Achievement in the Province of Ontario*, I (n.p., 1929), 15, 104, 146, 157.

families, and heirs with gifts of land. A supplementary act in 1801 increased the amount given and set aside a strip four and a half miles wide and forty-eight miles long in central Ohio as a "Canadian Refugee Tract." This reservation included twice as much land as was needed to satisfy the claimants, and although no figures are available by which the extent of the movement may be measured, the few hundred settlers that came from Canada present a startling contrast to the human tide that was flowing in the opposite direction.[63]

A careful analysis of the available evidence reveals that 6,800 Loyalists were in the old province of Quebec (then all of Canada) in 1785.[64] But the arrivals of 1783 and 1784 were not the only persons who had a fair claim to the title. Some others drifted in from Nova Scotia and New Brunswick where they had been disappointed in conditions and in their own prospects. Others were members of the very mixed group that continued to come from the United States during the latter half of the 1780's. They may not have been actively engaged in opposing the establishment of the revolutionary governments, but they claimed to have remained loyal to the allegiance in which they were born and, upon taking an oath renewing that allegiance, they were entitled to lands if not supplies. These immigrants were not above suspicion; indeed, the term "late Loyalist" was something of a gibe. A dramatic illustration of their mixed character is that the executioner of Major André received a Loyalist land grant at Kingston before being discovered and whipped out of town.[65]

63. Carl Wittke, "Canadian Refugees in the American Revolution," *Canadian Historical Review*, III (Toronto, 1922), 320–333. *Reports of Committee on the Petitions of Sundry Refugees from Canada and Nova Scotia* (Feb. 11 and 17, 1796). *Report of the Committee on Claims to Whom Was Referred . . . the Petition of Caleb Eddy* (1802). The last two are pamphlets in the Central Reference Library, Toronto.

64. A. L. Burt, *op. cit.*, 362–363.

65. *Ibid.*, 362n. This man had been a Loyalist prisoner who, in disguise, had acted as executioner under pressure from the American authorities and had been rewarded with his freedom; Winthrop Sargent, *The Life and Career of Major John André* (Boston, 1861), 393. These latecomers provide some excuse for the traditional, but exaggerated, estimate of 10,000 Loyalist immigrants into the old province of Quebec. A "Return of Disbanded Troops on King's Land in Quebec, 1787" gives a total of 5,628 men, women, and children; *P.A.C.R., 1891*, 17. It is estimated that by 1790, 3,000 settlers had

The Loyalist and accompanying migrations to Quebec fell off somewhat about 1790 because 1788 and 1789 were seasons of scarcity, governmental support had been withdrawn, and the early settlers had not yet fully adapted themselves to altered circumstances.[66] Yet, like the Loyalists of the Atlantic coast, these migrants had followed the natural avenues of expansion. It was true that, owing to official interference, they had passed over the fertile acres north of Lake Champlain, but except for that they had acted as forerunners for a mightier human tide to follow. Within New York State the land seekers who were working up the Hudson and Mohawk valleys were being kept out of the central and western sections of the state by disputes over land titles, by speculative grants, and by lack of roads. In contrast the broad lands of Canada lay invitingly open and Loyalist settlements in the former wilderness acted like magnets. North America was about to witness a thoroughly nonpolitical migration toward the north and west by pioneers who followed where the Loyalists had trodden, but did so with next to no thought of the boundary which the diplomats had laid down in 1783.

arrived at Niagara; *Niagara Historical Society Collections,* No. 10, 40. Since neither all of these nor more than a handful of the settlers in the Detroit region could properly be called additional Loyalists, the traditional total would have to include many quasi-Loyalists to be true even in 1790.

66. J. H. Thompson, *Jubilee History of Thorold Township and Town* (Thorold, Ont., 1897–98), 27, 29.

CHAPTER IV

THE FOLLOWERS OF THE LOYALISTS
1785–1812

For almost three decades following the peace of 1783 a current of migration flowed from the United States into the British provinces to the north. During the first years of that period observers had no difficulty in characterizing the nature of the movement. The emigrants were for the most part Loyalists, faithful subjects of George III, who for reasons of sentiment or policy believed that they would be happier or safer under the British crown. Often the change in residence was economically disastrous and their loyalty was the only philosophy that justified the change. But as the years passed, sentiment ceased to be the predominant factor. To settle in Canada became increasingly advantageous and as the opportunities were better known, loyalism waned and, finally, all but disappeared. The migration of the Loyalists gradually shaded off into a migration of pioneer farmers whose only motive was the traditional American search for better lands and a perfect home.

Even among the firstcomers between 1782 and 1785 there were some whose loyalty was not strong enough to compensate for hardships and uncertainty. This was particularly true among the motley crowd that had congregated in the refugee city of Nova Scotia, Shelburne. An official who visited that place in 1789 reported that two-thirds of its inhabitants had disappeared, many of them having gone back to the United States when the distribution of governmental provisions had ceased. They "were not much burthened with loyalty, a spacious name which they made use of," was his caustic description of some of the people who had gathered there.[1] It was, however, entirely natural that many of them should return. Nova Scotia had been easy of access from New York and the migration had not been particularly closely supervised. Many of those who

1. *P.A.C.R., 1921*, Appendix E: "Letters from Governor Parr to Lord Shelburne, Describing the Arrival and Settlement of the United Empire Loyalists in Nova Scotia, 1783–1784," 11.

came to Halifax were obliged to continue on a tedious land journey to other parts of the province or an uncomfortable sea voyage to the district that became New Brunswick. When it became necessary to move, it was inevitable that many should prefer to return to the old home instead of venturing into entirely new country.[2]

In the course of the population adjustment of the next years the southward drift continued. Edward Winslow, who was the contemporary chronicler of the Maritime Provinces, wrote in 1784: "All the great people of Halifax, men and women, have been and are still flocking to the States to visit their rebel brethern."[3] In later passages he records the outcome of these visits. At first the expatriate Tories were received with suspicion by their republican friends; on the second call a more cordial welcome was extended; and, finally, they remained and accepted citizenship in the new republic. It was shocking to his intense loyalism to note among them officers who were receiving half pay from the British government.[4] The hard years of pioneering in the later 1780's brought trying experiences for which many of the settlers had no preparation; and the fragmentary information dealing with the two decades that followed tells of farmers, tradesmen, and fishermen who decided that prospects for the future were brighter in the United States. During these same years there was taking place a considerable immigration from the British Isles into the provinces, particularly Cape Breton. These newcomers often caught the prevailing spirit of discouragement, which in their case was intensified by the unsatisfactory terms of land tenure that were offered, and they too joined in the southward trek.[5] The emigration which set in from Nova Scotia and New Brunswick toward Upper Canada about 1800 indicates that these provinces were losing their attractiveness to land seekers. The east-

2. *N.B.H.S.*, VIII, 256.

3. W. O. Raymond (ed.), *Winslow Papers A.D. 1776–1826*, 232.

4. *Ibid.*, 474–476. For a description of the corresponding emigration from New Brunswick, see P. Campbell, *Travels etc.*, cited, 282–284.

5. Cyrus Black, *Historical Records of the Posterity of William Black* (Amherst, N.S.), 188. H. A. Innis and A. R. M. Lower (eds.), *Select Documents in Canadian Economic History, 1783–1885* (Toronto, 1933), 392, 394. William Gregg, *History of the Presbyterian Church in the Dominion of Canada* (Toronto, 1885), 95. *P.A.C.R., 1895,* 42.

ward movement along the Atlantic coast had definitely come to an end.[6]

The only exception to this general statement was incidental to a new economic activity which ultimately was destined to influence the course of all population movements in the northeastern part of the continent. There nature had provided a fortune in the boundless forests of pine and spruce that stretched back from the rocky shores of New Brunswick and Maine. But the pioneer farmer in search of land did not consider the forests an asset; with him, in fact, fire played a conspicuous part in clearing them out of the way. Lumbermen, on the other hand, had been active in the region for many years, enjoying a moderate prosperity in time of peace, and profiting mightily when the navies of the world had need of their tall masts and stanch beams. This need arose forcefully and somewhat unexpectedly early in the nineteenth century when, as a result of the Napoleonic wars, England was no longer able to secure naval supplies from the Baltic and in its stead imported timber from her colonies.[7] This policy at once started a rage for cutting on the banks of the St. John and St. Croix and several settlements were formed in New Brunswick by frontiersmen from Maine who were adept in the handling of the ax. But the number was small and in no way compensated for the steady loss from the agricultural parts of the provinces.[8]

It was not in the vicinity of the Atlantic that the movement from the United States into Canada was apparent. That phase of population spread had now given way to a similar movement in an area

6. James H. Coyne (ed.), "The Talbot Papers," *R.S.C., 1907,* Sec. ii, 121, 134, 186.

7. W. O. Raymond (ed.), *Winslow Papers A.D. 1776–1826,* 638. A. R. M. Lower, "The Trade in Square Timber," *Contributions to Canadian Economics,* VI (Toronto, 1933), 40–61. D. G. Creighton, *The Commercial Empire of the St. Lawrence, 1760–1850* (Toronto, 1937), 148–150.

8. William F. Ganong, "A Monograph on the Origins of Settlements in the Province of New Brunswick," *R.S.C., 1905,* Sec. ii, 116, 156, 157. An indication of the steady influx into the timber region, much of which was in the disputed territory between Maine and New Brunswick, is given in W. O. Raymond (ed.), "State of the Madawaska and Aroostook Settlements in 1831. Report of John G. Deane and Edward Kavanagh to Samuel E. Smith, Governor of the State of Maine," *N.B.H.S.,* IX, 344–384.

that was one stage behind in development. The former had been an extension of settlement in coastal New England. The next resulted from the expansion of the vigorous communities that were steadily occupying the longitudinal valleys in the interior of New York and the New England states. Township by township the Yankees took possession of the fertile meadows that bordered either side of the Connecticut River and the American population which was deployed to the right and left of the upper river presented a front not unlike that of an army encamped along the international boundary and about to invade the territory on the other side of the line.

The territory which they faced was known as the Eastern Townships of Quebec. The first Loyalist refugees in the valley of the Richelieu had known the region and its advantages, but Governor Haldimand had stubbornly refused them permission to locate within its bounds; he foresaw with a clearer vision than most of his contemporaries possessed the time when the French of the St. Lawrence with a slower, although no less persistent, advance than that which the Yankees to the south exhibited would reach the townships by following the many tributaries of the St. Lawrence which drained the region.[9] The French, however, were still far distant. Large districts within the ancient seigniories along the river were still unpeopled and it was evident that a generation or two must elapse before their search for farms would bring them so far into the interior.[10]

Following the division of the old province of Quebec into Upper and Lower Canada in 1791, the administrators of each section embarked upon an energetic program of development. Above all they needed people, and in Lower Canada Haldimand's earlier policy of reserving lands for the grandchildren of the French was naturally discarded. Whoever the people might be, they were welcome; the New Yorkers and the New Englanders, ready to swarm over the boundary, were the most available and were waiting to be invited.

Americans had already made their appearance. The prohibition

9. A. L. Burt, *The Old Province of Quebec*, 367, 368.

10. Georges Vattier, *Esquisse historique de la colonisation de la Province de Québec, 1608–1925* (Paris, 1928), 38, 39. Ivanhoe Caron, *La Colonisation de la Province de Québec. Les Cantons de l'Est. 1791–1815* (Quebec, 1927), 11.

of settlement had not included the seigniories already established east of the Richelieu and on these estates a number of Loyalists from the Hudson and the Mohawk had found homes. Here they were joined by others from the old neighborhood who professed loyalty in varying degrees. From this base, during the 'nineties, the more venturesome among them, ignoring the established policy, moved onto the forbidden lands and selected the most promising sites, particularly those adjacent to Missisquoi Bay, the northeastern arm of Lake Champlain.[11] Farther to the east, during the same decade, Americans were also coming in from the New England states, squatting in true frontier style wherever their practiced eyes spotted a desirable location. If people were determined to come, the authorities reasoned, it would be better for the methods and conditions of settlement to be established officially than to allow the pioneers to choose what they wanted, trusting to the future for a confirmation of their claims.[12]

There was, in fact, no practical way of keeping them out. Two influential circumstances that usually fostered the settlement of an area were present in this case: accessibility and a market. The accessibility was provided by roads that began reaching out toward Lower Canada during the 'sixties and by a network of intertwining rivers; the market was found in Montreal. The natural window to the outside world for frontier Vermont and northeastern New York was provided by the St. Lawrence.

Instead of drawing the boundary along the watershed separating the rivers flowing to the south from those that emptied into the St. Lawrence, the negotiators of the treaty of 1783 had selected the forty-fifth parallel due west from its intersection with the Connecticut River. This cut across the system of communications that nature had provided. Easy portages led from one river system to another. The line bisected Lake Memphremagog, the long trough in the hills into which many of the minor streams of northern Vermont flowed. From the north end of the lake small tributaries provided paths

11. See above, pp. 57–58. C. Thomas, *Contributions to the History of the Eastern Townships* (Montreal, 1866), 15, 16. John P. Noyes, "The Canadian Loyalists and Early Settlers in the District of Bedford," *Third Report of the Missisquoi County Historical Society* (St. John's, P.Q., 1908), 90–107.

12. H. A. Innis and A. R. M. Lower, *op. cit.*, 13, 14.

leading to the St. Francis and the Yamaska, a second important water route of the British province. From the southern end another portage led to the Missisquoi River north of the British line, but the river flowed over into the United States, turned toward the north-west, and emptied into Lake Champlain at the boundary. Lake Champlain was drained by the Richelieu into the St. Lawrence. Geography had determined that in settlement this Canadian-American area was to be a unit.[13]

The market that the pioneers enjoyed was called into being by developments far distant from the hills of the Eastern Townships. The rapidly expanding textile industry of England called for bleaching and dyeing agents that the chemists of the day could pro-vide only by extracting them by crude processes from natural prod-ucts in which they were found in abundance. The "pot and pearl ashes" that were secured by the burning of many varieties of hard-wood yielded a high percentage of the chemicals, and the trees of the Eastern Townships seem to have been unusually rich therein. Every barrel transported to Montreal brought a cash price, and pioneer history records some fabulous sums obtained from the cutting on a single acre. When the clearing of land, which usually was nothing but the preliminary step toward the securing of an income, became a profitable venture in itself, the taking up of land was bound to pro-ceed with unexampled rapidity.[14]

The policy of encouraging settlement was inaugurated by a proc-lamation of Lieutenant-Governor Clarke on February 7, 1792.[15] A commission was appointed to receive applications for grants and to formulate the plan under which the lands would be actually disposed

13. W. A. Mackintosh, "Canada and Vermont: A Study in Historical Ge-ography," *Canadian Historical Review*, VIII, 9–30. John A. Dresser, "The Eastern Townships of Quebec; a Study in Human Geography," *R.S.C., 1935,* Sec. ii, 89–100.

14. John Lambert, *Travels through Canada and the United States of North America, in the Years 1806, 1807, and 1808,* II (2d ed., London, 1814), 526. Francis A. Evans, *The Emigrant's Directory and Guide to Ob-tain Lands and Effect a Settlement in the Canadas* (Dublin, 1833), 55, 94, 110, 111. *P.C.: App. to Jour. of Legislative Assembly,* X, No. V.

15. The proclamation may be found in Arthur G. Doughty and Duncan A. McArthur (eds.), *Documents Relating to the Constitutional History of Can-ada, 1791–1818* (Ottawa, 1914), 60–62.

of. Under their regulations a township would be granted to a leader acting for a group of settlers within a limited time. This was in its essential features the traditional New England system of town grants to a company of "proprietors" and probably because of their familiarity with the method, New Englanders were not slow in offering to engage in the enterprise, there being no restrictions in the matter of nationality either with respect to grantees or settlers. By July, 1793, warrants had been issued for the survey of 173 townships that had been petitioned for by 256 "leaders" and approximately ten thousand associates, most of them citizens of the United States.[16]

There were, however, many obstacles that delayed the actual process of settlement. Just as in New York, official privilege and private preëmption hampered the actual land seekers. Officials could not agree as to the scale of fees to be charged and there was uncertainty regarding the number of acres that the associates would be allowed to cede to the leader. Bona fide settlers who arrived found townships unsurveyed and no one on hand to administer the oath of allegiance that was demanded. Some returned to the United States; others remained as squatters in the hope of a speedy adjustment of their status. With the coming of a new lieutenant-governor in 1796 steps were taken by which order was finally established from the tangled state of affairs. Some of the townships in which systematic settlement had not begun were forfeited. In 1800 arrangements were confirmed by the Executive Council whereby the amount of land patented to any group of associates was made proportionate to the extent of the preparatory work which they had already carried through. The way was now open for the pioneers to secure a legal title and after 1800 the business of peopling townships with Yankee immigrants was remarkably brisk.[17]

From the local histories of the communities the general nature of the settlement can be outlined. Quakers located in two townships; among many others, a minority who claimed special concessions be-

16. Ivanhoe Caron, "Colonization in Canada under the English Domination from 1790–1796," *Statistical Year-Book of the Province of Quebec*, V (Quebec, 1918), 19–99.

17. Ivanhoe Caron, "Colonization in Canada under the English Domina-

cause of their Loyalist background congregated in the southwestern settlements; proprietors and settlers from Vermont outnumbered the Loyalists again in the more eastern sections.[18] There was, however, no regularity in the conditions on which the lands were held in spite of the proclamations and instructions. Some proprietors were rewarded for special services; others had borne the cost of survey and therefore received more favorable terms. Between 1796 and 1814 an estimated total of 2,203,709 acres was ceded, the greater amount before 1805.[19] In one feature there was uniformity: the actual tillers of the soil, whatever their politics or status, were predominantly American in blood and institutions. The officials had made no provision for the establishment of local government, but this neglect caused no confusion in the new communities. The settlers, with a tradition of more than a hundred years behind them, set about governing themselves.[20]

In the routine affairs of daily life the international boundary was, in fact, nonexistent. During the troubles of the Revolution many of the people of northern Vermont had considered themselves "neutrals" and in the uncertain years that followed, an influential group in the population had urged a union of the state with the British provinces as a step economically sound and politically acceptable.[21] Formal admission of that territory as a state of the Union in 1791 did not stifle the international spirit that prevailed along the border. Some settlers afflicted with typical pioneer restlessness moved back and forth across the line which they knew was somewhere in the

tion from 1796 to 1800," *Statistical Year-Book of the Province of Quebec,* VI, 582–648. Ivanhoe Caron, "Colonization in Canada under the British Domination (1800–1815)," *Statistical Year-Book of the Province of Quebec,* VII, 461–535. [John Cosens Ogden] *A Tour through Upper and Lower Canada by a Citizen of the United States* (Litchfield, 1799), 36. L. S. Channell, *History of Compton County and Sketches of the Eastern Townships* (Cookshire, P.Q., 1896), 166, 214.

18. Ivanhoe Caron, *La Colonisation de la Province de Québec. Les Cantons de l'Est. 1791–1815,* 178, 180, 234.

19. *Ibid.,* 219.

20. *Montreal Gazette,* Oct. 16, 1834, quoted in H. A. Innis and A. R. M. Lower, *op. cit.,* 34, 35.

21. W. A. Mackintosh, *op. cit.*

vicinity. Churches were constituted of members who lived on both sides of the boundary. Montreal was the natural market place of northern Vermont and no political regulations interrupted the trade. In local transactions stores and mills served a clientele that was made up of subjects of Great Britain and of the United States.[22]

The haphazard arrangements that prevailed in the granting of land explain the absence of any official figures adequate to measure the size of the American influx. In 1807 it was stated that approximately fifteen thousand had crossed the border to settle on the lands of the Eastern Townships.[23] Bishop Charles Stewart, writing at about the time of the outbreak of the War of 1812, estimated the total population at twenty thousand, derived almost entirely from American stock which, with the exception of the Loyalists from New York, had been drawn from New England.[24] The significance of the movement, however, is illustrated not so much by figures as by the predominance of the American element and by the cordial sentiments that the British authorities gradually came to entertain toward them. These were summed up in the words of Bishop Stewart: "In many respects they make the best settlers in a new country."[25] Pioneering was more important than politics and as pioneers they were welcomed and put to work.

That the influx into the Eastern Townships was far from being caused entirely by the generous policy that ultimately prevailed in the distribution of land is proven by the settlement that was taking place in the region that occupied a corresponding position west of the Richelieu River. Here no effort was made to encourage the coming of Americans; on the contrary, the proprietors looked upon them with disfavor. Nevertheless the Yankees came and those in authority were forced to compromise with a movement so vigorous in nature

22. Abby Maria Hemenway, *The Vermont Historical Gazetteer,* II (Burlington, Vt., 1871), 228, 232, 285; III (Claremont, N.H., 1877), 33. C. Thomas, *op. cit.,* 55, 100. Ernest M. Taylor, *History of Brome County, Quebec* (Montreal, 1908), 6, 7, 95, 263.

23. Hugh Gray, *Letters from Canada Written during a Residence There in the Years 1806, 1807, and 1808* (London, 1809), 349.

24. Charles Stewart, *A Short View of the Present State of the Eastern Townships in the Province of Lower Canada Bordering on the Line 45° North with Hints for Their Improvement* (London, reprinted 1817), 8.

25. *Ibid.,* 9.

that whatever opposition they could offer was doomed to be without effect.[26]

The triangle to the west of the Richelieu, bounded on the south by the forty-fifth parallel and on the northwest by the St. Lawrence, was early known as the District of Beauharnois and later as Huntingdon County. The Richelieu was the great road of commerce toward the north, carrying not only the trade of the Canadian settlements but most of the produce that the American pioneers sent down the rivers and creeks to Lake Champlain. Many flourishing villages and agricultural communities, some dating back to the French regime and others to Loyalist days, lined its banks and those to the west of it gradually extended toward the interior of the triangle. But difficulties were many and before the British subjects had made much progress through the swampy lowlands nearest the river, a swarm of American invaders had already taken possession of the most fertile meadows.[27]

This conquest on the part of the foreigners was facilitated by the topography of the region. It was drained by the Chateauguay River which flowed into the St. Lawrence but which originated in a score of sources on the American side of the boundary. These sources were enmeshed with the many tributaries of the rivers of northern New York, and when once the peopling of the northern wilderness got under way there was nothing to stop and much to encourage an advance down the valley of the Chateauguay.

Northern New York remained a wilderness much longer than other less favored and less accessible areas. Once the obstacle had been the presence of the French and their hostile Indian allies; then it had been a land policy that tied up many of the most desirable regions in the hands of speculators and large landholders. Ten towns had been laid out along the New York shore of the St. Lawrence River in 1787 but none of them flourished.[28] Not until ten years later when Nathan Ford, who had secured a large section in the vicinity of the present Ogdensburg, set out with the aggressiveness

26. Robert Sellar, *The History of the County of Huntingdon and of the Seigniories of Chateauguay and Beauharnois* (Huntingdon, P.Q., 1888), 35.
27. *Ibid.,* 14, 19–21.
28. Charles H. Leete, "The St. Lawrence Ten Towns," *Quarterly Journal of the New York State Historical Association,* X, 318–327.

of a modern land promoter to dispose of his holdings did the boom times of northern New York begin. The enthusiasm of his campaign affected other proprietors, encouraged the state to cut roads through the forest, and made the "Black River Country" a rival of the "Genesee Country" in popular favor.[29]

Ford concentrated his agents and propaganda in Vermont, and success attended the efforts. About 1799 a westward movement began to depopulate the towns of the Green Mountains and to send not only sons but families into what was to them a distant west. For several years the rush continued and as the fame of the new and fertile lands spread, all parts of New England and even Pennsylvania contributed to the migration.[30] Few, if any, of these pioneers had any thought of expatriating themselves, but those who had no definite destination in view scouted about for beaver meadows and millsites and in the course of such wanderings they often found themselves north of the unmarked latitude of forty-five degrees. Many of them considered the hardwood lands that they discovered in British territory to be better in quality and, in addition, the Montreal market for potash offered its great advantages.[31] Compared with the great column of settlers that was attacking the American forest this flank movement was a minor maneuver, but it turned Huntingdon County into another international zone where citizens of the United States concentrated upon earning a living and paid little attention to questions of jurisdiction.

Again the international character of a border settlement is illustrated by many of the affairs of everyday life as told in the pages of local history. Americans and Canadians crossed the boundary to have their grinding done in the nearest mills and all of them prepared potash and timber for the buyers of Montreal. Clergymen and physicians performed their duties on both sides of the line. Revolutionary soldiers went back once a year to collect the pensions that the United States government owed them. The terms which the

29. Franklin B. Hough, *A History of Jefferson County in the State of New York* (Albany, 1854), 127, 229, 234, 309.

30. Gates Curtis (ed.), *Our Country and Its People: A Memorial Record of St. Lawrence County, New York* (Syracuse, 1897), 392, 407, 519. L. D. Stilwell, *Migration from Vermont (1776–1860)* (Montpelier, Vt., 1937).

31. Robert Sellar, *op. cit.*, 15, 21, 33, 34, 39.

Canadian proprietors demanded of the settlers were somewhat severe, but otherwise residence in Canada was little different from that in the United States.[32]

Emigration from New England and New York into Lower Canada was not confined to farmers in quest of lands. The unending Yankee search for opportunities for making a living brought many others into the British province. Travelers record that almost without exception innkeepers in the river towns and along the post roads were Americans. The "American tavern" was an institution welcomed by every wandering European writer. The most prosperous and enterprising storekeepers, as, for instance, in the city of Montreal, were foreigners from New England. The country miller was usually an immigrant from the south; in fact, almost all the mechanics who could perform the duties of a new settlement were of Yankee origin; and the troupes of strolling players and "artists" who entertained the backwoods were on tour from the United States.[33] Upper Canada presented the same picture. Itinerant Methodist preachers and Yankee schoolmasters served the frontier settlements as far west as the Indian reservation on the Grand River.[34]

How far from home the New Englander would wander was illustrated by Philemon Wright of Woburn, Massachusetts. In 1797 he was exploring the banks of the Ottawa River, and there, opposite the site where later arose the capital of the Dominion, he discovered a location which pleased him. In the spring of 1800 he returned with his family and a small colony of artisans and farmers who became the pioneers of the town of Hull. But the enterprising leader had not come merely to cultivate the soil. He turned his attention to the

32. *Ibid.*, 29, 32, 178, 226.

33. John Lambert, *op. cit.*, I, 97, 496, 527; II, 2, 531.

34. *The Journal of Seth Crowell; Containing an Account of His Travels as a Methodist Preacher for Twelve Years* (New York, 1813), 12, 14, 31, 32. William Canniff, *An Historical Sketch of the County of York* (n.p., n.d.), xxi. J. Smyth Carter, *The Story of Dundas Being a History of the County of Dundas from 1784 to 1904* (Iroquois, Ont., 1905), 169. *Illustrated Historical Atlas of the Counties of Frontenac, Lennox, and Addington* (Toronto, 1878), 10. James Young, *Reminiscences of the Early History of Galt and the Settlement of Dumfries in the Province of Ontario* (Toronto, 1880), 35. H. H. Langton (ed), *Travels in the Interior Inhabited Parts of North America in the Years 1791 and 1792 by P. Campbell* (Toronto, 1937), 166.

surrounding forests, his settlers displayed their mettle as woodsmen, and in 1806 they sent their first raft down the river, thereby inaugurating a new era in the commercial history of the Ottawa Valley. Other Americans joined them in the neighboring townships, where they and their sons developed into the well-known Ottawa raftsmen who were to pilot logs down every river of the American north and west.[35]

The majority of the Loyalists who had departed to Quebec from the new republic had settled their families and fortunes in Upper Canada and it was to this province that the largest contingent of the emigrating Americans who followed them flocked. During its early stages this movement was not nearly so natural a phenomenon as the steady and normal expansion of settlement that brought Americans over the line into border counties farther to the east. Upper Canada was still far away from the frontier communities of the United States and the route was long, tedious, and dangerous. Loyalism, or at least homesickness for British institutions, remained a factor inducing and guiding the course of the influx for perhaps a decade longer than elsewhere. Not until almost 1800 was this current of migration drawn into and made an integral part of the continental westward movement of the time.

The Loyalists who had settled along Lake Erie, even after the early hardships of their adventure had been overcome, were far from satisfied with their lot and prospects. During the first trying years some, thoroughly discontented with conditions, returned to the United States and there is no evidence that any who remained urged others to join them. They were at that time residents of the old province of Quebec in which law, religion, and land relationships were all determined by the concessions that had been made to the

35. Andrew Picken, *The Canadas* (London, 1832), Appendix, xi–xxxiii: "An Account of the First Settlement of the Township of Hull, on the Ottawa River, Lower Canada, by P. Wright, Esq." Joseph Bouchette, *The British Dominions in North America* (London, 1831), Appendix, article "Hull." James Elliott Defebaugh, *History of the Lumber Industry of America,* I (2d ed., Chicago, 1906), 155–157. C. Thomas, *History of the Counties of Argenteuil, Que., and Prescott, Ont.* (Montreal, 1896), 25. A. R. M. Lower, *The North American Assault on the Canadian Forest* (Toronto, 1938), 164, 167.

predominant French element. Although they were assured that they would never be subjected to the feudal tenures of the French seigniories and would never see their political rights sacrificed in order to hold the allegiance of the French majority, these assurances were felt to be no more permanent than the authority of the administrators who made them.[36] The desire for a separate government was strengthened by a realization of these facts. The Colonial Office in London was made aware of the position of these new settlers and finally, by the Constitutional Act of 1791, Parliament authorized the division of Quebec into two provinces, the upper one being guaranteed a representative assembly and the holding of lands in "free and common socage."

A new activity was at once evident in all economic life. About this time, crops which for some years had been scanty became abundant in yield, and satisfaction over this change for the better coincided with the new contentment apparent in political affairs. Most of the Loyalists had relatives and friends still residing in the States and although they differed with them over the issues of the Revolution, they were interested in one another's personal fortunes and opinions. Letters and occasional visits kept their friendship alive and as the heat of political discussion cooled, interest was shifted to land, crops, and markets. In discussing these matters the Loyalists became more and more enthusiastic regarding the advantages of their province and, aided by some British sentiments still latent among their American friends, they succeeded in persuading some to return north with them.[37]

The Loyalists often had a practical motive to strengthen the enthusiasm which they expressed. Almost every family was tempted to become a real-estate jobber. Many had been endowed with more land than could be readily cleared and cultivated and every child upon reaching maturity would receive a grant of two hundred acres free from all expenses or fees. These grants usually lay at a distance from the family farm and since in these early days there was plenty

36. A. L. Burt, *op. cit.*, 384–399.

37. William Canniff, *History of the Settlement of Upper Canada*, 167, 196, 466, 585. Robert Gourlay, *Statistical Account of Upper Canada*, I (London, 1822), 248. *Illustrated Historical Atlas of the Counties of Frontenac, Lennox, and Addington*, 6.

to occupy the growing generation on the home acres, to sell them at a bargain price was the simplest disposition. The trade in certificates for unoccupied grants was a recognized branch of commerce in the Canadas and the smallness of the sum necessary to secure a choice farming location was a powerful magnet that drew Americans across the lake into the territory of a foreign nation.[38]

But these circumstances in themselves are insufficient to explain the numbers of immigrants. When the province received a new constitution, it also received a new lieutenant-governor who was a man of patriotism, vision, and energy. John Graves Simcoe was not content to rule over an undeveloped and sparsely populated wilderness.[39] The war conditions prevailing in Europe created a demand for products that Upper Canada could supply. It was his task to secure the people and provide the facilities for transportation that were essential if the market were to be satisfied. One of his first acts was to authorize the cutting of two great arteries of travel and trade through the forest: Yonge Street leading northward from York (Toronto) to Lake Simcoe and Dundas Street that proceeded westward from the head of Lake Ontario. Any history of the settlement of the province must begin with these two highways that opened up the interior by joining it to the route of the Lakes.[40]

In the matter of settlers Simcoe knew that Europe, troubled with revolution and the prospect of war, had relatively few to send; moreover, he realized that Europeans were not very capable of performing the services that pioneering entailed. He believed that many Americans were still British in sentiment, and on February 7, 1792, he issued a proclamation very similar to that which appeared on the same day in Lower Canada. In Upper Canada townships were granted to associations of settlers, and farm lots up to two hundred

38. *P.A.C.R., 1892,* 72. James Croil, *Dundas; or a Sketch of Canadian History and More Particularly of the County of Dundas* (Montreal, 1861), 135

39. Simcoe's plans for the province were outlined in a memorandum which he drew up in June, 1791. E. A. Cruikshank (ed.), *Correspondence of Lieut. Governor John Graves Simcoe,* I (Toronto, 1923), 27–34.

40. William H. Breithaupt, "Dundas Street and Other Early Upper Canada Roads," *Ontario Historical Society, Papers and Records,* XXI (Toronto, 1924), 5–11.

acres in extent to individual petitioners, with occasional grants up to one thousand acres. The only obligation that rested upon the recipient was to take an oath swearing to maintain the authority of King and Parliament.[41]

This proclamation was circulated throughout New York and New England, but American landlords were not willing to see it posted about in public places and ingenious methods had to be followed to bring it to the attention of interested persons.[42] There was some response. A considerable number of townships were assigned to various groups, and individual families were reported as coming from New England to claim the privileges offered by the proclamation.[43] But many of the immigrants probably would have come without any positive invitations because they were still tinged with loyalism, and the sense of allegiance that they still bore to the British crown was awakened by the anti-English spirit which broke out in the United States in 1793 and 1794 when the question of neutrality in the great European struggle of the day was thrown into the politics of the period.[44]

When the Americans who applied for lands were asked why they had chosen Upper Canada for their new home, they returned answers that illustrate that the migration was already related to the general conditions attending the westward movement. Land was cheaper in the Canadas. In the United States the government as well as private proprietors demanded a substantial price and a tract sufficient for a farm cost several hundred dollars. In Canada it was practically free. Indian difficulties still raged in the Old Northwest and even after the campaign of Anthony Wayne in 1793–1795 had defeated the tribes,

41. This proclamation is printed in E. A. Cruikshank (ed.), *Correspondence of Lieut. Governor John Graves Simcoe*, I, 108–109.

42. *Ibid.*, I, 124, 312.

43. La Rochefoucault-Liancourt, *Travels in Canada, 1795* (*Thirteenth Report of the Bureau of Archives for the Province of Ontario, 1916*. Toronto, 1917), 75.

44. L. J. Burkholder, *A Brief History of the Mennonites in Ontario* (n.p., 1935), 14–15. Justin Winsor (ed.), *Narrative and Critical History of America*, VII (Cambridge, 1888), 465, 466. This British loyalism is from time to time reflected in H. H. Langton (ed.), *Travels . . . by Patrick Campbell*, cited.

the fear of renewed hostilities acted as a discouragement.[45] Moreover, access to the territory that became the state of Ohio was difficult. It might be reached via Pittsburgh—but that was a roundabout journey for New Englanders. Not until about 1800 were the western settlements, then along the Genesee River, connected by road with the south shore of Lake Erie. Emigrants were obliged to travel down the river to Lake Ontario, to sail or walk along its coast to the Niagara River, then to pass onto Canadian soil, to proceed across the peninsula of Niagara, and finally to cross the waters of Lake Erie—if transportation could be found.[46] Every prospective migrant to the west who studied the route realized that Upper Canada could be reached more easily and more cheaply.

Presumably the desire for free political institutions was a factor of consequence that might have persuaded some Americans to endure the hardships of the longer journey in order to continue living in a republic. But their inquiries revealed that all the political rights that they treasured were also honored in the constitution of Upper Canada and in practical workings the government was less burdensome in its demands for service and taxes. King and Parliament were remote and, instead of demanding contributions from the colonists as assistance in bearing the expenses of empire, the mother country made appropriations for some burdens that had to be carried by the citizens in the United States.[47]

Perhaps as good a summary statement as any of what American

45. J. B. Brebner, "Canadian and North American History," *Canadian Historical Association Report for 1931* (Ottawa, 1931), 37–48. Isaac Weld, *Travels through the States of North America and the Provinces of Upper and Lower Canada during the Years 1795, 1796, and 1797* (4th ed., London, 1800), 286. E. A. Cruikshank (ed.), *Correspondence of Lieut. Governor John Graves Simcoe*, II, 109; III, 56. Robert W. Bingham (ed.), *Reports of Joseph Ellicott*, I (Buffalo, 1937), 164.

46. *History of Ashtabula County, Ohio* (Philadelphia, 1878), 25, 250. A. B. Hulbert, *Historic Highways of America*, XII, 95–100; a map of the roads of western New York in 1809 can be found on p. 122.

47. *The Canadian Antiquarian and Numismatic Journal*, Third Series, I (Montreal, 1898), 170. On pages 159–172 of this journal there is reprinted "A Letter from a Gentleman to His Friend in England, Descriptive of the Different Settlements in the Province of Upper Canada" which was published at Philadelphia in 1795.

immigrants thought of Upper Canada was provided by one of them who, having lost his possessions there owing to the War of 1812, could still write as follows in 1814 from his refuge in Virginia:

First, I am a native of the United States, was born in Pennsylvania, ten miles from Philadelphia, and in the year 1808 moved with my family to the province of Upper Canada, in order to obtain land upon easy terms, (as did most of the inhabitants now there) and for no other reason. I had not long remained in the province till I discovered that the mildness of the climate, fertility of the soil, benefit of trade, cheapness of the land, morals of the inhabitants, and equality of the government, so far exceeded my former expectations and the expectations of the public in general, that I deemed it my duty to make known the same; especially when I considered that there were many thousands of my fellow citizens of the United States, who were without land, and prospect of obtaining any in the United States upon such easy terms as they might in Upper Canada; nor had I then any expectation of war between the two countries.

Even during the war he had published three large editions of his booklet about Upper Canada and in 1814 was issuing it in enlarged form from a Baltimore press.[48]

The nature of the impulses that governed the migration is further illustrated by the experiences of some of the distinct groups whose history can be more readily traced. The attention of Governor Simcoe was early directed to the possibility of securing settlers from among the Quakers of Pennsylvania, whose experiences during the Revolution had been far from comfortable and many of whom still lived under the suspicion of their neighbors that they had been Tories at heart although they had maintained a neutrality during the war.[49] Some of them were so strongly suspected that their property had been confiscated and all of them felt the heavy burden of the taxes that weighed upon landed property.

Simcoe promised them freedom from two requirements that otherwise might have discouraged them from taking up lands in the prov-

48. Michael Smith, *A Geographical View of the British Possessions in North America*, Preface.

49. Ezra E. Eby, *A Biographical History of the Eby Family* (Berlin, Ont., 1889), 6.

ince. Instead of swearing to the necessary oath of allegiance they were allowed, as in Lower Canada, to make affirmation, and freedom from the usual compulsory militia service could be obtained by the payment of an annual fee. Persuaded by these concessions, an emigration to the north got under way which, like all the other Quaker migrations, continued over a long period of years and was more in the nature of a drift than a migration: families reuniting after a separation and members of one "meeting" joining friends that had preceded. Quaker colonies came not only from Pennsylvania but from the valley of the Hudson, Vermont, and New Jersey, and they formed a substantial element in the population that opened the lands off Yonge Street.[50]

A broader view of the establishment of these Quaker communities also reveals a relationship to the inevitable trend of continental population. All American Quakerdom was in a state of flux during the generation following the Revolution and when the Indian difficulties of the Northwest had been quieted, the movement known in Quaker annals as the "great migration" brought individuals and congregations from all parts into the southern and middle districts of Indiana. Compared with that later exodus the influx into Canada was only an insignificant flank movement, but it came early and confirms the hypothesis that even among migrations that were believed to be governed by specific and peculiar factors, the prevailing direction of population movement during any given time was faithfully reflected.[51]

Along with the Quakers came representatives of another religious group whose beliefs and experiences were very similar. The Mennonites and Dunkers in the eastern counties of Pennsylvania had also come through the Revolution under the shadow of disloyalty to the patriot cause. The scriptures to which they so confidently turned for guidance spoke to them more clearly of kings and kingdoms than

50. Michael Smith, *op. cit.*, 54, 55. James Bowden, *The History of the Society of Friends in America*, II (London, 1854), 361–362. *Friends' Miscellany: Being a Collection of Essays and Fragments, etc.*, III (2d ed., Philadelphia, 1845), 361–362. *Annual Report of the American Historical Association, 1896*, I, 613, 645, 647.

51. Arthur G. Dorland, *A History of the Society of Friends (Quakers) in Canada*, 53, 55.

of presidents and republics. Their creed of nonresistance had subjected them to many annoyances during the war; and the early years of the Republic, disturbed as they were by Indian uprisings and threats of domestic insurrection, promised little assurance of peace. Moreover, families increased rapidly in numbers and the prudent father who wanted to establish his sons as independent farmers saw no opportunity of doing so in a region which was already so crowded that the price of land was mounting rapidly. Some new agricultural location must be found, but none wanted to move to the south and southwest where the institution of slavery was being revived. For the time being their attention was turned to the north, which was accessible, where land was readily obtained, and where British rule reminded them of the stability of earlier days.[52]

A few of these Germans had come into Upper Canada with the Loyalists. The first distinct community was founded as early as 1786 in the Niagara peninsula at a place known as "the twenty," but its numbers never became very large. Within the next few years another and larger group arrived and settled in Welland County. In 1799, when the real emigration of the Mennonites got under way, it was directed toward the Grand River, where in Waterloo township, about the town of Berlin (now Kitchener), the largest and most prosperous settlement of Germans was gathered. In 1803, when some temporary doubts arose as to the validity of the titles under which they held their lands, a third colony was started at Markham, north of York. The stream of Germans to the Waterloo Settlement doubled its population during 1805–1807 and continued to add to it down to the War of 1812.[53]

Like the Loyalists, the Mennonites kept up a direct connection with the compatriots they had left behind. They often traveled back to the eastern counties of Pennsylvania, stopping every night, it was said, at the home of some Mennonite or Dunker, and this well-defined route facilitated a continual movement into the province which kept

52. L. J. Burkholder, "The Early Mennonite Settlements in Ontario," *The Mennonite Quarterly Review*, VIII (Goshen, Ind., 1934), 103–122. W. H. Breithaupt, "The Settlement of Waterloo County," *Ontario Historical Society, Papers and Records*, XXII, 14. L. J. Burkholder, *A Brief History of the Mennonites in Ontario*, 14, 15, 21, 24.

53. *Ibid.*, 29–37.

up until the main current of Mennonite migration, like that of the Quakers, was turned to Indiana and neighboring states. Not all of the Germans who moved into Canada subscribed to the religious tenets of those who had come first. The success of the pioneers induced other Pennsylvania Germans to follow and to take up lands in the neighborhood of the communities where their own tongue was spoken and where their own accustomed ways prevailed.[54]

Governor Simcoe proved to be far from successful in his handling of the land affairs of his province. Many of the townships which he arranged for were never settled and the grants had to be revoked. There was confusion in the conditions imposed upon individuals, and there was no regularity in fees.[55] When he retired from office in 1796 an effort was made to secure more uniformity in policy and administration and a stricter inquiry into the assets and desirability of petitioners was inaugurated. A charge for surveying was levied.[56] In spite of this more rigorous procedure the number of applicants increased and immigration swelled in volume.[57] This was, in fact, what was to be expected, because Upper Canada lay across the path of one of the main currents of population spread.

The population of west central New York had now reached the first stage of pioneer saturation at which some readjustment was necessary. First settlers and younger sons were ready to make beginnings elsewhere; restless families were ready to follow. They began to fill in rapidly the counties laid out in the western part of the state, to move along Lake Erie to the famed Western Reserve, and to cross the Niagara River onto the rolling lands that bordered that lake to the north. This last destination rapidly gained in popularity.[58] All of the advantages that the firstcomer had enjoyed were still

54. A. B. Sherk, "The Pennsylvania-Germans in Canada," *The Pennsylvania-German*, VIII (Lebanon, Pa., 1907), 101–104. W. H. Higgins, *The Life and Times of Joseph Gould* (Toronto, 1887), 24.

55. H. A. Innis and A. R. M. Lower, *op. cit.*, 73. E. A. Cruikshank, "An Experiment in Colonization in Upper Canada," *Ontario Historical Society, Papers and Records*, XXV, 32–78. E. A. Cruikshank (ed.), *Correspondence of Lieut. Governor John Graves Simcoe*, IV, 276, 277, 338.

56. *Ibid.*, 308.

57. For a description of the migration in 1799 see a letter from Fort Erie, Jan. 20, 1799, in *Ontario Historical Society, Papers and Records*, XX, 47.

58. George Heriot, *Travels through the Canadas* (London, 1807), 151,

in evidence and Upper Canada became known as the place where the poor man could most quickly work his way into the position of an independent landholder.[59]

Unfortunately, no one counted the immigrants that crossed the river and the only estimate that has been preserved placed the number of new families that settled in the province at five hundred per year.[60] Whatever the actual figures were, settlers came in such numbers that some worried Canadians began to fear the results of this invasion of republican radicals. By 1806 a strong prejudice against the growing strength of the American population was clearly evident and the desirability of continuing the liberal policy in disposing of the public lands was seriously questioned.[61]

Two men whose names rank high in the list of Canadian colonizers were already making efforts to organize an imperial scheme of settlement that would take the place of the planlessness that left the peopling of the province to a haphazard immigration from Great Britain and the overflowing from the American states. Thomas Douglas, the Earl of Selkirk, had first considered the problem of emigration from the viewpoint of a Scottish landlord and his initial effort resulted in the establishing of eight hundred Highlanders upon Prince Edward Island in 1803. Plans for settlements near Oswego, near Lake St. Clair, and at Sault Ste. Marie failed to materialize as he had hoped. When an attempt to found a similar community in the Niagara peninsula could not overcome the opposition of some of the authorities of Upper Canada, Selkirk turned his attention to the far Northwest. A grant made to him by the Hudson's Bay Company opened for colonization a tract of land almost as large as Great Britain, and in each year from 1812 to 1815 Selkirk sent out groups of settlers (including soldiers from a Swiss regi-

152, 182. Michael Smith, *op. cit.*, 12. David William Smyth, *A Short Topographical Description of His Majesty's Province of Upper Canada in North America* (2d ed., London, 1813), 27, 31. H. H. Langton (ed.), *Travels . . . by Patrick Campbell*, 189. *Friends' Miscellany*, II (2d ed., Philadelphia, 1836), 69.

59. D'Arcy Boulton, *Sketch of Her Majesty's Province of Upper Canada* (London, 1805), 3, 5, 8, 13.

60. *P.A.C.R., 1892*, 202.

61. *Ibid.*, 38.

ment) to the valley of the Red River of the north.[62] For more than a half a century this community, clustered about Fort Garry, remained an outpost of empire that was of importance only to soldiers and traders, but in time it became a focal point that more and more directed the course of population movement as the sweep of continental migration rounded the Lakes and advanced toward the Northwest.

Of more immediate significance was the settlement venture of Colonel Thomas Talbot, a man who had been associated with Simcoe and, like him, admired the pioneering qualities of the Americans; but he was also anxious to turn the current of British emigration away from the United States to the provinces. For some time the naval and commercial interests in England had been concerned over the increasing difficulty of securing an adequate supply of hemp, and Talbot convinced the colonial authorities that Upper Canada was a place where, with proper encouragement, it might be produced in abundance. The encouragement was extended in the form of a grant of five thousand acres on the north shore of Lake Erie and the promise of more. Talbot started operations in 1803, but for several years his activity was limited to preparatory work and the people he introduced were laborers and mechanics. Actual settlement began in 1809 with an influx of farmers from Pennsylvania, New Jersey, New York, the Maritime Provinces, and England.[63] The influence of the project was, however, far wider than any catalogue of families would indicate. Upper Canada was advertised as a desirable place of residence by his agents throughout the eastern states, the mills that were constructed served all settlers, and Talbot Road, which was opened up along the shore of Lake Erie, long remained one of

62. Chester Martin, *Lord Selkirk's Work in Canada* (Oxford, 1916), 21–36. H. I. Cowan, "Selkirk's Work in Canada," *Canadian Historical Review,* IX, 299–308. A. S. Morton, "The Place of the Red River Settlement in the Plans of the Hudson's Bay Co., 1812–1825," *Canadian Historical Association Report for 1929* (Ottawa, 1930), 103–111. L. A. Mills, *Ceylon under British Rule* (London, 1933), 12, 13.

63. James H. Coyne, *op. cit.,* 38–40. Gilbert C. Patterson, "Land Settlement in Upper Canada, 1783–1840," *Sixteenth Report of the Department of Archives for the Province of Ontario, 1920* (Toronto, 1921), 188–190. *Reminiscences of Early Settlers* (St. Thomas, Ont., 1911), 86–87. N. Macdonald, "Hemp and Imperial Defence," *Canadian Historical Review,* XVII, 385–398.

the great highways through the province which were followed by pioneers in quest of lands.

The migration to the Canadas, instead of decreasing, gained in strength. From 1807 to 1809 the policy of the United States government swelled the number. Jefferson's embargo, in prohibiting the export of the American products of which Europe was in such urgent need, ceded to the British provinces the advantages that the Republic had formerly enjoyed. American commerce came to an immediate standstill. Sailors loitered about the empty docks; teamsters who had been busy hauling to the ports the products of the fields put up their wagons; and throughout the countryside enterprising farmers saw their barns and granaries choked with harvests for which there was no sale.[64]

The effects of the embargo were felt from the Atlantic to the Great Lakes. Nova Scotians in the fishing industry were faced by such a grand opportunity that the authorities considered the possibility of encouraging New England fishermen to move to the province.[65] The stagnation in agriculture, trade, and forest industries of the northern states was in gloomy contrast to the hopeful activity apparent along the St. Lawrence, on Lake Ontario, and in the forest clearings of Upper Canada. There was an immediate and unprecedented export demand in Montreal and Quebec for flour, lumber, and fish. Large quantities of these articles were smuggled over the border from the states and at the same time an impulse was given to their protection within the provinces. In 1816 the editor of the *Montreal Gazette*, looking back over the administrations of Jefferson and Madison, wrote: "If the two last Presidents are entitled to the honour of monuments, anywhere upon the globe, it surely is at Montreal."[66]

Settlement in Canada now became even more advantageous than it had been before and an extraordinary influx of able and proper-

64. John Lambert, *op. cit.*, II, 294.

65. *P.A.C.: C.O. 217/80 (N.S. A138)*, No. 146: Wentworth to Castlereagh, Feb. 3, 1806; *C.O. 217/84 (N.S. A142)*, No. 24: Provost to Castlereagh, Nov. 4, 1808; *C.O. 217/82 (N.S. A140)*, No. 185: Wentworth to Castlereagh, March 28, 1808.

66. H. A. Innis and A. R. M. Lower, *op. cit.*, 233. The quotation is found on page 235.

tied Americans crossed into a country where their efforts would not be stifled by governmental policy. From the embargo to the outbreak of the War of 1812 the trade of the United States with Europe was never normal. As a result land sales fell off at home while the emigration of Americans to Canada continued, and the volume would have been even greater had some of the Canadian officials not discouraged the solicitation of settlers on the other side of the line and had some proprietors not refused to receive Yankees upon their lands.[67]

Although no census or other official document records the extent of the immigration during the twenty years preceding 1812, the writer of an authorized gazetteer of the province estimated that in that year eight out of every ten persons in Upper Canada were of American birth or of American descent. One fourth of that number were the Loyalists and their children, but these firstcomers were concentrated on the north shore of Lake Ontario and in the Niagara peninsula. The townships recently settled along Lake Erie and in the upper valley of the Thames River were peopled almost entirely by pioneers from Pennsylvania, New Jersey, and New York.[68] Since there had been originally less than six thousand Loyalists in the region and the population was now about one hundred thousand, the province seemed more American than British to its anxious officials and military leaders.[69] When war began many observers on both sides of the line believed that the inevitable result of the conflict would be to make Canada wholly American.

67. James H. Coyne, *op. cit.*, 41. David Anderson, *Canada: Or, a View of the Importance of the British Colonies* (London, 1814), 47, 49, 99. R. W. Bingham (ed.), *Reports of Joseph Ellicott*, I, 394.

68. Michael Smith, *op. cit.*, 51. The townships settled from the United States are listed in Michael Smith, *Geographical View of the Province of Upper Canada and Promiscuous Remarks on the Government* (New York, 1813), 9–17.

69. For the Loyalists, see A. L. Burt, *op. cit.*, 362–363. For the population of Upper Canada, 1806, 1811, 1814, see *Seventh Census of Canada, 1931*, I (Ottawa, 1936), 146–7.

CHAPTER V

PIONEERS AND IMMIGRANTS
1812–1837

THE outbreak of war between Great Britain and the United States in June, 1812, resulted in innumerable complications in the everyday life of the thousands of Americans settled in Canada. Their presence created a problem which at first caused the colonial authorities as much concern as the exposed military position in which both Upper and Lower Canada were placed. The two circumstances were, in fact, closely related. Many of the belligerent "War Hawks" in Congress had openly expressed the belief that the conquest of the provinces would be the first achievement of American arms, and even after what proved to be an inglorious campaign had begun, former President Jefferson wrote to a correspondent: "The acquisition of Canada this year, as far as the neighborhood of Quebec, will be a mere matter of marching."[1] These patriotic hopes were brightened by the belief that Canadian settlers of American birth and descent would rise in revolt and welcome the invading armies as liberators.[2]

The events of the three years that followed were a happy surprise to the governors of the two provinces. Disloyalty was evident, but it never became organized as an effective threat. Faulty American strategy, the blundering of the American commanders, the vigilance of the British military leaders and the colonial officials, and the apathy of the settlers who were located at the most strategic points were responsible for the unexpected American failure to conquer the Canadas.

The apathy was most noticeable in the lower province. Had American strategy organized a campaign toward the St. Lawrence to seize Quebec or Montreal and thus cut off the British forces operating in the west, the coöperation of the Americans living in the Eastern Townships and in Huntingdon County would have been an

1. H. A. Washington (ed.), *The Writings of Thomas Jefferson*, VI (New York, 1854), 75, 76: Jefferson to Colonel Duane, Monticello, Aug. 4, 1812.
2. William Dunlop, *Recollections of the War of 1812* (Toronto, 1905), 19.

essential factor in any resulting success. Such a campaign was not organized. In the matter of land operations, as in the agitation for aggressive action, the war was primarily a western affair. Neither the political leaders nor the people of the New England states and New York were eager for any northern conquests and their half-hearted response to the calls for militia to serve in the Federal forces is a well-known chapter in the political history of the United States.[3]

In Nova Scotia, Lieutenant-Governor Sherbrooke on July 3, 1812, issued a proclamation ordering the inhabitants of his province not to molest or disturb those Americans who were fishing if they offered no sign of hostility. His final words—"It is therefore my wish and desire, that the Subjects of the United States, living on the Frontiers may pursue in peace their usual and accustomed Trade and occupations, without Molestation"—indicate the lack of animosity on the coastal borders of the two countries. One week later Lieutenant-Governor Smyth of New Brunswick issued an almost identical statement.[4]

Governor Prevost of Lower Canada, however, unaware of the actual state of public sentiment, issued a proclamation on July 9, 1812, ordering all Americans who would not take an oath of allegiance to leave the country within fourteen days.[5] This alternative offered a painful choice to the majority of settlers. Some departed, some took the oath, and others did neither. The last class suffered no molestation because of their disobedience. The governor had intended none. Along with the proclamation he had sent to the commissioners authorized to administer the oath secret instructions directing them to insist upon a declaration of allegiance only in the case of those whom they suspected of disloyalty or treasonable intentions.[6]

After the first excitement attendant upon the beginning of hos-

3. Henry Adams, *History of the United States of America during the Administration of James Madison,* VIII (New York, 1930), 212–238.

4. W. Wood (ed.), *Select British Documents of the Canadian War of 1812,* I (Toronto, 1920), 204, 205. *P.A.C.: C.O. 188/18 (N.B. A21)*: Proclamation of G. S. Smyth, July 10, 1812.

5. *P.A.C.R., 1921,* Appendix B: Proclamations of the Governor of Lower Canada, 1792–1815, 158.

6. Robert Sellar, *The History of the County of Huntingdon and of the Seigniories of Chateauguay and Beauharnois,* 26, 61–63.

tilities, the border communities of Lower Canada and of New England and New York settled down to a routine of life which they described as one of "neutrality." In the panic days of the summer of 1812, many had abandoned their farms and carried off their property, but in time they drifted back to the homes they had cleared and, far from the scene of war, carried on the normal social and business intercourse which had hitherto disregarded the international boundary.[7] Even the military expedition of Governor Prevost, which in the late summer of 1814 advanced along the Richelieu River until it was checked and turned back at the Battle of Plattsburg on Lake Champlain, did not disturb the settlements that were remote from the river. After the war refugee Americans came back and met little hindrance except on one of the proprietorships in Huntingdon County where the agent of the estate burned the cabins, tore up bridges, and obstructed the roads to prevent the return of the deserters. But his actions, the local historian explains, were not the result of patriotic feeling; his motive was to keep rightful claimants out in order that he might appropriate the lands and improvements for his own personal use.[8]

In Upper Canada the prewar population was more mixed, and anti-American feeling had been becoming more bitter with each year. The American settlements were not like those in Lower Canada, international communities that straddled an artificial boundary; they were located in the interior and were often remote from the frontier. A self-imposed neutrality was out of the question. With news of the declaration of war there arose a general desire on the part of Americans to retire to the land of their birth, many of them, undoubtedly, in the belief that they would return with the victorious army from the south. Although the authorities found the presence of these aliens a perplexing problem, they were not ready to permit an exodus of those who would take to the enemy's army information of the greatest military value or return as guides in the ranks of invaders.

In fact, the authorities were caught in a medley of conflicting motives. They did not want to lose the substantial American settlers

7. B. F. Hubbard, *Forests and Clearings: The History of Stanstead County, Province of Quebec* (Montreal, 1874), 5, 30. Abby Maria Hemenway, *The Vermont Historical Gazetteer*, III, 32.

8. Robert Sellar, *op. cit.*, 131.

and hoped that their stake in the country would induce them to be at least benevolently neutral. On the other hand, they could not openly countenance wholesale retention of avowed Americans, or risk their concerted hostile action. Men without property were better out of the province, it was felt, as were the clergy and other potential molders of public opinion. The plan adopted, therefore, in the proclamation of November 9, 1812, by General Roger H. Sheaffe was to require every person in Upper Canada who claimed exemption from military service because of American citizenship to report to a board in his district.[9] Here a certain amount of discretion was exercised in granting passports to those who proved their status and either wanted to leave or were thought better away. Guards were placed at the principal points of exit to regulate the movement. Naturally enough, some desirable settlers either had their lands confiscated or abandoned them. Some of these returned to their former homes in the United States, but others found the Western Reserve to the south of Lake Erie an attractive destination for able North American pioneers. At the same time, the war produced something of a converse movement, for a number of French- and English-speaking Canadians found it advisable or congenial to return to the shelter of the British flag.[10]

In the meantime all Americans in the province had awaited with interest the action of the army under General Hull that had gathered at Detroit. But the proclamation that Hull issued after crossing the river, in which he advised all the inhabitants to remain at home and threatened that there would be no quarter in case any of them

9. Michael Smith, *A Complete History of the Late American War with Great Britain and Her Allies* (Lexington, Ky., 1816), 34. *P.A.C.: C688B;* Proclamation of R. H. Sheaffe, Nov. 9, 1812; *C688B;* Instructions . . . to the President of the Board Appointed at Niagara . . .; *C688B;* Report of the Board at Kingston, Dec. 13, 1812.

10. W. W. Williams, *History of the Firelands, Comprising Huron and Erie Counties, Ohio* (Cleveland, 1879), 456, 506. *History of Sandusky County, Ohio* (Cleveland, 1882), 590, 704, 705. Thad W. H. Leavitt, *History of Leeds and Grenville, Ontario, from 1749 to 1879*, 83. *History of Ashtabula County, Ohio*, 238. The difficulties experienced by an American family settled in the province are described in "A Narrative of the Sufferings in and Journey from Upper Canada to Virginia and Kentucky, of M. Smith, Minister of the Gospel" in Michael Smith, *A Complete History*, 229–287.

were found fighting along with the Indian allies of Great Britain, alienated many.[11] The rout of the army after it had advanced a few miles into the province and its subsequent capture together with the post of Detroit in August, 1812, put an end to all immediate concern on the part of the officials. A year later when an invading army again appeared upon Canadian soil, the Americans who remained had become committed to the cause of the country in which they lived and their attitude was no longer a questionable factor.[12]

But the experiences of the war and fears arising from it were bound to influence subsequent policy with regard to a matter which was fundamental in determining the course of immigration—the disposition of land. That less encouragement would be held out to Americans in the future was evident from a law adopted in March, 1814, which decreed that the lands of all settlers who had come from the United States and had returned there without the prescribed passport would be forfeited.[13] No encouragement was to be held out to induce the deserters to come back. But that their nationality as well as the act of desertion was a factor was indicated in January, 1815, when Lord Bathurst, the Secretary for the Colonies, directed Governor Drummond of the province to refuse any grants of land to persons of American nationality and to prevent their coming in so far as possible.[14]

This regulation dammed up the stream that had hitherto brought into Upper Canada most of its incoming settlers, and lowered the price of land because there were fewer purchasers. "This was the deadliest thrust ever made by folly at the prosperity and welfare of Upper Canada" was the opinion expressed a few years later.[15] It

11. Hull's proclamation of July 12, 1812, may be found in *Niles Weekly Register* (Baltimore), II, Aug. 1, 1812, 357, 358.

12. Michael Smith, *A Complete History*, 38, 45. The disappointment of the pro-American element in Upper Canada over the outcome of Hull's surrender is described in Donald M'Leod, *A Brief Review of the Settlement of Upper Canada* (Cleveland, 1841), 40–46.

13. *Collection of the Acts Passed in the Parliament of Great Britain Particularly Applying to the Province of Upper Canada* (York, 1818), 317, 318 (54 Geo. III, c. 9).

14. The letter of Lord Bathurst is printed in William Wood (ed.), *Select British Documents of the Canadian War of 1812*, III, 507–509.

15. Robert Gourlay, *Statistical Account of Upper Canada*, II, 421.

provoked a discontent which reached such a point in 1817 that a series of resolutions was brought forward in the Assembly to censure the government's policy in this respect, and these proceedings were halted only by the prorogation of the legislative body after the first two resolutions had been adopted by the House.[16] The dissatisfaction grew from realization of the fact that many of the citizens of the Republic were ready to join their friends who had gone to Canada before the war just as soon as peace was reëstablished, and that presumably the momentous westward movement that agitated New England and western New York in the years after 1815 would have swept many land seekers around the north shore of Lake Erie. Some did come. An official report referred to their arrival as a "rush," but no other contemporary evidence indicates that the movement was one of any considerable proportions.[17]

In addition to the hostile official reception that awaited him, the prospective settler from the Republic faced an uncertain status with regard to the possession of landed property. The laws governing naturalization in the British colonies dated back to the reign of George II (13 Geo. II, c. 7). This ancient legislation decreed that an alien was obliged to live seven years in a province before he would be entitled to hold land. On the other hand, by an imperial statute passed after the Revolution and by Simcoe's proclamation in 1792 the only qualifications for holding land and for general admission to the rights of British subjects were those of taking an oath of allegiance to the Crown and declaring the intention of residing permanently in the province.[18] Thus the strict regulation of naturalization had been generally neglected, but when the hostilities were over it was deemed desirable that the old law be enforced and an order issued by the Colonial Office in November, 1817, directed the authorities of Upper Canada to dispossess persons holding lands illegally. But who was in illegal possession? Were people aliens who had been born before 1783 in the colonies that later became the United States and who had lived in the States thereafter for some years

16. *P.A.C.: G186,* Bagot to Stanley, No. 76, April 9, 1842.
17. *P.A.C.R., 1896,* "State Papers of Upper Canada: Calendar," 20.
18. 30 Geo. III, c. 27. For a succinct account of the alien question, consult Aileen Dunham, *Political Unrest in Upper Canada, 1815–1836* (London, 1927), 67–78.

before settling in the British dominions? If they were not aliens were their children, born after 1783, aliens? These questions, if raised before, had received no judicial decision. Now it was desirable that settlers already established and those who proposed to come should know what their position was. The Executive Council, accordingly, referred the problem to the law officers of the Crown and all concerned could do nothing but patiently await a decision.[19]

In the meantime any American who was content to endure a possible seven-year wait for the confirmation of his title was able to secure a temporary grant of land. In the spring of 1817 the strict prohibition of two years earlier was modified by a circular which prescribed an oath of allegiance to be administered by appointed commissioners to settlers from the United States who had been specially designated as eligible by the lieutenant-governor. This put the control of immigration entirely in the hands of an official who could be guided by his own ideas as to the class of people who should be encouraged to enter the province.[20]

The instructions of 1815 and the slight modification they received in 1817 should not be judged as an ill-considered act of pique directed against persons who had been lately alien enemies. For the first time in the history of British Canada, the colonial authorities had adopted a positive policy of settlement: Americans were to be discouraged from entering, but the coming of trusted British subjects was to be fostered and, if necessary, subsidized. No longer was a vital frontier of the empire to be endangered by the uncertain loyalty of its people.[21]

The return to Great Britain of troops from Canada in the spring of 1815 made possible a generous offer. The transports that normally would go out from England empty could be put to service in the carrying of settlers; here would be an opportunity of removing to the New World with little expense some of those families in the distressed regions of Great Britain who for a decade or more had been petitioning for assistance in crossing the Atlantic. Moreover,

19. Arthur G. Doughty and Norah Story (eds.), *Documents Relating to the Constitutional History of Canada, 1819–1828* (Ottawa, 1935), 1–9.

20. Robert Gourlay, *op. cit.,* II, 426, 439, 440.

21. A. R. M. Lower, "Immigration and Settlement in Canada, 1812–1820," *Canadian Historical Review,* III, 37–47.

they would go to strengthen a British colony instead of the United States. Scottish people were considered more tractable than Irish and therefore more desirable as subjects for experimentation. In February, 1815, announcement was made in the Edinburgh newspapers of the liberal terms to be offered: transportation, free grants of a hundred acres, rations for eight months, tools at less than cost. In return, the prospective settler was obliged to present evidence of good character and (what was more difficult and sometimes impossible) deposit eighteen pounds as security that he would stay by the venture—this amount to be returned to him in two years.

No one accounted the experiment a success. The escape of Napoleon from Elba and the Waterloo campaign, the unwillingness of the Admiralty to coöperate in providing transports at the proper time, the late arrival in the colony with the subsequent wintering in government barracks, and delay in surveying the allotted district resulted in uncertainty and grumbling. A year after sailing from Scotland the settlers finally reached their lands and then began to experience all the hardships and discouragements of pioneering. Complaints from the colony regarding administration, and from the Treasury regarding expense, led to an abandonment of all thoughts of continuing the scheme, and in 1816 and 1817 discharged soldiers alone were offered transportation and the customary grant. Civilian emigrants received nothing but land.[22] A modified scheme in 1818 provided that any person of capital who would guarantee to take out ten individuals or more would be rewarded by the grant of a hundred acres for each and that space would be allotted on government vessels. The support of the emigrants on board ship and during the period of settlement would be borne by the enterpriser. Only three groups were located in Canada under this plan, and in 1819 and after it was applied only in the case of British emigrants proceeding to the Cape of Good Hope.[23]

The greatest obstacle to the success of Canadian colonization was recognized by everyone. It lay in the popular preference for the

22. Helen I. Cowan, *British Emigration to British North America, 1783–1837* (Toronto, 1928), 66–74. *P.A.C.: G7,* Bathurst to Drummond, June 13, July 12, 1815.

23. Helen I. Cowan, *British Emigration,* 74–82.

United States that prevailed among those who were directly interested in emigration. With the return of peace and the onset of profound economic depression in Great Britain, the methods that had already launched tens of thousands of immigrants into the Republic were restored. Ship captains began to circularize the rural districts in the vicinity of the British ports. Redemptioner agents enrolled penniless young men for service in the prospering states of America. Landowners sought out yeomen farmers and persuaded them that their modest capital invested in America would yield a fortune for their children. As a result, from 1816 to 1819 a postwar exodus brought into the United States upwards of 150,000 Europeans, a migration the parallel of which had never before been witnessed.[24]

Those among them who were favored with capital, skill, and good fortune discovered the future that they sought. But that was not the lot of all. Many did not possess the resources or courage to proceed beyond the ports where they landed. New York and Philadelphia, in particular, became congested with unemployed artisans and laborers and farmers who could not find a suitable job or location. Even during 1817 and 1818 when every evidence of prosperity was apparent in the country at large, distress and suffering were a problem for private charity; and in 1819 when the boom times collapsed, it proved impossible to satisfy hunger and provide shelter for all in need.[25]

The continental European immigrants of the time had been of a substantial class who could provide for themselves. The majority of the recent arrivals who suffered most from the emergency were persons who still owed allegiance to King George, and they visited and

24. No official statistics of immigration were kept until September 1, 1819. The total of 150,000 is derived from estimates made by Hezekiah Niles. *Niles Weekly Register*, IX, Oct. 19, 1816; XIII, Sept. 13, 27, 1817; XVII, Sept. 18, 1819.

25. John Bristed, *America and Her Resources* (London, 1818), 440. *The Second Annual Report of the Managers of the Society for the Prevention of Pauperism in the City of New York* (New York, 1820), 18, 20, 24. William T. Harris, *Remarks Made during a Tour through the United States of America in the Years 1817, 1818 and 1819* (London, 1821), 29, 35, 77. J. Knight, *Important Extracts from Original and Recent Letters,* Second Series (Manchester, 1818), 21, 34, 40.

sometimes stormed the British consulate begging for assistance or passage back to the country of their birth.[26] The consul at New York was James Buchanan, brother of A. C. Buchanan, the British emigrant agent at Quebec. The two were in accord as to what should be done. Let the distress be an object lesson to those who contemplated leaving the protection of the British government and let that government show its paternalism by forwarding the stranded expatriates to the colonies where they should have gone in the first place. As early as December, 1816, Consul Buchanan had been authorized to incur an expense not exceeding ten dollars per person in forwarding British subjects who wanted to proceed from New York to the colonies to the north.[27] During the first year more than 1,600 were sent to Kingston and York and by 1819 the number totaled over 3,500.[28] But when the real depression began, the authorization was revoked by the officials who undoubtedly feared that a great expenditure would be incurred not only for transportation but also for the support of the destitute people when once they reached the provinces.[29] An offer was made by the government of free land to British citizens in England and the United States, but the added prudent note that a certain amount of capital was necessary served to make the offer of no particular value to those most in need.[30] Thus left to themselves, the immigrants were obliged to shape their own course. Some found the means of returning to the country from which they had so hopefully departed; others, with the aid of charity, found a place in the economic structure of the community in which they were located; and others struck out to wander over the countryside until some chance opportunity provided employment and a home.

The disfavor into which the United States now fell and the increased demand for assistance in emigration that was expressed in

26. *P.R.O.: F.O. 5/144:* Letters of William Dawson, Baltimore, June 1, Sept. 1, 1819; letter of George Manners, Boston, Feb. 4, 1819; letter of Gilbert Robertson, Philadelphia, July 1, 1819.

27. *P.R.O.: F.O. 5/116:* Letter of Foreign Office to Buchanan, Dec. 4, 1816.

28. *P.R.O.: F.O. 5/125:* Letter of Buchanan, New York, Nov. 5, 1817. Helen I. Cowan, *British Emigration,* 125.

29. William F. Adams, *Ireland and Irish Emigration to the New World from 1815 to the Famine* (New Haven, 1932), 265, 266.

30. *P.A.C.: G414,* Richmond to Bagot, Feb. 13, 1819.

the petitions that flooded the Colonial Office persuaded the authorities to venture into some new schemes of directed emigration.[31] Many emigration societies had been formed among the distressed weavers of Scotland and in negotiations with the Colonial Office it was agreed that land and equipment would be provided for them upon arrival in Canada, but that the expense of passage had to be borne by the individuals or jointly by the society, and the settlers were pledged to reimburse the government for some of the expenditures. Several hundred families were established in the colony under these regulations.[32] In 1823 and again in 1825 the British government, thinking not so much of finding people for the provinces as of relieving the congested rural system of Ireland out of which, it was believed, most of the agrarian disorders of the time arose, sent out several shiploads of Irishmen and planted them in colonies north of Lake Erie.[33]

Had all these Scottish and Irish arrivals remained where official bounty placed them, they would have had only a distant connection with a discussion of Canadian-American population relations. But rumors were frequent that many of the emigrants sold the supplies and equipment that they had received and slipped off to the United States. Naturally the public officials were emphatic in their declarations that only a few, and those the least desirable, had decamped.[34] It is certain, nevertheless, that a number left the settlements and took employment upon the public works in Canada, and of these it is likely that a large proportion were finally drawn over the line by the higher wages paid to laborers upon the canals and roads in the States.[35] Others who had relatives located in the Republic were persuaded to join them, and it was generally believed that so long as the government demanded reimbursement for the supplies and equipment that had been advanced to emigrants, the temptation to escape

31. Scores of petitions sent to the Colonial Office are filed in *P.R.O.: C.O.* *384/6, 384/7.*

32. Helen I. Cowan, *British Emigration,* 84–95.

33. William F. Adams, *op. cit.,* 146, 147, 275–283.

34. T. C. Hansard, *The Parliamentary Debates,* N.S., XII, 1358–1361 (April 15, 1825); XVI, 475–513 (Feb. 15, 1827).

35. *United Kingdom, Parliamentary Papers, 1826,* IV, "Report from the Select Committee on Emigration from the United Kingdom," 18.

the obligation of repayment would persuade many to follow the same route.[36]

The uncertainty that surrounds this point is only a reflection of the greater uncertainty that must prevail in any attempt to measure the flow of population across the boundary line, toward the north as well as toward the south. In the years immediately following the panic of 1819, although there was a great deal of rather aimless drifting about on the part of unemployed workers, the strong current of westward migration which had in itself been one of the most influential of the factors leading to the speculation of the times was in abeyance. Eastern farmers could not sell their lands and western banks could extend them no credit. So the prospective "movers" remained where they were.[37] Every spring the frontier communities eagerly awaited the "immigration season" in the hope that the renewal of settlement would put life into stagnant business, but it was not until 1825–1826 that a decided and persistent movement again got under way.[38]

But during the preceding years there had been a considerable and necessary readjustment in population distribution. Friends and families were reunited and every crossroads village in the new country received its complement of useful artisans. Any person who did possess ready funds could buy up a partially improved farm at an attractive price and in so doing he brought to the West a little of that capital which the new territory needed.[39] This readjustment, like the other population movements, ignored the boundary that the governments had drawn. New Englanders continued to cross over into the Eastern Townships and take up the sites that remained uncleared.[40] Some Americans persuaded the officials of Upper Canada

36. *The Quebec Mercury*, Jan. 10, Aug. 26, 1826.

37. *Detroit Gazette*, April 28, 1820; Nov. 16, 1821.

38. *Ibid.*, May 10, June 7, 14, 1822; Feb. 28, May 23, Oct. 3, 1823; March 26, 1824; April 26, May 10, 24, June 28, Sept. 13, 1825; Jan. 3, May 23, June 20, 1826.

39. John Pearson, *Notes Made during a Journey in 1821 in the United States of America* (London, 1822), 9, 19, 30, 49. [? Capt. Blaney], *An Excursion through the United States and Canada during the Years 1822–23 by an English Gentleman* (London, 1824), 434.

40. C. Thomas, *Contributions to the History of the Eastern Townships*, 249, 326, 368.

that they could be safely accepted as settlers and to such grants were made. Others bought lands from earlier private holders. The complaints regarding the "swarms of mechanics and laborers" from the United States who overran the country indicate that ambitious North American artisans were paying little attention to political allegiance when in search of a job.[41] Another group, the ubiquitous Yankee schoolmasters and the popular circuit preachers from the United States, aroused fear as well as dislike among the officials of the Canadas because they might easily instill "republican" principles.

When the westward tide was resumed about 1825–1826, conditions on both sides of the line determined that the western states rather than Upper Canada, which was still far from settled, should be the popular destination. The provincial authorities were slow in making up their minds as to what attitude should be followed with regard to American settlers. Under instructions from the Colonial Office, the legislation of George II's reign, demanding seven years of residence and sundry oaths and declarations before naturalization, was still in force, but the natural inclination of American settlers to elect their own kind to the Provincial Assembly provoked a crisis in 1821.[42] There ensued six or seven years of the greatest confusion, not only because the Loyalists were anxious to circumscribe the political rights of Americans whose citizenship was open to question, but because the authorities involved in the matter were the British courts and legislature as well as the Upper Canadian, and final authority resided with the former.

Disregarding the long and confusing sequence of court decisions, Assembly resolutions, rival colonial representations in London, and inappropriate legislation,[43] the rather unsatisfactory outcome can be

41. Isaac Fidler, *Observations on Professions, Literature, Manners and Emigration in the United States and Canada* (New York, 1832), 124, 183, 194. Robert Gourlay, *op. cit.,* I, 425. *P.A.C.: Q410,* Part II, Arthur to Glenelg, No. 111, Dec. 18, 1835; *Q410,* Part II, Bishop of Montreal to Arthur, Nov. 20, 1838; *G42,* Horton to Maitland, Oct. 7, 1826.

42. The case of the Bidwells, father and son; see A. Dunham, *op. cit.,* 69–71.

43. The principal documents in this matter may be found in Doughty and Story, *op. cit.,* and a narrative in A. Dunham, *op. cit.,* 68–78. A typical pamphlet concerning the American cause is *An Abridged View of the Alien Question Unmasked by the Editor of the Canadian Freeman* (York, 1826).

summarily indicated.[44] In 1826, the British Parliament passed an act (7 Geo. IV, c. 68) to the effect that all persons naturalized by act of the legislature of Upper Canada should be deemed capable of sitting in the Assembly, voting, and being members of the council. At the same time, the Upper Canadian Assembly was instructed to legislate for the immediate naturalization of those Americans who had seven years of residence and naturalization was authorized for the others when their seven years were complete. This was done in an unsatisfactory way early in 1827, but this act was disallowed and a new one was passed early in 1828 which was much more pleasing to resident Americans. It declared that all persons who had received grants of land from the government, or who had held any public office, or who had taken the oath of allegiance and had been settled in the province before 1820, should be admitted to the privileges of British birth, while others should receive similar privileges on the completion of seven years of residence. It did not, however, provide for future arrivals, who could, therefore, be naturalized only by special acts of the provincial or the British legislature. It is a tribute to the irresistible trends of North American migration that Americans continued to pour into a province where the law was hostile and where some of them could normally acquire lands only by private purchase.

The long-protracted discussion brought out many proposals unfavorable to American settlers and raised many doubts as to what their fate might be. Particularly in 1827, when the nature of the oath that a naturalized alien would take was under consideration, many disquieting rumors were afloat. It was generally believed that an oath entirely different from any that had preceded would be demanded, one in which the taker not merely recognized the authority of King and Parliament as before but swore perpetual allegiance to the Crown. The inference that Canadians of non-Loyalist American origin who had for years not thought of themselves as Americans were somehow a "lesser breed" who needed to take special oaths to become respectable citizens was so offensive to some that, according

44. A retrospective and full discussion of the alien problem is to be found in *P.A.C.: G186*, Bagot to Stanley, No. 76, April 9, 1842.

to contemporary accounts, they preferred to return to the United States.[45]

There is no evidence that any extensive departure of patriotic Americans took place as a result of this legislation. Yet among potential immigrants from the United States it could be considered only as a victory for the anti-American element[46] and, accordingly, it added another to the circumstances that tended to keep the New Englanders and New Yorkers who were seeking new homes on their own side of the line, thereby diminishing what might have been a larger movement to Canada.

These circumstances were related to the new conditions that attended the settlement of the West. The completion of the Erie Canal in 1825 had opened up an "all-American" water route from the interior to the Atlantic, and now residence in Canada, which had meant preferential treatment in the use of the St. Lawrence, ceased to possess one of its strongest advantages. As a natural response to the creation of this new outlet to the sea, a great stimulus was given to commerce upon Lake Erie. Steamboats and sailing vessels multiplied in numbers, and emigration to the West, which had once meant long and wearisome journeys upon rough roads and down winding rivers, was shortened and made more comfortable.[47] All the new states and territories, eager to become part of the great network of commerce, entered upon ambitious schemes of development, thereby offering employment for laborers and promising openings for investment. In this new chapter in the expansion of settlement, to set out for Indiana, Michigan, or Illinois was as logical as twenty-five years before it had been to take the road to Ohio or the Canadas.

Although the destination of most westward-moving Americans was American territory, some found it more convenient to reach their new homes by passing through Upper Canada. Because of the impassable condition of the swamps of northwestern Ohio, pioneers bound for Michigan were obliged to use the Canadian roads if they

45. *Detroit Gazette*, May 1, 22, 1827.

46. *P.A.C.: G69*, Goderich to Colborne, Jan. 10, 1832, indicates the official attitude toward the entrance of Americans.

47. Emay R. Johnson, *History of Domestic and Foreign Commerce of the United States*, I (Washington, 1915), 221, 230.

traveled during the winter season when traffic on Lake Erie was suspended, and so steady was the traffic that as early as 1828 a stage line connecting the Niagara River with Detroit was organized which brought passengers through in four days. Even after communications on the American side had been improved, emigrants from New England bound for Michigan continued to follow the shorter foreign route.[48]

Within the British provinces, as in the United States, consolidation of population was accompanied by growth of a sense of political identity. Each country was now provided with a vigorous stock of pioneers which in time (although it might be only in the course of several generations) would occupy the vacant lands within its bounds. The process was actively under way. In Nova Scotia and New Brunswick the families established beside the coast and along the rivers were sending their sons into the interior to found new homes.[49] The children of the Eastern Township Yankees were moving down the rivers flowing toward the St. Lawrence to meet the waves of French Canadians coming up from the seigniories.[50] In Upper Canada the patches of settlement between the Ottawa River and Lake Ontario were growing together and in the western part of the province settlers were taking possession of the vacant spaces on either side of the government roads and pioneers were beginning to advance into the Huron tract and adjacent regions to the north.[51] In the colonization of their domains neither the United States nor British North America was obliged to call in helpers from the territory of the other.

Had the westward movement been the only feature characterizing

48. *Detroit Gazette,* Jan. 30, May 22, 1818; Feb. 28, 1823; March 5, 1824; April 28, 1828. "From Vermont to Vermontville," *Burton Historical Collection Leaflet* (Detroit, 1923), 61–76. *St. Lawrence Republican and General Advertiser* (Ogdensburg, N.Y.), May 7, Sept. 24, 1833; April 15, 29, 1834.

49. William F. Ganong, "A Monograph on the Origins of Settlements in the Province of New Brunswick," *R.S.C., 1904,* Sec. ii, 84–88.

50. Georges Vattier, *Esquisse historique de la colonisation de la Province de Québec,* 42.

51. C. Schott, *Landnahme und Kolonisation in Canada am Beispiel Sudontarios* (Kiel, 1936), 136, 137.

the population history of North America at the time, the relations between the two peoples might be dismissed with the generalization that for the present they had ceased to be interdependent. But the native North Americans who were filling up the back country were not the only pioneers of the decade between 1827 and 1837. The same forces of expansion and opportunity that summoned them into the interior drew Europeans across the Atlantic and the immigration of the period was as international in its nature as the course of internal migration had ever been.

The emigrant ships of the 1830's, although they left no ruts in their wake, followed routes almost as distinct as those cut a decade later by the prairie schooners on the plains. In both cases commercial considerations had as much or more to do with determining routes and destinations as the wishes of, and opportunities open to, intending emigrants. There was an imperative interplay between human freights and other cargoes. In this sense, Canadian commerce influenced the character of the immigration that reached the United States and in many cases affected its distribution; and, to a lesser degree, the commerce of the city of New York left an imprint upon the human influx into Canada.

The northern part of the continent produced only one staple commodity of which Great Britain stood in constant need. The navy and the mercantile marine, the factories and the building industry of the kingdom gradually came to rely upon the timber of the northern provinces, and New Brunswick was the first of the colonies to profit from the growing market. Every spring a fleet of timber vessels set out from the ports of Great Britain to bring back the winter's cut, and these vessels, which otherwise would have gone out empty or almost empty, offered convenient and cheap accommodation to passengers who would feed and care for themselves on the voyages.[52] For a few days after arrival at Miramichi, St. John, and the many timber landings on the St. Croix, the immigrants enjoyed remunerative employment in loading the ships with lumber and deals (softwood boards of special British specifications), but after the fleet had sailed

52. Andrew Picken, *The Canadas*, 25. *The Advantages of Emigrating to the British Colonies of New Brunswick, Nova Scotia, etc. by a Resident of St. John's, New Brunswick* (London, 1832), 32–34, 43.

prospects darkened.[53] None had the skills required to go into the forest and become axmen; few had the courage to undertake agriculture on the stump farms of the province. Of other employment there was little to be found. There was no alternative but to pass on and here, again, commerce had prepared the way.

A lively coasting trade had grown up between the ports on the Bay of Fundy, the islands in Passamaquoddy Bay, and the eastern cities of the United States as far south as Baltimore. As a whole, the fishing stations and lumber camps of the north could not be adequately supplied by the farms of New Brunswick and Nova Scotia, and a fleet of hundreds of small sailing craft was employed in bringing wheat and corn from American farms to this market. On the return trips they carried fish, grindstones, and gypsum in the hold and immigrants on deck, the latter paying only a dollar or two for passage.[54] Until the 1840's, when the export trade in New Brunswick lumber declined, this route was recognized as providing the cheapest method by which the poor of the British Isles might reach the United States and it was followed, in particular, by the first immigrant invaders of New England who gave to the cities and industrial villages of the section their Irish cast.[55]

Timber became a staple export from the St. Lawrence also. In June and July of each year the harbor of Quebec was full of vessels and the streets of the city were crowded with new arrivals. Some tem-

53. *The Nautical Magazine*, II (London, 1833), 136. *The Quebec Mercury*, March 15, 1831.

54. *P.R.O.: F.O. 5/228:* Letter of Gilbert Robertson, Philadelphia, May 4, 1827; *F.O. 5/274:* Letter of James Buchanan, New York, Jan. 2, 1832; letter of Gilbert Robertson, Philadelphia, Dec. 31, 1822; *F.O. 5/304:* Letter of J. Sherwood, Portland, Jan. 5, 1835. *Dublin Morning Post*, Aug. 1, 1821: Letter from Halifax on the trade of the Maritime Provinces. *Eastport Sentinel and Passamaquoddy Advertiser*, June 15, 20, 1822; June 20, 1832. *Eastern Democrat* (Eastport, Me.), June 8, 15, 1832. G. S. Graham, "The Gypsum Trade of the Maritime Provinces," *Agricultural History*, XII (Washington, 1938), 209–223.

55. *P.R.O.: F.O. 5/285:* Letter of George Manners, Boston, Jan. 4, 1833; *F.O. 5/324:* Letter of J. Sherwood, Portland, Dec. 31, 1838; *C.O. 384/35:* Letter of Lieutenant Friend, emigrant agent at Cork, June 30, 1834. A. C. Buchanan, *Emigration Practically Considered* (London, 1828), 59, 60. *The Emigrant's Guide; Containing Practical and Authentic Information* (Westport, 1832), 96.

porary labor was available about the docks, but during the summer all but the very poorest and those who were ill continued up the river, passed along the Lakes, and were absorbed by the many enterprises that in the latter part of the decade of the 1820's gave to the business of the country a hitherto unknown activity.[56] In its early attempts to further the settlement of Upper Canada, the Colonial Office had struggled with the problem of providing the capital which in a new community was essential if the penniless immigrants were to get established. That problem it did not solve, as the failure of its earlier schemes indicates. But a new era in the life of the colony began in 1826 when the Canada Company was chartered. To this corporation were ceded the area east of Lake Huron known as the Huron tract and scattered holdings elsewhere; British capitalists put up funds for what was considered a promising investment; and in the years between 1827 and 1832 several thousand settlers were aided in transportation, in getting established upon the lands, and in learning the art of pioneering.[57] The organization was favored with vigorous leadership. Roads were opened, stores were established, and the new district was brought to the attention of the world. Although the investors did not gain the profits for which they had hoped, the company stimulated neighboring communities and the government to engage in similar undertakings. During the first years of the decade of the 'thirties every able-bodied arrival in the colony was assured of employment.[58]

As a result, much of the prejudice that the emigrating classes of

56. *The Quebec Mercury,* July 25, 1826; May 20, 1828; March 17, 1829; Feb. 20, May 18, June 12, 1830; April 30, May 12, 1831. *P.A.C.: M173, Evidence of A. C. Buchanan, Dec., 1828; Minutes of Evidence Taken . . . Jan. 1832, Evidence of A. C. Buchanan.*

57. A map showing the possessions of the Canada Company appears in Oscar D. Skelton, *The Life and Times of Sir Alexander Tilloch Galt* (Toronto, 1920), 16. For the company's activities see C. Schott, *op. cit.,* R. K. Gordon, *John Galt* (Toronto, 1920); J. W. Aberdeen, *John Galt* (London, 1936).

58. *Statistical Sketches of Upper Canada, for the Use of Emigrants,* by a Backwoodsman (London, 1832), 21. Thomas Dyke, *Advice to Emigrants* (London, 1832), 33. *Canada in the Years 1832, 1833, and 1834,* by an Ex-Settler (Dublin, 1835), 16. *The Quebec Mercury,* May 4, 1830, March 27, 1832.

Great Britain had always entertained against the British provinces was dissipated, and the course of their movement was deflected to the St. Lawrence. Most of them turned their hands to the simple muscular tasks that they could perform: the digging of canals, the construction of roads, and the handling of freight. They all hoped to gain funds and experience and finally arrive at every immigrant's ideal: the position of an independent landowner. But so long as a day's work would bring wages they were inclined to postpone the hour when the clearing in the bush had to begin.[59]

Along with the laborers came the small propertied farmers who had also caught the enthusiasm which the news of a prosperous Canada had inspired in the Old Country. That the province was their deliberate choice and the destination not accidental is proven by the fact that many of them came to their new homes via the United States by a route that was the reverse of that followed by the poor emigrant who had centered his future in the Republic. Again the conditions of an established commercial route provided an influential factor. The vessels in the timber trade were the most unsatisfactory afloat; they were often the refuse of all the commercial routes of the world.[60] Discomfort and danger had to be considered part of the cost of passage and every season reported a heavy toll of shipwrecks in the foggy channels that led up the St. Lawrence. Anyone who could afford to travel by some other route was urged by emigrant advisers to ensure safety by paying a higher rate.[61]

The finest ships upon the Atlantic were the packets bound for New York and although steerage passage was double that on vessels sailing directly for Quebec, the yeoman farmer was willing to bear the cost. The American customs regulations allowed the effects of settlers destined for Canada to pass through without the payment of duty and the Canada Company maintained an agent in the city to

59. *P.R.O.: C.O. 384/35:* Letter from A. C. Buchanan, Quebec, July 22, 1834. *The Quebec Mercury,* May 12, 28, Oct. 15, 1831.

60. John Rebans, *Observations on the Proposed Alteration of the Timber Duties* (London, 1831), 24. *United Kingdom, Parliamentary Papers, 1840,* V, "Report from the Select Committee on Import Duties," 23.

61. Thomas W. Magrath, *Authentic Letters from Upper Canada* (Dublin, 1833), 29. *Canada in the Years 1832, 1833, and 1834,* by an Ex-Settler, 36. *P.R.O.: F.O. 5/294:* Letter of James Buchanan, New York, June 14, 1834.

assist the travelers on their way and, undoubtedly, to see that they were not argued out of their plans.[62] From New York they started along the regular settlers' highway to the West, up the Hudson and along the Erie Canal, branching off to cross Lake Ontario or the Niagara River into the province of Upper Canada. It was generally stated that the number that came to Canada by this route was equal to the number that continued from Montreal and Lake Ontario to the western states. The one group balanced the other.[63] But along with the former were found immigrants who had been residents in the United States for a period of months or even years and who now, disappointed in their fortune or with Yankee life, had determined to try British territory.[64]

The vigorous British interest in Upper Canada was not without some response from the Americans of the eastern states. The land offices and journalists of the province joyfully called attention to the arrival of numbers of American citizens, but how long they had been Americans no information indicates.[65] Some exchange of people was inevitable as a result of the family connections that had been established a generation before. The situation was well summed up in 1831 by a New Yorker who, in speaking to a traveler regarding the possibility of war between the United States and Canada, said: "Well, sir, I guess if we don't fight for a year or two we won't fight at all, for we are marrying so fast, sir, that a man won't be sure but he may shoot his father or brother-in-law."[66]

Not all of those who arrived at Quebec were determined to remain in the provinces. They had chosen a cheap route by which to reach

62. On the relative cost of passage see *The Quebec Mercury,* July 17, 1830; *P.R.O.: F.O. 5/294:* Letter of James Buchanan, New York, Sept. 1, 1834; Thomas W. Magrath, *op. cit.,* 112; *Official Information for Emigrants Arriving at New York, and Who Are Desirous of Settling in the Canadas . . . as Issued by A. C. Buchanan, Esq.* (Montreal, 1834).

63. *Hints to Emigrants Respecting North America* (Quebec, 1831), 7. *The Quebec Mercury,* Dec. 11, 1830.

64. *Ibid.,* July 13, 1830.

65. Thomas Dyke, *op. cit.,* 21. *The Emigrant's Guide; Containing Practical and Authentic Information,* 73. Isaac Fidler, *op. cit.,* 205.

66. Adam Fergusson, *Practical Notes Made during a Tour in Canada and a Portion of the United States in MDCCCXXXI* (2d ed., Edinburgh, 1834), 147–148.

the rising states of the West. Travel by the St. Lawrence and the Lakes to Ohio and Michigan was considered as convenient and quick as via New York and the Erie Canal. The number who reached the province merely en route to the United States was variously estimated, sometimes as high as two-thirds of the total, but there was no way of judging and the proportion varied from year to year.[67] The Canadian administrators would not admit that the immigrants pushed on to the United States because of their disappointment with the colony, and they accused agents of American land companies of traveling along with the groups of immigrants on the St. Lawrence boats and persuading them to continue farther west by false stories of hardships in Canada and glorious opportunities in the States.[68]

Not only did many of the individual immigrants who reached Canada in any given season pass directly into the United States, but settlers whose destination had been the colony of the Canada Company crossed over the border as well. One route to the Huron tract passed through Detroit, where the company planned to meet the arrivals and transport them to Goderich in a steamer maintained for the purpose. But the management was not of the best and one observer complained that because of neglect in meeting the passengers on schedule, several hundred families who had been destined for the colony remained in Michigan or moved still farther to the west.[69] Dissatisfaction with the company's terms and conditions caused others who did take up lands to desert the enterprise and seek a country where the soil was considered more fertile and the price more reasonable and stable.[70]

Toward the middle of the decade of the 'thirties the popularity of Upper Canada began to wane. Contemporaries blamed the decline in the number of arrivals upon many superficial conditions: the shipwrecks in the St. Lawrence, the growing opposition among many of the natives to the presence of paupers and sick, the threat of restrictive legislation on the part of the Assembly of the lower province

67. Helen I. Cowan, *British Emigration*, 236. *P.A.C.: M173, Minutes of Evidence . . . Jan., 1832. Evidence of A. C. Buchanan.*

68. J. E. Alexander, *Transatlantic Sketches*, II (London, 1833), 218.

69. *The Seventh Report from the Select Committee of the House of Assembly of Upper Canada on Grievances* (Toronto, 1835), 26.

70. *P.R.O.: C.O. 384/36:* Letter of G. I. Call, Bideford, July 12, 1834.

where the French element feared the growing power of the British settlers.[71] A broader view, however, suggests that the time for a readjustment had come. A state of congestion had resulted from the rapid development of land and resources, and disappointment was the inevitable reaction among many. The United States, however, continued to enjoy a prosperity that became more exuberant with each year, and an increase in the migration southward across the border was noticed by those who took a critical view of the situation and was exaggerated by those who used it as evidence of the inadequacy of the government of the day.[72]

While this confused crossing and recrossing of the paths of the pioneers and immigrants was taking place, one migration was under way which had no relationship to the fundamental patterns of the population history of the continent.

Negro slaves had been brought into Upper Canada by Loyalist settlers, but the institution was not destined for a long life. A law of 1793 prohibited all future introduction of slaves and provided for the gradual emancipation of those who were in service. The soil of the province was no "freer" than that in the states of the Union that were adjoining, but it was beyond the operation of the fugitive slave laws which kept every runaway Negro in the western states in constant fear. Moreover, here were no laws that placed disabilities upon the economic and social activities of those who had been legally emancipated, as was the case in many of the states. Canada became the desirable refuge for fugitive Negro and freedman alike.

So different was life on the frontier farms from plantation routine that the individual Negro was lost. Only through coöperation with men of the same color could he acquire economic independence. Land was given to him on generous terms by the authorities, and in 1833 the Assembly decreed that no Negro could be extradited to the United States except for larceny, murder, or crimes of the same violent nature. With this encouragement and under this protection, several settlements were founded that, when established, offered shel-

71. *P.R.O.: C.O. 384/38:* Letter of A. C. Buchanan, Liverpool, Nov. 20, 1835. *The Quebec Mercury,* March 11, May 1, 6, 1834.

72. Fragmentary statistics dealing with immigration into the United States from Canada indicate a doubling of the movement after 1832. Walter F. Willcox, *International Migrations,* I (New York, 1929), 401–409.

ter and a practical education for every new refugee from the States. These settlements were scattered along the Thames River and eastward from Detroit along the edge of Lake Erie. Growth was slow. The "Underground Railroad" was not yet functioning with the success that twenty years later was to make it an issue in the domestic politics of the Republic and to swell the number of Negroes in the British province to a total that might ultimately cause not a little concern.[73]

For the time being, however, the presence of the Negro was no problem. Even had it been, any difficulties that he could have caused would have been overshadowed by the vexing political disputes that were beginning to disturb the peace that many had taken for granted. In Upper Canada land-hungry pioneers looked with jealousy upon the clergy reserves that set aside for the minority in the established churches some of the choicest locations; a strong reform party found fault with every policy of the authoritarian government; descendants of the first settlers failed to coöperate with those recently arrived from the mother country. In Lower Canada disputes regarding language, land, taxation, and representation were approaching the point of violence. Before any of these difficulties were to be resolved, rebellion was destined to take place in both provinces and to inaugurate a new period in the course of population movement.

73. W. R. Riddell, "The Slave in Upper Canada," *Journal of Negro History,* IV (Washington, 1919), 372–395. *Reminiscences of Levi Coffin* (Cincinnati, 1876), 250, 251.

CHAPTER VI

THE BEGINNING OF THE SOUTHWARD MIGRATIONS
1837–1861

WITH the passing of the year 1837 the wavering balance of population movements as between the United States and Canada began sharply to favor the southern country. The attractions of the Republic, with the immense scale of such enterprises as canal building and its wide stretches of available lands, had for some time been drawing a few native-born Canadians and many recent immigrants into the nation across the border; but on balance compensation for their departure had been provided by the arrival of Europeans who traveled to the Canadas via New York and of Americans from the eastern states who still considered the prospects offered by the north more attractive than those available in their own west. But during the hard times that followed the panic of 1837, the influx of European immigrants by all routes greatly declined and there was little motive for Americans to move either to the north or to the west. Special conditions in the Canadas, however, induced a marked southward movement of their peoples, and when, in the middle 'forties, prosperity returned to the continent of North America, it set under way such vigorous activity in the industry of the eastern states and such hopeful development of the agriculture and transportation of the western states that for the time being the advantages to be found in the provinces were almost eclipsed. Then Canadians joined with Americans in the great expansion of settlement into the Mississippi Valley and beyond that did much to stamp indelibly upon American consciousness an infectious faith whose historical name is "Manifest Destiny."

The first of the circumstances which favored Canadian emigration were the political rebellions in both provinces which occurred in 1837 and 1838.[1] These arose from the inadequacy of the representa-

1. For a brief discussion see W. P. M. Kennedy, *The Constitution of Canada* (London, 1922), 114–115, 152–154, 156–166; also Antoine Roy,

tive government which had been established in 1791 when measured against parliamentary reform in Great Britain and Jacksonian democracy in the United States. The executive branch of government was so securely entrenched as to be able largely to disregard the ambitions of the representative branch in the matter of such long-seated grievances as the conflict between business and agriculture, favoritism in the land system, and the landed endowment and educational monopoly of an established church whose adherents were in a minority. In Lower Canada these circumstances were intensely aggravated by the fact that the French-speaking population and the English-speaking group who dominated them politically and economically were separated by deep differences in outlook and in general cultural heritage. The marvel is that the number of rebels and of overt clashes with authority was so small, but the relatively minor proportions of the rebellions were not reflected in a moderate official attitude once they were suppressed. A stern policy of punishment drove into exile all the participants who could escape, and the uncertainty that at once grew up about the future of the provinces and their governmental policies persuaded others to transfer their families and movable property into the United States, where they found sympathy and protection.[2]

The refugee who found safety in the United States came with no intention of forgetting politics in following the peaceful career of a settler. The United States was to serve as a base for offensive operations, and during the three years that followed, the border was constantly disturbed by raids and demonstrations organized by the exiles and their American sympathizers.[3] When the hope of success had faded, they settled down to make the Republic, which had been

"Les Evénements de 1837 dans la Province de Québec," *Bulletin des recherches historiques,* XXXVII (Lévis, P.Q., 1931), 75–83; *Canadian Historical Association Report for 1937* (Toronto, 1937), *passim.*

2. *Plattsburg Republican* (Plattsburg, N.Y.), Extra, Dec. 9–16, 1837. *Troy Budget* (Troy, N.Y.), Dec. 25, 1837; Jan. 5, 1838.

3. This is the subject of a study by A. B. Corey which is to appear in the Carnegie Endowment series. *Detroit Journal and Courier,* Jan. 9, 1838. Victor Morin, "Une Société secrète de patriotes canadiens aux Etats-Unis," *R.S.C., 1930,* Sec. i, 45–57. *P.A.C.: Q250,* Fox to Palmerston, Nos. 9, 10, 28. This entire volume contains material on the rebels along the border.

the model of their endeavors, their permanent home, and when a partial amnesty in 1843 and a general amnesty in 1849 permitted a return to the provinces, only a few took advantage of their terms.[4]

More important as a factor in inducing emigration was the stagnation that in the winter of 1837–1838 settled down upon all business enterprise. The "hard times" that came as the aftermath of the panic of 1837 throughout North America and Europe were responsible in part; the depression was intensified in the Canadas by the prevailing fear that insurrection would again break out. Shipbuilding, which had been the usual winter employment for carpenters and laborers in the St. Lawrence cities, was at a standstill. All plans for public improvements were dropped by the government. Immigration, which normally brought in the capital of substantial farmers as well as the muscle of mere laborers, fell off in the ensuing season, and the Canada Company was obliged to curtail the varied activities by which it had stimulated the trade of the more remote sections.[5] Many of the recent comers who had been in doubt as to whether to remain in the British dominions or pass on to the United States now chose to follow the latter course. The superior popularity which for a decade Canada had enjoyed among the emigrating classes of Great Britain now came to an end.[6]

The departure of the people who had not attached themselves permanently to the economic life of the provinces had always aroused concern, but it was to be expected. Now, however, the emigration of native-born Canadians was a phenomenon that reflected the discouragement of the times and the dissatisfaction felt even by many citizens who had no sympathy with rebellion. In the spring of 1838 the spirit of uneasiness gave rise to many rumors in Upper Canada: the United States government was favorably inclined toward setting aside a large tract of land for those who were willing to change allegiance; an emigration society was being formed to found a colony in the newly established territory of Iowa; many whose patriotism could

4. Charles Lindsey, *The Life and Times of William Lyon Mackenzie,* II (Toronto, 1862), 290, 292.

5. *The Quebec Mercury,* Jan. 27, Oct. 23, 1838; May 11, 1839.

6. *P.R.O.: C.O. 384/52:* Letter of T. F. Elliot, July 27, 1839. Patrick Matthew, *Emigration Fields: North America, the Cape, Australia and New Zealand* (Edinburgh, 1839), 34, 39.

not be questioned were becoming interested in schemes that involved expatriation.[7]

The scattered items concerning these inducements that appeared in the newspapers indicate that, although no encouragement was actually held out by officials of the United States and no organization directed the movement, the emigration assumed disturbing proportions. A thousand persons a week were reported as crossing the Niagara River into the state of New York during July, 1838; and from Detroit came similar accounts describing the extent of the exodus during that and the succeeding year.[8] From Iowa came the statement that Canadian settlers were arriving not by the hundreds but by the thousands.[9] Later information revealed that, like most migrations, its numbers were exaggerated in the public mind; but the local histories of the counties in Michigan adjacent to Canadian territory indicate that many of their pioneers came from the upper province during the troubled years of 1838 and 1839.[10]

Perhaps some of the most pessimistic forebodings of the time might have materialized had the imperial authorities not taken strenuous action to learn the true state of affairs. The appointment of the liberal Lord Durham to the post of governor-general was a reassuring gesture and his report, which admitted the presence of the evils which had been the cause of the most bitter complaints on the part of the reformers, seemed to promise an improvement in the tone of the politics of the colony. In the report, the failure of the colony to hold the great proportion of the newly arrived immigrants and the emigration of well-established residents were recognized as circumstances that should be remedied.[11] All awaited eagerly the

7. Egerton Ryerson, *The Story of My Life* (Toronto, 1884), 184.

8. Fred Landon, "The Duncombe Uprising of 1837 and Some of Its Consequences," *R.S.C., 1931*, Sec. ii, 83–99. R. S. Longley, "Emigration and the Crisis of 1837 in Upper Canada," *Canadian Historical Review*, XVII, 29–41. *Burlington Free Press* (Burlington, Vt.), May 31, 1839.

9. *Niles National Register*, LV, Oct. 20, 1838, 55, 115.

10. *Portrait and Biographical Album of Sanilac County* (Chicago, 1884), 454. George N. Fuller, *Economic and Social Beginnings of Michigan* (Lansing, Mich., 1916), 149. *North American* (Swanton, Vt.), July 10, 1839.

11. *Report of the Earl of Durham, Her Majesty's High Commissioner and Governor-General of British North America* (London, 1902), 3, 105–111, 122, 148–155, 201–203.

legislative program that would assure a new era in economic as well as political life.

The most far-reaching results of the investigation were the creation of a new constitutional framework and the promise of a large British loan to be expended upon public works. Upper and Lower Canada were merged into the one Province of Canada, with a single governor and a single legislature. Not until this new regime went into operation in 1841 could other promises be fulfilled. Two pronouncements promptly outlined the attitude of the new administration to matters of population. A land law authorized free grants of fifty acres to anyone who would actually clear ten acres and construct a house and barn. By this disposition of crown lands it was believed that more of the immigrants would stay in the province and that the attractiveness of the United States where land had to be paid for would be dimmed.[12] On the other hand, an effort to increase the influx by encouraging the settlement of American citizens whose pioneering talents were unquestioned met a determined, almost sharp, rebuff from the governor-general. The new Canada was neither to give its people to the neighboring republic nor to receive many settlers from the States.[13]

This officially desired independence was not achieved. Forces stronger than any publicly proclaimed policies were in operation. During the next twenty years the United States went through a fundamental transformation: it acquired an empire in the west that stretched to the Pacific; millions of fertile prairie acres were offered for settlement; industry supplanted agriculture as the predominant economic activity in many sections of the northeast; and on both the Atlantic and Pacific oceans a new era in commerce launched hundreds of vessels to carry the products of the farms and factories. Each of these changes and developments resulted in shifts of population that affected all parts of the continent and the people of the British provinces reacted in much the same way as the Americans

12. *Statutes of the Province of Canada,* 4 and 5 Vic., c. 100. Hugh Mackenzie Morrison, "The Principle of Free Grants in the Land Act of 1841," *Canadian Historical Review,* XIV, 392–407. *P.A.C.: G421,* Arthur to Thomson, June 19, 1840.

13. *P.C.: Jour. of Legislative Council,* I, App. No. 23, 507. *P.A.C.: G390,* Sydenham to Russell, No. 179, Oct. 12, 1840.

who were engaged in the same pursuits. But so varied were the conditions under which British Americans lived that no single group of causes explains the migration that crossed the international boundary southward, from the Maritime Provinces in the east to the territory of the fur traders in the west.

The Maritime Provinces escaped the political disturbances of 1837 and 1838 and until the revolution in British imperial trade policy that came in the middle of the 1840's, a satisfactory if not abundant prosperity favored Nova Scotia and New Brunswick. The only inhabitants to suffer notably were the fishermen, who found it difficult to meet the competition of the New England vessels whose skippers succeeded in exercising a broad interpretation of the terms of the treaty of 1818 which permitted them to carry on some of their operations within the territorial waters of the provinces. The presence of the Yankee fleets resulted in a constant drain on the man power of the villages along the coast, a loss that continued throughout the century. The American ships were larger, provided with better equipment, and, most important of all, they enjoyed the advantages of a large and protected market in the States. Each member of the crew fished on shares, turning over to the owner a proportion of his catch, but receiving for his own the American price. This system offered obvious advantages to the Nova Scotians who were willing to become a part of it. Many of them, leaving families at home, went to Boston and Gloucester and signed up on the foreign vessels, returned to the waters with which they were well acquainted, and when the season was over remained in the province. Local observers declared that upwards of a half and probably more of the men on the American fleet were Nova Scotians, and an even larger percentage of the captains were, in the words of their more patriotic neighbors, "white-washed Yankees." In time, they tended to adopt the nationality of the ship in which they sailed and took their families to the southern ports. It was a slow but persistent emigration that foreshadowed a much larger movement to follow.[14]

What fishing meant to the coastal regions of Nova Scotia, the timber trade and shipbuilding meant to New Brunswick. The for-

14. *N.S.: App. to Jour. H. of A., 1844,* No. 28, 49, 50; *1853,* No. 4, 115; *1854,* No. 2, 23, 27–30. *N.S.: App. to Jour. of Legislative Council, 1852,* No. 3, 46, 47; No. 9, 81, 82.

ests were so extensive and the demand so steady that farming became a part-time occupation for the owners of land and most of the laborers and artisans were employed either in the cutting of trees or in the construction of vessels. Agriculture was neglected and the province was dependent upon imported food. So long as the forest industries flourished this situation caused little concern.[15] The steady flow of immigrants into St. John and their passing on to the United States gave constant rise to suggestions for encouraging farming, but no results came out of the agitation.[16] When the economic collapse did come, it struck with a suddenness that revealed how essentially vulnerable the organization of life in the province had been. In 1842 and again in 1846, reductions in the British timber duties opened the market to the almost neighboring Baltic countries, a step that quickly reduced the demand for the New Brunswick product and lowered the price of the smaller quantity that was sold.[17]

Commission merchants and landowners, woodcutters and rivermen, many of whom were already in debt, were ruined by this far-reaching change. And the future held no brighter prospects for New Brunswick because the mother country seemed firmly committed to a program of free trade.[18] But logging and lumbering were skilled professions and in the tariff-protected United States, where rapidly growing cities and an expanding marine called for all kinds of forest products, every man who was expert with the ax or could pilot a raft down a river was assured of employment. The Aroostook country of Maine was the first destination of a large part of the discomfited New Brunswick woodsmen, and out of this area many of them ultimately moved on to wherever forests were being felled, a few to the southern Appalachians, Pennsylvania, and New York, but the majority to the "big woods" that surrounded the Great Lakes.[19]

15. *Letters from Nova Scotia and New Brunswick, Illustrative of Their Moral, Religious, and Physical Circumstances, during the Years 1826, 1827, and 1828* (Edinburgh, 1829), 156.

16. Abraham Gesner, *New Brunswick; with Notes for Emigrants* (London, 1847), 318, 372, 373.

17. James Elliott Defebaugh, *History of the Lumber Industry of America*, I, 107. Adam Shortt and Arthur G. Doughty (eds.), *Canada and Its Provinces*, V (Toronto, 1914), 203, 204.

18. *N.S.: App. to Jour. H. of A., 1849*, No. 30, 279.

19. James F. W. Johnston, *Notes on North America*, I (Boston, 1851),

Soon after this dispersion from New Brunswick had started, a succession of short crops afflicted Nova Scotia, and the province, which even in the most satisfactory of years was obliged to secure some of its food elsewhere, was forced to pay exorbitant prices for imports. This situation coincided with the opening of the islands of the British West Indies to American trade, and the resulting glut of northern fish and wood products in the markets there reduced the value of the exports that the Nova Scotians counted on to balance accounts abroad. Commercial towns at once felt a sharp decline in the demand for shipping. Halifax, in particular, fell into a depression that gave no promise of improvement so long as the British Empire continued its policy of free trade. Real estate declined in value and empty houses testified to the withdrawal of capital that sought the larger interest yield offered by the expanding economic structure of the United States.[20]

Along with capital went people. Young men of enterprise sought the possibilities to be found in New England and the west. It was estimated that more than a thousand left in 1847 and by 1848 the number of young men and young women emigrants was estimated at eight thousand.[21] Many of these, it is true, were gone for only a season to engage in summer work, but this temporary migration often developed into a permanent absence and to emigrate as soon as one grew up became the accepted custom in many communities. From the towns, apprentices who had served their time and learned a trade carried their skill to the cities and rapidly rising villages of the south; and farmers who were troubled by the prospect of seeing their children leave were inclined to dispose of what property was salable and, like many New Englanders of the time, to seek the western states.[22]

37, 99; II, 146. For two interesting lives of migratory New Brunswick lumbermen, see Isaac Stephenson, *Recollections of a Long Life* (Chicago, 1915), and J. E. Nelligan, "The Life of a Lumberman," *Wisconsin Magazine of History*, XIII (Madison, 1929–30), 3–65, 131–185, 241–304.

20. *N.S.: App. to Jour. H. of A., 1849,* No. 30, 277.

21. Abraham Gesner, *The Industrial Resources of Nova Scotia* (Halifax, 1849), 12, 66.

22. *N.S.: App. to Jour. H. of A., 1853,* No. 45, 359, 360; *1857,* No. 71, 413, 415, 421; *1858,* No. 47, 368. *The Christian Messenger* (Halifax), Oct. 6, 1848, Sept. 7, 1849.

The departures from the Maritime Provinces, although large, were taken somewhat philosophically because of almost a century of population interchange with New England. Far different were the alarm and official interference that arose in French Canada when the sons of the habitants began to leave. Their emigration was not only a loss of friends; it was a weakening of vital French-Canadian strength that neither the Catholic church nor the political leaders would accept without opposition. The continuation and increase of the movement, in spite of the naturally vigorous efforts made to stem its flow, illustrate the deep-seated nature of the continental forces that were operating.

It was not an unusual thing for descendants of the French *voyageurs* who had revealed and exploited so much of the continent to stray far from the seigniories along the St. Lawrence. They were still the traders and trappers of the west and at every frontier post beyond the Lakes a small colony of French Canadians kept alive many of the traditions of the old empire.[23] It was not, however, to these remote villages where the old language and religion were preserved that the young men were departing. New England was now the magnet and there, in the enthusiastic Americanism of the times, the characteristics that had been maintained in Quebec for more than half a century in spite of English rule seemed about to be lost by every emigrant who crossed into the young republic.

Long-continued repetition has established a historical tradition that the first French-Canadian emigrants were the refugees from the rebellion of 1837.[24] But these exiles were not the pioneers. The early settlers of towns in northern New York often depended upon Montreal for a labor supply. A traveler in 1806 discovered two young Frenchmen working for the season on a Vermont farm, and in 1815 a Canadian family were living in Woonsocket, Rhode Island, where

23. For this persistence to our own time, see J. M. Carrière, *Tales from the French Folk-lore of Missouri* (Evanston, 1937).

24. Marie Louise Bonier, *Débuts de la colonie franco-américaine de Woonsocket, Rhode Island* (Framingham, Mass., 1920), 74. E. Hamon, *Les Canadiens-Français de la Nouvelle Angleterre* (Quebec, 1891), 164, 165. Abby Maria Hemenway, *The Vermont Historical Gazetteer*, II, 298, 299. Alexandre Belisle, *Histoire de la presse franco-américaine* (Worcester, 1911), 10, 11.

they were joined by other families during the 1820's. In 1825 Father Matignon of Boston baptized several children of French parents at Burlington, Vermont, and in 1831 there were about thirty families at Lewiston, Maine, which they had reached by following the "Kennebec Road" from the north.[25] Undoubtedly there were many more scattered individuals and communities which escaped the observation of travelers or priests.

After 1837 a marked increase in the movement began to attract the attention of Canadians and Americans alike. In it political and economic motives were mingled, as they had been in the situation that had brought on the revolt. Stated very briefly, a rapidly growing French-Canadian population was finding that good new lands within their old province had either almost disappeared or were in the hands of Anglo-Canadian proprietors whose advantageous position was closely related to their entrenched political privilege. French Canada therefore embarked upon three activities that were to continue for a century. Some of the population grimly tried to develop marginal and submarginal farms. Others were lucky enough to discover a few undeveloped regions where land was cheap and where its fertility, combined with favorable climatic conditions, made a profitable agriculture possible. Still others began to spill over into the former Upper Canada, into northern New York and New England, and into northern or western New Brunswick, either to accumulate a little capital in forest, farm, or factory employment, or to take up farm land which others were anxious to dispose of before moving farther west, but which was better value for the money than could be obtained in the French homeland.

Few observers realized that the basic trouble was that old Quebec could not support the growing number of her children, for there were many secondary consequences of this which more easily caught the inquiring eye. For instance, many commentators blamed the emi-

25. John T. Smith, *A History of the Diocese of Ogdensburg* (New York, n.d.), 77, 78. John Lambert, *Travels through Canada and the United States of North America, in the Years 1806, 1807, and 1808,* II, 523. Marie Louise Bonier, *op. cit.,* 79. Louis de Goesbriand, *Les Canadiens des Etats-Unis* (n.p., n.d.), 2. R. J. Lawton, J. H. Burgess, H. F. Roy, *Franco-Americans of the State of Maine* (Lewiston, Me., 1915), 31. A. Desrosiers and Abbé Fournet, *La Race Française en Amérique* (Montreal, 1911), 218.

gration on scanty harvests without going behind them to investigate the reasons for soil exhaustion. The habitant, like his ancestor in France, made bread the staple of his diet and his continued cultivation of wheat with no rotation of crops and little attempt at adequate fertilizing brought about a steady decline in the yield. In the meantime families increased and the size of farms dwindled with the division of the small holdings among many heirs. Attempts to encourage more scientific methods met no popular response. Many a farm could be held as a family unit only if some of the sons and daughters found employment for wages elsewhere during some months of every year.[26]

The demand for laborers in New England, which was already filling the mill towns and railroad camps with Irish immigrants, began to draw young French Canadians across the border.[27] They hired out on the farms of Vermont and New Hampshire where the attractions of the city had depleted the household of young people;[28] they joined the lumbermen from New Brunswick on the rivers of Maine;[29] and some, more adventurous, packed family belongings into a French cart and set off on a several weeks' journey that brought them to the industrial centers of Massachusetts and Rhode Island.[30] The building of factories and long streets of tenement houses gave an impetus to the manufacture of brick. In the brickyards young Canadians, who were already inured to heavy labor in heat and cold, who had the requisite skill, and who wanted only a seasonal job, made up the majority of the workers.[31]

By 1849 members of the legislature of Canada were so worried that they authorized an investigation which revealed not only the extent of the exodus but also the circumstances that set it in motion. An estimate of seventy thousand was considered too high, but the

26. Henry Taylor, *The Present Condition of United Canada, as Regards Her Agriculture, Trade and Commerce* (London, Canada West, 1849), 6, 7, 8. E. C. Hughes, "Industry and the Rural System in Quebec," *Canadian Journal of Economics and Political Science*, IV (Toronto, 1938), 341–349.

27. *P.A.C.: Q260*, Part I, Colborne to Normandy, No. 113, Sept. 16, 1839 (enclosure).

28. *L'Evolution de la race française en Amérique*, I (Montreal, 1921), 65.

29. Isaac Stephenson, *op. cit.*, 48.

30. Marie Louise Bonier, *op. cit.*, 87.

31. *Ibid.*, 74. Alexander Belisle, *op. cit.*, 4.

investigating committee agreed upon twenty thousand as being a conservative figure to represent the number of French Canadians who had emigrated during the preceding five years. Priests who appeared as witnesses gave evidence regarding the unfavorable conditions that caused emigration from their parishes: the higher wages offered in the States, the decline in lumbering operations along the tributaries of the St. Lawrence, the difficulty of securing good land in the vicinity of the old villages, and the unwillingness on the part of the sons of proprietors to step down into the class of laborers. One regrettable feature of recent years had been the increase in the number of family groups that had gone—not to the industrial centers of the east, but to the prairies of the west.[32]

The question was repeatedly asked: why don't these young men and families settle on the vacant lands so abundant in the remoter parts of the province? This question was answered two years later when a second legislative investigation made clear the difficulties that hindered colonization of this nature, especially in the unoccupied portion of the Eastern Townships which was always pointed to as the logical field for settlement. Here were large tracts of the most desirable townships, but they were in the hands of speculators who demanded a high price. Clergy reserves also helped to obstruct the logical advance. Communications were nonexistent in many parts and even the through roads that had been built at great expense were not kept in a passable state. Finally, the British-American Land Company, which had been chartered in the hope that it would foster the development of the region in the way that the Canada Company had improved the counties near Lake Huron, had title to much of the unoccupied land but imposed terms that no penniless settler could afford.[33]

The realization of the existence of these conditions had already set under way an agitation that for the next half century was to be

32. *Rapport du comité spécial de l'Assemblée législative, nommé pour s'enquérir des causes et de l'importance de l'émigration qui a lieu tous les ans du Bas-Canada vers les Etats-Unis* (Montreal, 1849). *Le Canadien émigrant par douze missionaires des Townships de l'Est* (Quebec, 1851), 16, 18, 24, 25.

33. "The French-Canadian Emigrant; or Why Does the French Canadian Abandon Lower Canada?" *P.C.: App. to Jour. of Legislative Assembly,* X, No. V.

closely associated with the French emigration and in time was to influence both its nature and its course. The Catholic clergy had been disturbed not only over the loss of parishioners, but by the realization that those who took service with British and American farmers in the Eastern Townships were surrounded by influences that encouraged them to lose the faith into which they were born.[34] Efforts had been made to provide "colonization priests" who would keep in touch with the individual settlers and laborers, but the latter were too scattered to be served satisfactorily. A program of supervised settlement, it was believed, would aid the poorer colonists in getting established and it would lead to the formation of compact communities that would support the churches and schools to which they were accustomed. In the spring of 1848 a colonization association was organized under the presidency of the Bishop of Montreal and the priests of the province became active agents in furthering the formation of local societies that would undertake the enrolling of settlers and sponsor their activities.[35]

As yet, however, assisted Canadian colonization on a scale that could in any way affect the progress of emigration was a remote ideal. Residents on the north bank of the St. Lawrence had for some time been sending their children to the valley of the Saguenay, first to exploit the forests and thereafter as settlers. The region immediately to the north and east of Montreal was being colonized by expansion from the river villages between 1830 and 1850.[36] But the habitants on the south bank hesitated to cross into the wilderness on the other side so long as they saw behind them a fertile and forested area which they considered their birthright. The inertia of the government and the difficulties attending pioneering without roads and without resources hindered settlement in these townships, whereas short crops and distress discouraged movement to the Saguenay during the 1850's.[37] Though ineffective at the time, the early considera-

34. *Mélanges religieux, scientifiques, politiques et littéraires*, V (Montreal, Feb. 24, 1843), 291.

35. *Ibid.*, XI (March 21, April 7, 1848), 187, 188, 208, 209. *Montreal Weekly Witness*, April 17, 1848.

36. Georges Vattier, *Esquisse historique de la colonisation de la Province de Québec, 1608–1925*, 42–44.

37. *Le Canadien*, Feb. 7, March 26, 1849; April 5, 1850; April 14, July 7, Sept. 10, 1852.

tion of preventive measures that could be employed against emigration yielded useful results at a later period when political was added to religious influence in forcing the adoption of an official program.

During the decade of the 'fifties the colonization agitation had to face the counterappeal of a more popular solution. Many observers believed that emigration was inevitable and that effort given to directing its course would be more effective than plans for damming at the source. Not in emigration but in the fate to which most emigrants were condemned lay the danger. As day laborers in cities and factory towns they lost everything that Canadians held highest: religion, language, nationality—all of which might be preserved under the American as well as the British flag if the emigrants were concentrated in farming communities, preferably in the West where society was still in the process of being formed.[38]

The champions of this policy could point to the success that already had attended some unorganized pioneering. The interest in the West that was apparent in all parts of North America in the late 'forties did not leave Lower Canada untouched. Many so-called "Americans" of the Eastern Townships sold their farms (often to French Canadians) and joined in the current that for a time threatened to depopulate the hills and valleys of northern New England.[39] French Canadians also caught the spirit of the times and, like all proceeding to the West, first sought Chicago, which still possessed the nucleus of a French community in a group of retired *voyageurs*, traders, and their children.[40]

But it was not Chicago that was to become the new French Canada of the West. Fifty miles south of the rising metropolis on the border of the great central prairie of Illinois, a region where French North Americans had been living since the end of the seventeenth century,

38. *Mélanges religieux, etc.,* XIV (Aug. 22, 1851), 373, 374.

39. Henry Taylor, *Journal of a Tour from Montreal thro' Berthier and Sorel, to the Eastern Townships* (Quebec, 1840), 29, 32. C. Thomas, *Contributions to the History of the Eastern Townships,* 140, 228, 369. Georges Vattier, *op. cit.,* 41. L. S. Channell, *History of Compton County and Sketches of the Eastern Townships,* 35. *Montreal Weekly Witness,* Sept. 24, Oct. 22, 1849; July 22, 1850.

40. *Mélanges religieux, etc.,* XII (Nov. 17, 1848, May 22, 1849), 74, 303. *Le Canadien,* Dec. 7, 1849.

lay the marshes of the Kankakee which had long been the resort of hunters and trappers. Here, in the 'thirties, a French trader and his Indian wife lived in frontier splendor as the owners of thousands of acres of tribal lands that had come into their hands. These lands were acquired by some more energetic promoters, who set out to dispose of their holdings to settlers, but in this process the area did not lose its original French character.[41] One French family after another joined the community, and inquiring Canadians who were uncertain as to where to locate were advised, upon reaching Chicago, to proceed to the Kankakee country. During the last half of the decade of the 'forties approximately a thousand French families had located in the vicinity and were engaged in constructing a flourishing replica of the society from which they had come. This was a model to encourage a greater enterprise.[42]

The moving spirit in this project was a priest already recognized as a crusading reformer. Father Charles Chiniquy was the Canadian "apostle of temperance" honored in all the villages along the St. Lawrence for his zeal for social betterment. On a visit to the United States he was impressed by the difference between the squalor in which the laborers of the east were obliged to work and the independent comfort which the farmer of Kankakee enjoyed. After returning he devoted his energies to the encouragement of emigration to Illinois and announced that he would himself settle on the prairies to aid in the development of a prosperous and happy community to which all who were forced to leave the old home could come in the assurance that they were not giving up everything.[43] Father Chiniquy carried out his plans, settling at St. Anne in the midst of two hundred families who followed him from Canada. In 1856 he claimed that his parish numbered six thousand souls.[44] The ultimate results,

41. Charles Lindsey, *The Prairies of the Western States* (Toronto, 1860), 80–92.

42. *Le Canadien*, Jan. 29, April 3, 1850. Charles B. Campbell, "Bourbonnais; or the Early French Settlements in Kankakee County, Illinois," *Transactions of the Illinois State Historical Society, for the Year 1906* (Springfield, 1906), Part II, 65–72.

43. Letter of Father Chiniquy in *Le Canadien*, Sept. 22, 1851.

44. *Le Canadien*, July 14, 1854. *Les Annales de la propagation de la foi*, XXIX (Lyon, 1857), 120–128.

however, were far from a realization of first hopes. A quarrel with church authorities ended in a complete break with the ecclesiastical organization, and finally the priest and many of his parishioners abjured the old faith to become Presbyterians.[45] This apostasy shocked the Catholic hierarchy in Canada into developing a closer control over the French emigrants by advising them before departure and providing clergymen for the communities in which they settled. In the meantime, the vogue of Illinois continued. Several other settlements, with no particular religious affiliation, were established, and small colonies were sent out from the older towns to become in turn places to which incoming French Canadians directed their course.[46]

Illinois was not the only destination of the emigrants from the St. Lawrence. Before 1860, comparatively few had gathered about the textile factories of New England where so many thousands were to assemble in the future. In the three northern states of the region they were lumbermen, farm hands, and laborers. The city of Troy was the center from which the thousands who came down the historic route via Lake Champlain spread into the active towns that bordered the Erie Canal. Ogdensburg and its neighboring towns on the St. Lawrence were the homes of several thousands.[47] In the west, Michigan was receiving an increasing number, many of whom came, not from the old province, but from the French villages in Essex County (the district opposite Detroit) to which Michigan was the natural field of expansion.[48]

Two forms of economic activity that during the decade of the 'fifties were enjoying an unusual expansion affected the distribution of French Canadians, men from the Maritime Provinces, and to a lesser degree emigrants from Upper Canada. By the middle 'forties

45. John G. Shea, *History of the Catholic Church in the United States, 1844 to 1866* (New York, 1892), 618–619.

46. James Caird, *Prairie Farming in America, with Notes by the Way on Canada and the United States* (London, 1859), 34, 36, 39, 63.

47. *Les Annales de la propagation de la foi*, XIX, 461, 465. *Mélanges religieux, etc.*, XIV (July 15, 1851), 331. *Le Canadien*, Sept. 19, 1851. *Montreal Weekly Witness*, Feb. 11, 1850. *St. Lawrence Republican and General Advertiser*, April 12, 1842.

48. Telesphore St. Pierre, *Histoire des canadiens du Michigan et du Comté d'Essex, Ontario* (Montreal, 1895), 221.

settlement had reached the treeless prairies where, when a home was to be built, lumber had to be imported from the northern forests.[49] This demand stimulated a vigorous activity on the upper tributaries of the Mississippi and along the rivers that flowed into Lake Huron and Lake Michigan. Bay City was the first of the distinctive "sawmill" towns in which Canadians gathered in large numbers and the succession of lumber ports that appeared on the east shore of Lake Michigan attracted many across the peninsula. Canadians coming to Chicago in search of work learned of the opportunities in the woods and mills for which their earlier life had provided a training. Many of the proprietors of timberlands were Canadian capitalists who had foreseen the coming market and had shifted, along with their resources, the skilled woodsmen already in their employ.[50] Sailors from the Maritime Provinces followed the rivermen and took command of the lumber vessels that multiplied so rapidly on the waters of the upper lakes.

In Wisconsin the industry followed a similar course both in development and personnel. The Green Bay region was the first to attract attention, and here lumbermen from New Brunswick and Maine put to use the methods invented in the Aroostook country. Milwaukee and Chicago were the markets of this area.[51] Then, since the settlements being formed in southern Minnesota and Iowa could be reached more conveniently by the Mississippi, cutting began along the Chippewa and St. Croix rivers to meet this need. Again local history records the predominance of Canadians and Yankees in the camps and on the rafts. Around each sawmill arose a hamlet and logged-over lands were cleared of stumps to become the homes of lumbermen who retired to the more permanent calling of farmers.[52] In 1850, slightly over eight thousand Canadians were resident

---

49. *History of Muskegon County, Michigan* (Chicago, 1882), 21–24.

50. Augustus H. Gansser, *History of Bay County, Michigan and Representative Citizens* (Chicago, 1905), 123, 464. David D. Oliver, *Centennial History of Alpena County, Michigan* (Alpena, Mich., 1903), 85. *History of St. Clair County, Michigan* (Chicago, 1883), 242, 503, 554, 570–572. *Detroit Free Press*, Feb. 17, 1854; Feb. 7, 1855. Telesphore St. Pierre, *op. cit.*, 222, 223.

51. Isaac Stephenson, *op. cit.*, 79–82, 104–105.

52. John G. Gregory, *West Central Wisconsin; a History* (Indianapolis,

in the state and the census a decade later indicates an increase of ten thousand. They were particularly numerous in the counties where logging activity was brisk.[53]

North of the timber belt the beginning of copper mining along the south shore of Lake Superior also attracted Canadians. This was more of an accident than the result of any technical ability that they possessed. French Canadians who were making a far from satisfactory living in the rapidly declining fur trade willingly accepted the employment that the opening of the mines offered.[54] The first great influx of prospective miners came in 1845 and after two years of boom times the current settled down to a quieter annual addition to the population.[55] It may well have been that the incoming French Canadians found less employment in the mines than in the carrying trade and fishing industry with which they were acquainted and both of which received an impetus from the increased population of the district. With the opening of the canal around the Sault Ste. Marie rapids in 1855, access to Lake Superior was possible to sailing craft and steamboats from the lower lakes. This development modernized transportation upon Lake Superior and put an end to the regime of the bateaux and *voyageurs*. But it was also accompanied by an increased activity in the mines and a greater demand for laborers that employed all the hands that could be found available in the forests and about the lake and attracted workers from the remote villages in Lower Canada.[56]

1933), 211, 218, 245, 250. A. B. Easton, *History of the St. Croix Valley* (Chicago, 1909), 495.

53. *The Seventh Census of the United States, 1850* (Washington, 1853), Table XV. *Population of the United States in 1860 Compiled from the Original Returns of the Eighth Census* (Washington, 1864), Table V. The distribution of Canadians in Wisconsin in 1850 by counties is indicated in a table prepared by the staff of the Wisconsin Historical Society from the original schedules. A copy was kindly furnished by Dr. Joseph Schafer, the superintendent of the Society.

54. *Detroit Daily Advertiser*, April 6, 1844.

55. John Harris Forster, "Early Settlement of the Copper Regions of Lake Superior," *Report of the Pioneer Society of the State of Michigan*, VII (Lansing, Mich., 1886), 183–192.

56. *Lake Superior News and Miners' Journal* (Copper Harbor, Mich.), July 11, 1846. *Detroit Free Press*, April 26, May 23, 1854; June 28, Oct. 30,

In the public mind developments along Lake Superior were over-shadowed by the spectacular news that came from California. Every European nation and every state was represented in the crowds that rushed to the diggings. It may be assumed that among the 5,437 Canadian-born Californians listed in the census of 1860 were miners who came from every province.[57] Many of them had been early upon the scene because among the first arrivals had appeared such large bands of adventurers from the old trading settlements north of the Columbia River that those posts were in danger of losing all able-bodied residents.[58] On the whole, however, the number of Canadians was not large and although Canadian newspapers were filled with the contemporary accounts of the golden Eldorado on the Pacific there are only a few items referring to actual departures.[59] One reason may be found in the revival which the events of the decade brought about in the shipbuilding industry. More than six hundred vessels were withdrawn from the Atlantic to carry on the new commerce of the Pacific and every yard that could lay a keel was engaged in the construction of ships to make good the loss.[60]

During the next thirty years, until the northern part of the continent was spanned by the Canadian Pacific Railway, the Pacific coast, British and American, was bound together into one unit in trade and population. Evidence of this was provided in 1858 when a

1855. *P.C.: App. to Jour. of Legislative Assembly*, XV, No. 47: "Report of the Special Committee on Emigration."

57. *Population of the United States in 1860 Compiled from the Original Returns of the Eighth Census*, Table V. John Carr, *Pioneer Days in California* (Eureka, Cal., 1891), *passim.* Carr spent his boyhood in Brockville, Canada, which he revisited in 1852. "Out of one hundred and twenty or thirty apprentices who served their apprenticeship during the time I was one, but four were left in the town when I got back. Such is the way in which Uncle Sam absorbs the bone, sinew and youth of British America." He also reveals that the famous "Arkansaw Dam" on the Trinity River at Weaverville was actually built by a gang of New Brunswick men.

58. *Les Annales de la propagation de la foi*, XXII, 155–159.

59. *Le Canadien*, April 4, Sept. 24, Oct. 3, 1849; Nov. 6, 1850. *Montreal Weekly Witness*, Oct. 1, 15, 1849. *The Calais Advertiser* (Calais, Me.), Dec. 18, 1850, June 11, 1851; *Frontier Journal* (Calais, Me.), Feb. 6, Nov. 17, 1849. *The Christian Messenger*, Nov. 2, 1849. James F. W. Johnston, *op. cit.*, II, 216.

60. *The Anglo-American Magazine*, III (Toronto, 1853), 569.

consignment of gold dust from the Fraser River in British Columbia reached San Francisco. The British authorities were more than willing that Americans should take part in the exploitation of the precious metal.[61] More than seventeen hundred miners who were dissatisfied with their fate in California sailed for the north in a single day and in the course of the first season approximately twenty-five thousand persons representing all the nationalities that made up the motley population of the state, as well as many from the Puget Sound region, joined in the northward movement.[62] But with the collapse of the first hopes a return exodus almost as precipitous set in which brought many of the adventurers back into the United States to await the excitement of the next British Columbian gold discovery, which followed rapidly eighteen months later.[63] The Cariboo region did not leap quite so rapidly into prominence as had the Fraser River, but in 1860 rumors were abroad of the gold to be found there. Some were wary, having learned a bitter lesson from the earlier rush, but many from California and Oregon went north again. Those from Oregon had a head start in the provision and packing trades and it was here that many were found. The second rush gathered force in 1861 and by 1862 had reached large proportions, drawing more heavily, however, from the northern coast region than had the earlier excitement.[64] The importance of these movements along the coast lies not only in the extraction of gold from British soil by American miners, but also in the exploration and knowledge of the regions south of British Columbia, much of which led to later settlement by homeseekers from both sides of the line.

61. *P.A.C.: G335,* Lytton to Douglas, No. 2, July 1, 1858.

62. *Daily Alta California* (San Francisco), March 9, April 17, 21, 30, May 3, 23, June 5, 11, 21, 22, 24, 1858. Henry de Groot, *British Columbia; Its Condition and Prospects, Soil, Climate, and Mineral Resources, Considered* (San Francisco, 1859), 4, 13, 19. F. W. Howay, *British Columbia from the Earliest Times to the Present,* II (Vancouver, 1914), 14–18. Adam Shortt and Arthur G. Doughty (eds.), *Canada and Its Provinces,* XXI, 134, 140.

63. *Daily Alta California,* Aug. 2, 6, 9, 21, Sept. 6, 7, 14, Oct. 14, 1858; June 17, Dec. 10, 1859. *British Colonist* (Victoria, B.C.), Dec. 13, 1859.

64. *Ibid.,* Sept. 15, 1860. *Daily British Colonist* (Victoria), Dec. 21, 1860; Jan. 10, Feb. 13, 14, March 2, 11, Oct. 8, 15, Nov. 14, 1861; Jan. 21, May 9, 15, 1862.

As yet, however, the Pacific coast was not the scene of the most significant exchanges of population between territory that was British and that which was American. The settlement of the Middle West was a necessary preliminary to any further advance of the agricultural frontier and in this process farmers from Ontario mingled with farmers from Ohio and the East. And here it must be remembered that Canada had no Middle West of her own. The great inhospitable mass of the Laurentian Shield, which towered above the fertile alluvial lands of the St. Lawrence and Ottawa valleys, came down to form the very shores of Georgian Bay, Lake Huron and Lake Superior, and did not give way to arable acres until the Manitoba Basin was reached. In spite of gallant, ill-calculated efforts to drive roads across its rocky, shallow soil and filigree of lakes and rivers, the Laurentian Shield neatly deflected Canadian expansion to the south of Lake Huron and Lake Superior, and, until the westward tide of population swung around these lakes into the Red River corridor to the north, one great Canadian frontier of settlement was in the United States.[65] Probably because his career was less exciting than that of the gold seeker and less colorful than that of the lumberman, the coming of the Canadian in search of a farm home left little record on the pages of the local chroniclers. But this was the objective, for instance, of the majority of the eight thousand natives of British America who in 1860 were living in Iowa and the nine hundred recorded in Kansas.[66]

Although the trend was so decidedly out of Canada into the United States, Americans continued to drift into that part of the provinces that had been Upper Canada. All of the townships that had been first settled by Quaker and Mennonite pioneers about the year 1800 still showed, in the enumerations of 1851 and 1861, a much larger percentage of American-born residents than did the

65. A. R. M. Lower, "The Assault on the Laurentian Barrier, 1850–1870," *Canadian Historical Review*, X, 294–307. J. B. Brebner, "Canadian and North American History," *Canadian Historical Association Report for 1931*, 37–48.

66. *Montreal Weekly Witness*, Oct. 22, 1849; July 22, 1850. *Burlington Free Press*, May 31, 1839. *The Calais Advertiser*, May 15, 1850. *The Christian Messenger*, Oct. 6, 1848. *Population of the United States in 1860 Compiled from the Original Returns of the Eighth Census*, Table V.

districts by which they were surrounded. These sectarian townships were still a magnet that attracted surplus population from the parent communities. Another band of townships in which the American percentage was noticeable stretched from the Niagara River to the Detroit River along the north shore of Lake Erie. This paralleled the overland route by which many settlers proceeding from the eastern states to those of the west reached their destination. The figures probably represented some that "dropped off" by the way, although others may be the American-born children of British immigrants who had tarried for a time in the Republic before continuing to the British possessions.

One group of Americans was living under the British flag, not because of any accidental choice, but because they wanted the protection that it offered. With the increasing bitterness of the slavery controversy and the development of facilities for escaping forever from the threat of being returned to their masters, the number of Negroes in Canada increased rapidly. The passage of the Fugitive Slave Act in 1850 made many thousands of presumably free Negroes living in the northern states liable to seizure on suspicion, with the possibility of being sent back into bondage. They now wanted the security to be found on the other side of Lake Erie. The immigration of so many families who had no immediate means of support created a problem that the residents met by organizing several charitable societies, among which the Canadian Anti-Slavery Society founded in 1851 was the most important. For the next decade these groups were active in providing for the refugees. No statistics of arrivals were possible when people whose coming was naturally surreptitious were involved; but the estimate of sixty thousand Negroes in Upper Canada in 1860 (including, as it does, those who were born in the province) does not appear to be an exaggeration.[67]

Several thousand Negroes were residents of the Maritime Provinces in 1860, but almost without exception these persons were descendants of the eighteenth-century refugees, slave and free, who had fled from New York with the Loyalists. A few fugitives had

67. Fred Landon, "Negro Migration to Canada after the Passing of the Fugitive Slave Act," *Journal of Negro History*, V, 22, 35. Carter G. Woodson, *A Century of Negro Migration* (Washington, 1918), 35, 36.

found refuge in the Eastern Townships, coming in from New England. It was in Upper Canada, and particularly in that part which bordered the Detroit River, that the runaway Negroes were concentrated in the greatest numbers. Being conveyed across the river under cover of darkness was an exciting experience, but, in spite of the existence of organizations pledged to care for them, the trying days were not over upon landing on territory that was unconditionally free. The majority settled in the counties adjacent to the border; some became members of the colonies that attempted to provide a community life; and a few drifted into the cities.[68]

After 1857 a number of Canadian emigrants who were on the way to becoming Americans returned to the land of their birth. The economic crisis of that year ushered in another period of hard times when construction ceased, day laborers were discharged, the westward movement halted, and farm produce found no market. From Nova Scotia to the remote townships of the West, outward migration ceased and expatriates came back to parents and friends.[69] It was, however, only a pause in a movement that was to attain even greater proportions. But before it was resumed a bloody war was destined to inaugurate a new era in the development of the Republic and to set up new inducements to tempt Canadians from the allegiance in which they had been born.

68. Benjamin Drew, *A North-Side View of Slavery* (Boston, 1856), gives material on the previous history, entrance, and concentration of Negroes in Canada at this time. *Detroit Free Press*, Feb. 4, 1854. W. H. Siebert, *The Underground Railroad* (New York, 1899), 201–205, 218–225. Fred Landon, "Negro Colonization Schemes in Upper Canada before 1860," *R.S.C., 1929*, Sec. ii, 73–78.

69. *N.S.: App. to Jour. H. of A., 1858*, No. 47, 366. *P.C.: App. to Jour. of Legislative Assembly*, XVI, No. 41: Emigration Report for 1857.

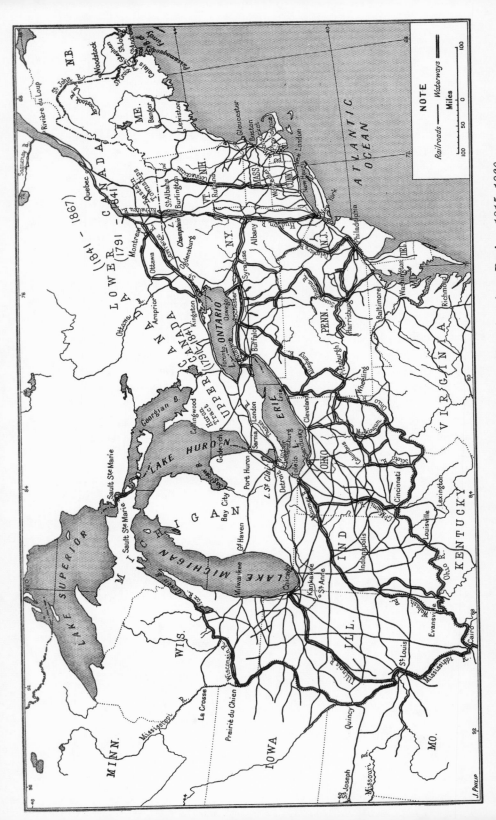

Transportation and Settlement in the Eastern Canadian–American Region, 1815–1860

CHAPTER VII

THE INTERLUDE OF THE CIVIL WAR
1861–1865

By the middle of the nineteenth century so close were the relations, business and personal, between the British Provinces and the United States that any violent change in the internal organization or domestic affairs of the one created repercussions that would be felt in the most remote districts of the other. Such an event occurred in 1861 and the shock was felt all the more because during the preceding decade the ties of mutual dependency had been made even stronger. In 1854 a series of reciprocity agreements between the United States and the provinces (each of which, at that time, determined its own tariff arrangements) provided for a mutual free exchange of natural products. To the American west this meant access to the commerce of Europe through the Great Lakes and the St. Lawrence; to the Canadian east it opened the markets of New England and New York for the fish, eggs, butter, potatoes, and oats of Nova Scotia, New Brunswick, and Prince Edward Island. New England received privileges in the North Atlantic fisheries which she had long claimed as of right; and the Canadians traded freely north and south across the Lakes as well as east and west with Montreal and Europe.[1] Financial connections paralleled the routes of trade; merchants and farmers crossed and recrossed the boundary buying and selling wherever the greatest advantage could be found. The freedom in transit that had characterized movements of population was now extended to business and, as the latter widened its contacts, the flow of people became an even more normal and everyday phenomenon.

During the autumn of 1860 every prospect foreshadowed a complete recovery from the "hard times" of 1857 as soon as the uncertainty of politics had been settled by the November presidential election. But the choice of Abraham Lincoln brought secession and war instead of peace. The disruption of the "southern trade" resulted in

1. *N.S.: App. to Jour. H. of A., 1863,* No. 18. *The Islander* (Charlottetown), Dec. 28, 1860. *Montreal Weekly Witness,* Sept. 4, 1868. D. C. Masters, *The Reciprocity Treaty of 1854* (London, 1937).

bankruptcy to hundreds of American commercial houses and banks, and only those few factories that produced goods that were in demand for the army camp or battlefield continued in operation. All building construction and public improvements were suspended and until the vessels on the Lakes and the railroads of the North could adjust themselves to the situation created by the blocking of the Mississippi, the products of the western farms piled up in the warehouses. In the cities and in the country, the winter, spring, and early summer of 1861 were a period of unemployment and inactivity that troubled Canada as well as the States.[2]

An almost complete cessation of emigration from Europe to the New World was the natural result of the threatening state of affairs.[3] Canadians also were advised by their American friends to remain at home until chances for employment were improved, so that during the season of 1861 migration across the border sharply declined.[4] After the outbreak of hostilities a legal barrier added to the inconvenience. An order from the Department of State required all travelers entering or leaving the United States by sea to be provided with passports.[5] To the majority of British North Americans a passport was an unknown document and not until January, 1862, were facilities provided in various towns in the provinces for the issuance of certificates that would serve the purpose.[6] In March of

2. *The Merchants' Magazine and Commercial Review*, XLIV (New York, Jan.–June, 1861), 414, 665, 787, 791; XLV (July–Dec., 1861), 105, 216, 301, 434, 546. *P.C.: Sess. Pap., 1863*, III, No. 5: "Report of the Commissioner of Crown Lands." The situation among the laboring classes of the city of New York is described in *The Eighteenth Annual Report of the New York Association for Improving the Condition of the Poor* (New York, 1861), 14, 15, 17, 70.

3. *Senate Reports*, 38th Congress, 1st Session, Doc. No. 15, 2.

4. A letter from Boston published in *The Islander*, July 5, 1861, warns Canadians to remain at home. For the decline in emigration see *P.C.: Jour. of Legislative Assembly, 1862*, App. No. 1: "Report of the Select Committee on the Colonization of Wild Lands in Lower Canada."

5. Frank Moore (ed.), *The Rebellion Record: A Diary of American Events*, III (New York, 1862), 92.

6. *Dom. Can.: Sess. Pap., 1869*, No. 75: "Correspondence with the Imperial Government in Reference to the Outlay Incurred in Canada on the Frontier in 1863–4," 28. *P.A.C.: G229*, Lyons to Monck, Nov. 28, 1861.

that year the order was rescinded, but aliens were warned that arrest would be made of any person "who may reasonably be suspected of treason against the United States."[7]

Residents of the United States of British and Canadian birth were well aware of these conditions and this realization as well as the unemployment prevailing during the first months sent a steady stream of dissatisfied persons northward into British territory. Some were French Canadians who returned from the factory towns of New England in the hope that the colonization projects devised for the peopling of the Eastern Townships would assist them; some were Irish and English artisans and laborers who readily found work; some were Canadian-born farm hands whose American experiences were an asset, giving them the preference among applicants for positions. Others who traveled home as rapidly as possible were the Canadians who often went south for the winter months to work in the shipping or lumbering industries in the Gulf and Atlantic ports, but who with the coming of the war found themselves without money and had to be assisted on the way.[8] This movement continued until 1863 when employment conditions in the States changed and the current reversed its course.

The war in its military aspects was responsible for some more direct movements, both to the north and to the south. The abolitionist element in the Federal states had a considerable following in the provinces where the Canadian Anti-Slavery Society was engaged in active propaganda for the cause. Negro refugees arriving destitute and frightened were well-known figures and a constant source of sympathy. *Uncle Tom's Cabin* was as popular a book as it was in the States; it was translated into French, published at Quebec, and enjoyed a wide circulation in the French communities. The outbreak of a war in which the institution of slavery was the most evident issue was bound to enlist active participants in what seemed to be a crusade for freedom.[9]

7. *N.S.: App. to Jour. H. of A., 1862,* No. 31.

8. *P.C.: Sess. Pap., 1863,* III, No. 4: "Annual Report of the Minister of Agriculture and Statistics," App. No. 8. *P.A.C.: G166,* Newcastle to Head, No. 135, Aug. 6, 1861 (enclosure). *Daily British Colonist,* Feb. 1, 1861.

9. Fred Landon, "Canadian Opinion of Southern Secession, 1860–61," *Canadian Historical Review,* I, 255–266. For a comprehensive study, see

Early reports indicated that companies of volunteers would be formed in various Canadian cities, but apparently none of them were actually organized.[10] A royal proclamation issued in London on May 13, 1861, announced the neutrality of the empire in the impending civil war and attention was directed to the Foreign Enlistment Act of 1818 and the penalties to which anyone would be liable who undertook the enlistment of British subjects for foreign service.[11] Nevertheless individual Canadians crossed the border and joined the regiments being formed in every northern city. Even in the early months the officials were far from satisfied that this volunteering was entirely spontaneous, and a formal communication from the American Secretary of War in October that no governmental authority had been delegated to anyone to seek recruits abroad did not entirely allay suspicion.[12]

Some undoubtedly did enlist out of sympathy, among them Negroes from the refugee settlements who traveled to Massachusetts to join the colored regiments that were mustered into service in that state.[13] Some, in particular young French Canadians, sought the excitement offered by the campaigns as a welcome break in the routine of life.[14] Others were tempted by the liberal bounties that any man enrolling in the forces after the first year of the conflict could expect to receive.

It was, in fact, the bounty system that set in motion the migration that attracted most attention. Lincoln's first call for volunteers met a satisfactory response, but when successive calls had drained the communities of the young men with the most enthusiasm or the fewest responsibilities, it became difficult for the states and counties to

Helen G. Macdonald, *Canadian Public Opinion on the American Civil War* (New York, 1926).

10. *Chicago Press Tribune,* June 15, 1861.

11. *British and Foreign State Papers,* LI (London, 1868), 165. *P.A.C.: G229,* Lyons to Head, Oct. 25, 1861 (enclosure).

12. *Dom. Can.: Sess. Pap., 1869,* No. 75, 7.

13. *Buffalo Express,* April 9, Nov. 13, 1863. *The Globe* (Toronto), Feb. 25, 1864; Feb. 2, 1865.

14. *P.C.: Sess. Pap., 1865,* No. 6: "Report of the Minister of Agriculture of the Province of Canada for the Year 1864," 23. Calixa Lavallée, composer of the Canadian national anthem, was member of a Rhode Island regiment. E. Lapierre, *Calixa Lavallée* (Montreal, 1938).

fill the quotas assigned to them.[15] But state and local pride demanded that the number asked for be delivered and enlistment was encouraged by the offering of "bounties" that would enable recruits to meet their outstanding obligations or provide them with a tidy capital that would be an advantage with the return of peace. The competition of one district with another forced the amount upward, and before the close of the war the volunteer might expect bounties (national, state, county, and sometimes city) totaling up to a thousand dollars.[16]

By the summer of 1862, however, the modest bounties then being paid could not fill the ranks with the hundreds of thousands of men that the military situation demanded. The Federal administration decided to resort to a draft upon the militia of the states, but adopted a law which allowed the citizen called into service to provide a substitute who would not be subject to the draft.[17] This was the alien's opportunity. Whatever financial arrangement the conscript made with his substitute was no concern of the officials and the man who could afford to pay for release could afford to have a representative found for him. The broker who dealt in men was the response to this need and his business increased after March, 1863, when a more severe and direct conscription act was passed.[18]

Soldiers of fortune from all parts of the world and healthy foreigners who were willing to take the risk appeared. The trade in Europeans was carried on briskly in New York.[19] Canadians found their market in the border cities. Buffalo, in particular, was the center of much activity but Detroit and northern New England were busy with foreign recruitment as well.[20] Young men from the Cana-

15. Fred A. Shannon, *The Organization and Administration of the Union Army, 1861–65*, I (Cleveland, 1928), 259–263.

16. *Ibid.*, II, 49–99.

17. Act of July 17, 1862. *United States Statutes at Large*, XII, 597.

18. Act of March 3, 1863. *United States Statutes at Large*, XII, 731. *Kennebec Journal* (Augusta, Me.), Oct. 28, 1864. *The Rutland Courier*, Aug. 14, 1863. *Montreal Witness*, April 19, 1865. *Detroit Free Press*, July 24, 28, 1864; Jan. 6, 18, 1865. *P.A.C.: G233*, Lyons to Monck, Aug. 8, 17, 1864.

19. *The Globe*, Jan. 16, 25, 1864. *Allgemeine Auswanderungs Zeitung* (Rudolstadt), March 3, June 2, 1864.

20. *Montreal Witness*, April 9, May 4, June 8, 1864. *Detroit Free Press*, April 24, 1863.

dian side of the Niagara River had no difficulty in making the necessary contacts. A newspaper advertisement illustrates the eagerness with which they were sought:

Substitutes Wanted. On account of the great and increasing demand made for substitutes, the subscribers are ready to pay the *highest price for aliens* willing to take the places of conscripts. For such men as may not have permanent residence in the city, the subscribers will furnish board and lodging up to the time of their being sworn into the service.[21]

So long as the aliens came voluntarily, the business of the broker caused no difficulties, but when his activities had to be extended across the boundary in the search for likely young men, complications of a serious international nature arose, very much like those of 1855 when Joseph Howe of Nova Scotia tried to recruit in the United States for the British Army in the Crimea.[22] Fences and walls in the Canadian cities were plastered with notices describing the opportunities for employment that existed in the States. Undoubtedly some of these were legitimate; others were nothing but bait to lure the applicant into a situation where to enlist was his only recourse, and warnings were printed cautioning those who accepted them as valid to investigate carefully before going to the United States.[23] Personal solicitation was an effective but more dangerous method. According to the opinion expressed by the British consuls and the colonial authorities, soldiers in the military forces stationed in Canada were encouraged to desert.[24]

The newspapers were outspoken in their reports, complaining of the steady depletion of the garrison stationed in the border city of

21. *Buffalo Express,* Aug. 15, 1863.

22. J. B. Brebner, "Joseph Howe and the Crimean War Enlistment Controversy," *Canadian Historical Review,* XI, 300–327. Interestingly enough, one of Howe's sons enlisted in the Union Army.

23. *Montreal Witness,* Aug. 13, Oct. 25, 1862; May 2, 1863; Jan. 13, March 2, Nov. 30, 1864. *Detroit Free Press,* July 24, 1862. *The Globe,* Jan. 12, Feb. 2, 23, March 16, April 29, Nov. 3, 1864. *P.C.: Sess. Pap., 1864,* III, No. 32, Part III: "Report on Immigration to Canada for the Year 1863," App. No. 4. William F. Roney, "Recruiting and Crimping in Canada for the Northern Forces, 1861–1865," *Mississippi Valley Historical Review,* X (1923), 21–33.

24. *Dom. Can.: Sess. Pap., 1869,* No. 75, 10.

Kingston, of the assistance given the runaways in the neighboring American towns, and of the willingness with which they were accepted in the volunteer regiments where no questions were asked.[25] Mere boys, it was charged, were induced to leave home for the life of army adventure.[26] Liberal rewards were offered for the apprehension of the agents and occasionally one was caught. But the majority were too wary, passing themselves off as buyers of stock or employers in search of laborers.[27] Their methods became bolder in 1864 and the early months of 1865.[28]

The charges made by Canadian newspapers were countered by the complaints of American army officers that many of those who enrolled of their own volition and collected the liberal bounties decamped at the first opportunity, slipped into Canada, and returned for another profitable enlistment as soon as they thought it safe. Some were accused of several transactions of this nature. Proof of such charges was difficult, but "bounty jumping" was such a fundamental defect of the whole system that it cannot be doubted that aliens who had a place of refuge at hand availed themselves of the chance of making some easy profits.[29] In 1864, when the American government was confronted with the protests of the British ambassador regarding alleged recruiting activities, the Secretary of State replied that, far from authorizing agents, the government did not know of their existence; aliens in large numbers, it was true, served in the Federal army, but they had entered the country as immigrants and service in the military forces was their own choice.[30]

25. *The Globe,* Jan. 13, Feb. 3, 12, 23, March 1, July 18, Aug. 20, Sept. 28, 1864. *Montreal Witness,* March 15, May 28, Aug. 13, 16, 1862; May 23, Aug. 1, 1863; Feb. 3, 10, 13, 17, March 4, 30, 1864.

26. *The Globe,* Jan. 6, 1864.

27. *Ibid.,* Jan. 11, 12, 14, 18, 27, Feb. 2, 16, 23, Sept. 8, Nov. 1, 1864. *Montreal Witness,* Jan. 20, March 2, Sept. 21, 1864.

28. *The Nova Scotian* (Halifax), Jan. 30, 1865. *The Christian Messenger,* April 13, 1864.

29. J. M. Callahan, "The Northern Lake Frontier during the Civil War," *Annual Report of the American Historical Association for the Year 1896,* 358. *The Globe,* March 16, 1864; March 3, 1865. *The Rutland Courier,* Aug. 28, 1863.

30. *War of the Rebellion: Official Records* (Washington, 1880–1901), Series III, Vol. IV, 455–457.

Whether volunteers, substitutes, or bounty jumpers, tens of thousands of soldiers of Canadian birth served in the northern forces. How many there were that came directly from Canada cannot be stated with any certainty. The standard authority on the nativities of the soldiers serving in the Federal armies (an investigation based upon state and regimental records) lists 53,532 as being born in the British-American provinces. New York led with about 20,000 and Illinois with 4,400 was second. Most of the other border states had about 3,000 enrolled in their forces. Many of these aliens, however, were domiciled in the United States before enlistment, and these figures can provide no evidence as to the extent of the influx during the course of the war nor information regarding which provinces contributed most liberally to the man power of the northern army.[31]

Without question, French Canada sent many more than any other part of British America. Several of the Catholic bishops enjoined their parish priests to warn the young men in their congregations against the dangers of foreign military service,[32] and three statements made at the close of the conflict emphasize the preponderance. One of them estimated that out of 40,000 enlistments, 36,000 were French Canadians; and another placed the proportion at 35,000 out of 43,000.[33] Ferdinand Gagnon estimated the number as 40,000 in the northern army.[34] It was natural that the region that sent the most emigrants in peace should contribute the most soldiers in war; and in some of the regiments formed in northern New England so many of the privates were from Quebec that French was the prevailing tongue.[35]

Although Canadians appeared in Boston to volunteer or offer themselves as substitutes, there is little evidence that the Maritime Provinces sent any considerable number of their sons into the conflict.[36] The four years of war were four years of prosperity for

31. Benjamin Apthorp Gould, *Investigations in the Military and Anthropological Statistics of American Soldiers* (New York, 1869), 27.

32. Helen G. Macdonald, *op. cit.*, 133. *Montreal Witness*, April 30, 1864.

33. *The Nova Scotian*, March 6, 20, 1865.

34. *Le Travailleur* (Worcester, Mass.), Oct. 31, 1879.

35. *The Globe*, March 1, April 29, 1864.

36. *Buffalo Express*, Aug. 3, 1863.

them. Any young man who craved excitement needed only to join the crew of one of the many blockade runners that swarmed out of Halifax and St. John. Those that wanted work and attractive wages could secure employment in fishing and lumbering, mining, shipbuilding, and farming. The conditions imposed by the maritime war gave an impetus to the first two of these industries. American schooners and American seamen were needed for other tasks, so that the fishing grounds were left to be exploited by Nova Scotians. The closing of the ports in the southern states prevented any of the timber of Georgia and the Carolinas from reaching the market and lumbering enjoyed a renewed activity.[37]

When the war began, Nova Scotia was living in the midst of a gold excitement that had started in 1860 when miners who had returned from California and Australia discovered paying lodes in geological formations similar to those that they had learned to recognize on the shores of the Pacific. No frantic rush of adventurers followed the discovery, although a few restless Yankees appeared upon the scene. Nevertheless, for several years the mine shafts yielded gold in paying quantities and able-bodied men never needed to be without a job.[38] The coal mines of Cape Breton received a stimulus that was more directly a consequence of the war. The high rates of wartime transportation lifted the price of coal in New England and New York to a level at which the provincial mines could profitably export to the United States. American capital and experienced American workers moved north to seize the opportunity, and from 1863 to 1865 coal was exported in increasing quantities to the cities down the coast.[39] Finally, farming also reaped its share of the financial harvest. Agricultural exports had never been large, but potatoes, the staple of New Brunswick and Nova Scotia, and oats, the staple of Prince Edward Island, were needed to feed the men and horses engaged in war, and all kinds of craft were loaded with these products

37. S. A. Saunders, "The Maritime Provinces and the Reciprocity Treaty," *The Dalhousie Review*, XIV, 355–371. *The Globe*, Jan. 8, 1864. *Eastport Sentinel*, April 29, Oct. 21, 1863. *Kennebec Journal*, Nov. 6, 1863.

38. *N.S.: App. to Jour. H. of A., 1863*, No. 6.

39. *N.S.: App. to Jour. H. of A., 1863*, No. 14, 15. *Annual Report on Foreign Commerce, Year Ended Sept. 30, 1866* (Washington), 71, 72 (hereafter *A.R.F.C.*).

and sent off to the wharves of Boston and New York.[40] It was not the excitement of war, but the dull times that came with peace that caused the "down-Easter" to leave his home.

The draft policy adopted in the summer of 1862 set in motion a second current of migration that aroused as bitter comment in the United States as the first had caused in Canada. Draft dodgers were soon dubbed "skedaddlers" because of the unanimity with which they sought to put themselves out of the reach of the provost marshal by flight across the boundary. Every subsequent order of conscription provoked another wave in the current and in the public mind the fugitives were classed along with actual military deserters who also took refuge outside the jurisdiction of the government at Washington.[41] Desertion and draft dodging were noticeably prevalent in the border states of Maine, New Hampshire, New York, Wisconsin, and Minnesota; and the streets of Montreal, Windsor, and Amherstburg swarmed with these temporary, and in many cases undesirable, residents.[42]

At first their presence caused little concern. The majority were active young men, acquainted with American agricultural routine and experienced in all the work that a farm demanded. There already was a shortage in labor caused by the great decline in immigration from the British Isles, and Canadian landowners welcomed the coming of hands who could be trusted with tasks that a "green" worker could not perform. The early comers arrived in time to assist in the harvest of 1862 and their presence materially reduced the exorbitant wages that the farmers had expected to pay.[43] But by the next year the comments were not so cordial. A few of the refugees were able to buy or rent farms, but the majority, even of those who

40. *The Islander,* Nov. 13, 1863; Nov. 25, 1864. *The Nova Scotian,* Feb. 20, 1865.

41. *War of the Rebellion: Official Records,* Series III, Vol. II, 329, 370; Vol. III, 425, 426, 485. *Buffalo Express,* March 27, 1863. *Eastport Sentinel,* Aug. 13, Nov. 11, 1862. *The Rutland Courier,* Aug. 8, 1862; March 13, 1863. *Kennebec Journal,* Nov. 4, 1864. *Detroit Free Press,* Aug. 10, 12, 14, Sept. 13, 1862; Feb. 12, 1863. *Montreal Witness,* April 29, 1863.

42. *P.C.: Sess. Pap., 1864,* III, No. 32, Part III: "Report on the Immigration to Canada for the Year 1863," App. No. 4. Ella Lonn, *Desertion during the Civil War* (New York, 1928), 207.

43. *P.C.: Sess. Pap., 1863,* III, No. 4, App. No. 6.

had passed through the customhouse, had no baggage but a half-filled carpetbag, and it was suspected that the much greater number who came in surreptitiously possessed even less. By 1863, and to a more marked degree in 1864, skedaddlers and deserters were so numerous and so uniformly spread throughout the central and western parts of the province of Canada that reports ran that native workers found it difficult to compete with them in wage jobs and that farmers could obtain all the helpers they wanted by promising nothing but shelter and board.[44]

Estimates of their number ranged up to fifteen thousand, and angry American comment was aroused.[45] A background for this feeling was provided by the belief that sentiment in the provinces was decidedly pro-Confederate, and the reception given the refugees, however proper under the accepted rules of international law, was interpreted as a harboring of outlaws. The failure of the legislature of Canada to take action in 1863 providing for the compulsory return of all deserters from the United States Army intensified the dissatisfaction.[46] Congress, however, was anything but vindictive. In March, 1865, when the value of every man who could serve in civilian or military pursuits was rated high, a law was passed authorizing the President to issue a proclamation giving all deserters sixty days during which they would be pardoned upon returning to their regiments and prescribing the loss of citizenship as punishment for failure to comply.[47]

Canada was the home of another type of refugee whom the Northerner feared as well as hated. During the prosperous years of the 1850's many cotton planters who came north for the summer passed through the states in which abolitionist sentiment was strong and lived for the season in the pleasant towns along the St. Lawrence. The personal connections thus formed were remembered when civil

44. *P.C.: Sess. Pap., 1864,* III, No. 32, Part III: "Report on the Immigration to Canada for the Year 1863," App. No. 3; *1865,* III, No. 6, 127, 138. *The Rutland Courier,* April 3, 1863.

45. Ella Lonn, *op. cit.,* 202.

46. *Buffalo Express,* April 27, 1863.

47. *United States Statutes at Large,* 38th Congress, 2d Session, C. 79, Sec. 21. The proclamation is to be found in John G. Nicolay and John Hay, *Abraham Lincoln: Complete Works,* II (New York, 1894), 660–661.

war began. Men too old to fight, families of planters who were in active service and, in time, veterans invalided out of the army gathered in Montreal and elsewhere, where they were welcomed into the most select circles of society.[48] Here they were joined by Confederate sympathizers who brought with them capital and experience with which they set up many kinds of business enterprise.[49] Residents on the American side of the border had at first nothing to fear from these gentlemen, but when the Confederate government sent military agents to Canada to rally escaped Confederate soldiers and others there for raids on the United States, the civilian refugees shared with them the full wrath and angry protests of the North.[50]

Until the year 1863, military considerations had been predominant in determining the population relations of the United States and British North America. After years of conflict, economic factors began to operate. By that time the business structure of the states that remained in the Union had been adjusted to the new relationships that existed among the different parts of the country; an army at the front had developed into a market to take the place of the one that the manufacturers had lost in the secession of the southern states; and crop shortages in Europe led to an export demand for every bushel of wheat that the West could spare. A hitherto unknown confidence in the successful outcome of the struggle was an incentive to housing, factory, and railroad construction.[51] In eastern industrial centers and in western farming communities the one requirement that had to be satisfied before economic demands could be met was more labor. Wages began to rise early in 1863, and by

48. J. E. Collins, *Life and Times of the Right Honorable Sir John A. Macdonald* (Toronto, 1883), 268. Fred Landon, "Canadian Opinion," 255–266.

49. *P.C.: Sess. Pap., 1864*, III, No. 32, Part III: "Report on the Immigration to Canada for the Year 1863," App. No. 1. *The Globe*, April 29, 1864. *Montreal Witness*, April 30, 1864.

50. *War of the Rebellion: Official Records*, Series I, Vol. XLIII, 930–935. For a full account of the border problems during the Civil War see C. P. Stacey, *Canada and the British Army, 1846–1871* (London, 1936), 117–178.

51. Edward Dicey, *Six Months in the Federal States*, II (London, 1863), 139, 140. Emerson D. Fite, *Social and Industrial Conditions in the North during the Civil War* (New York, 1910), 17–154. S. M. Peto, *Resources and Prospects of America* (New York, 1866), 47.

1864 skilled and unskilled workers demanded and received a scale of payment that employers felt to be an insupportable handicap to production.[52]

The traditional American solution for this problem was a call sent to Europe. The governor of Michigan expressed the need and policy: "We want men, we want settlers; and the true interest of the whole state requires that immigration should be encouraged and fostered by needful legislation."[53] Secretary of State Seward wrote: "The government frankly avows that it encourages immigration from all countries."[54] No longer, however, was the plain news that labor was needed sufficient to attract all who could be employed. Encouragement and advertisement were necessary. Some of the states appointed commissions to draw as many of the newcomers as possible in their direction, and in 1864 the Federal government set up its own board, which was instructed to facilitate the influx of Europeans and to use all means available to swell the incoming tide.

These beckonings to Europe could be successful only with time. Meanwhile the Canadians who came into the Republic did so in response, not to official blandishments, but to the inviting labor market that existed. An exchange in population was the first phenomenon. Skedaddlers and deserters had glutted the labor markets in the provinces and the resultant decline in wages there made American high wages all the more noticeable. A "counteremigration" of Anglo-Canadian workers set in, and as their success became known, neighbors followed and immigrants recently arrived from Great Britain joined in the movement.[55] French Canada also responded, perhaps even earlier, because the contacts that bound the American industrial districts to the St. Lawrence seigniories were many and frequently personal. The current began to flow particularly strongly in the summer of 1863, and instead of ceasing as was usual in the

52. For the high wages paid to agricultural laborers see the county by county survey printed in the *Third Annual Report of the Secretary of the State Board of Agriculture of Michigan for the Year 1864* (Lansing, Mich., 1865), 14–51.

53. *Joint Documents of the State of Michigan for the Year 1862,* Doc. No. 2, 12.

54. *War of the Rebellion: Official Records,* Series III, Vol. IV, 456.

55. *Buffalo Express,* March 27, April 13, 1863.

fall of the year, it continued during the winter, attaining a new and hitherto unknown volume in 1864. Habitants deserted the villages and residents on the colonization lands abandoned clearings.[56] A bishop visiting his diocese that summer was much concerned to meet on the roads caravans of carts filled with families and baggage moving down to the New England cities where every hand could find employment.[57]

Fortunately for the prairie farmers of the Mississippi Valley states, farm machinery was steadily reducing the need for hired men, and there are no contemporary accounts of any large influx of agricultural laborers, although every one that appeared could have counted upon immediate employment. But independent farmers from Canada did come. Some settled in Kansas; some chose Missouri, where the adoption of a law emancipating slaves seemed to promise a new era in development; and others (perhaps the majority) moved over into the neighboring state of Michigan, which could offer inducements of a particularly favorable character.[58] To this state there had been granted by Congress large areas of so-called swamp lands which the state, in turn, had disposed of to speculative buyers. Ownership was represented by scrip which in the absence of purchasers for several years had fallen in price. The prudent Canadian landowner who wanted a larger estate was in a most advantageous situation. His Canadian dollar, still on a gold basis, could be exchanged for two or more "greenback" dollars, and the latter were used to buy up depreciated scrip. Excellent land could be secured at prices that varied from twenty to thirty cents in gold per acre.[59]

Another advantage was the insistent demand which the war produced for all manner of easily accessible Michigan products. For a decade the exploitation of its timber resources had employed men and capital; the war broadened the nation's needs. Southern secession and the blockade cut off the sources from which most of the

56. *P.C.: Sess. Pap., 1864,* III, No. 32, Appendix: "Report on the Colonization Roads in Lower Canada"; Part III: "Report on the Immigration to Canada for the Year 1863." *Montreal Witness,* April 30, 1864.

57. Louis de Goesbriand, *Les Canadiens des Etats-Unis,* 3.

58. *Buffalo Express,* March 23, 1865. *A.R.F.C., 1867,* 141. *The Globe,* April 7, 1864.

59. David D. Oliver, *Centennial History of Alpena County, Michigan,* 115.

rosin, turpentine, tar, and pitch, so essential in the day of wooden vessels, had come. In six months price quotations in New York advanced more than 200 per cent.[60] The pine of Michigan, including even the stump heretofore discarded, yielded these products satisfactorily, so that the pioneer could sell the stumps which he pulled from his cut-over lands. Meanwhile he had no difficulty in disposing of his harvest of grain and other crops in the mill towns of the Saginaw Valley.[61] These mills did not merely cut lumber and shingles. The geologists had discovered the strata of salt that lay a thousand or two feet below the surface of the soil, and every sawmill was neighbor to a "salt-block" down into which its exhaust steam was forced, later to be pumped up as brine and evaporated. Laborers as well as farmers flocked into the valley, where typical boom times held sway.[62]

Capitalists, loggers, and rivermen who wanted to pass over Michigan could find opportunities almost as alluring in the forests of northwestern Wisconsin. The prairie settlement that went on in spite of the war created a demand for the lumber that even the humblest homesteader had to secure before he could build the rudest sort of a shack. Every raft of logs that was floated down the St. Croix or the Chippewa was soon cut up in the mills along the Mississippi and transported by railroad and wagon to the straggling frontier settlements. In 1864 and 1865 the expansion of the industry was checked by the need for more helpers; wages in the pineries and on the rivers were high and more lumbermen from Maine, New Brunswick, and Quebec appeared to join the gangs of loggers and crews of raftsmen.[63]

The second important industry of the then far Northwest was mining. As in other phases of economic life, the first shock of civil war resulted in a stagnation which within two years gave way to an unprecedented activity. The spring of 1862 found many of the Lake

60. *The Merchants' Magazine and Commercial Review,* XLV (July–Dec., 1861), 439.

61. David D. Oliver, *op. cit.,* 93, 94.

62. Augustus H. Gansser, *History of Bay County, Michigan and Representative Citizens,* 163.

63. Frederick Merk, *Economic History of Wisconsin during the Civil War Decade* (Madison, Wis., 1916), 60, 76, 108, 109. *Transactions of the Wisconsin State Agricultural Society,* VII (Madison, 1868), 50.

Superior mines closed. The price of copper was low and prospects uncertain. It was reported that the miners had departed "in droves."[64] But in the middle of the summer came a favorable reaction. A great increase in the demand for iron and copper reopened the mines and called back the French Canadians who constituted a large part of the working force. In spite of the tardy beginning, the year 1862 was the most prosperous that the region had experienced and each of the two years that followed witnessed an increase in production over the preceding twelve months. Wages followed the course of production, rising with each year and attracting laborers from wherever they could be found.[65] The permanency of these mines seemed now assured and communication with the industrial world was facilitated by the construction of a "military road" that reached the western section, while a branch line of the Northwestern Railroad tapped the easternmost mines. Along with these improvements new wedges of settlement were laid out.[66]

Although the expansion of population and the development of industry in the Lake and upper Mississippi region were remarkable for a period of war, the achievements actually fell short of what would have been accomplished had not the red man brought war to the adjacent frontier. The Sioux uprising of 1862, resulting in the massacre of scores of pioneers, frightened away settlers who were already taking up lands, and retarded the peopling of the American part of the fertile valley of the Red River.[67] On the other hand, it brought into prominence the advantages of settlement north of the forty-ninth parallel, where British relations with the Indians were conducted with less hostility, and the presence of an army of Hud-

64. *P.C.: Sess. Pap., 1863,* III, No. 5, App. No. 43: "Report on the Mines of Lakes Huron and Superior."

65. *Joint Documents of the State of Michigan for the Year 1862,* Doc. No. 13: "Annual Report of the Superintendent of the St. Mary's Falls Ship Canal for the Year 1862," 7, 8; *ibid., 1863,* Doc. No. 10, 4; *ibid., 1864,* Doc. No. 14, 4, 5. Conditions in the Lake Superior mining region are described in a letter in the *Northwestern Christian Advocate* (Chicago), July 2, 1862.

66. Robert M. Dessureau, *History of Langlade County, Wisconsin* (Antigo, Wis., 1922), 21, 263.

67. *History of the Red River Valley,* I (Chicago, 1909), 73. A. H. Moehlman, "The Red River of the North," *Geographical Review,* XXV (New York, 1935), 79–91.

son's Bay Company traders and half-breed trappers provided a welcome market.

The advantages that would result from the settlement of the lands adjacent to Fort Garry were well known to British colonial authorities, but the way in which it was being accomplished was far from encouraging. Access from the province of Canada via Lake Superior and the chain of rivers and lakes that had been the fur traders' route was not practical for settlers, who were usually burdened with a heavy load of belongings. The few who did move from the eastern possessions of the British crown to those in the west traveled through the United States and often gave up the journey to locate in one of the new American communities. In the meantime, residents of Minnesota were passing over the lands of their own frontier and taking possession of the promising locations along the river in British territory. Observers realized that these pioneers were merely the forerunners of the irresistible line of settlement that was steadily, though slowly, advancing across the continent. Unless it was checked by the planting of loyal subjects, the area that should be the connecting link between the British soil on the Atlantic and that on the Pacific would fall into the possession of the land-hungry Yankee and, if annexed by the United States, would destroy all hopes of a dominion stretching from ocean to ocean.[68]

The new province of British Columbia, although firmly attached to the empire by political, naval, and military bonds, was in commerce and population a part of the Pacific region which had its center at San Francisco. Agricultural resources remained undeveloped. Food and supplies of all kinds came up the coast from California, Oregon, and Washington. Fully three-fourths of the fifteen thousand miners who in 1864 made up the principal element in the population were Americans, and half of the business houses were branches of American establishments.[69] Before the close of the war the gold-mining interest began to decline and a return movement into the states, which by 1867 was to reduce the population to no

68. *P.C.: Sess. Pap., 1863*, I, No. 29: "Copies of All Communications Made or Orders in Council Passed in Relation to the Opening of a Route to Red River or British Columbia and the Pacific"; VI, No. 33: "Memorial of the People of Red River to the British and Canadian Governments."

69. *A.R.F.C., 1862*, 147.

more than six thousand souls, was already under way.[70] British Columbia no less than the territories of the Hudson's Bay Company was rapidly becoming a problem that was to test the statesmanship of the empire builders. Unless they made a vigorous effort to shape the future, within a generation the westward and northward movements and the annexationist ambitions of Americans threatened to remove it from their sphere.

These problems, realized and discussed early in the 1860's, were pushed into the background by international complications that demanded vigilance and skillful diplomacy. By 1864 the adventurous Confederate refugees domiciled in Canada were ready to open a war of terrorism against the unprotected towns of the northern states.[71] An attempt to seize Johnson's Island in Lake Erie, where several hundred Confederate officers were imprisoned, was frustrated.[72] A small band of refugees and sympathizers crossed over into Vermont and raided the town of St. Albans.[73] An effort to burn the city of New York was checked.[74] These incidents, although largely chimerical, forced upon the administration of the Federal states a realization of the dangers that might grow out of the complacency with which they had accepted the unprotected and unguarded northern frontier. The answer was a new policy in relation to migration.

On December 17, 1864, an order was issued directing all persons entering the United States except those coming by sea to be provided with passports. The exception was in favor of European immigrants whose coming there was no reason to check. The purpose was clearly stated in the sentence: "This regulation is intended to apply especially to persons proposing to come to the United States from the neighboring British provinces."[75] Journalists explained that the object was to compel the Canadian authorities to be more careful in

70. *Ibid., 1867,* 204–206.

71. *War of the Rebellion: Official Records,* Series II, Vol. VIII, 525.

72. *Ibid.,* Series I, Vol. XLIII, 932–933.

73. John G. Nicolay and John Hay, *Abraham Lincoln,* VIII (New York, 1890), 24–26.

74. John W. Headley, *Confederate Operations in Canada and New York* (New York, 1906), 274–307.

75. *War of the Rebellion: Official Records,* Series III, Vol. IV, 1020.

the observance of neutral duties along the border.[76] American citizens passing into Canada were also compelled to show their passports before they were allowed to leave the country. To the many citizens of both nations who were constantly moving over the frontier the order was an irritating nuisance. The phrases in which Canadian editors expressed their disgust illustrate how nonexistent realization of the international boundary had been. One characterized the order "a piece of stupidity" and another described it as "a disgrace . . . an excrescence of despotism, which no country pretending to be free would tolerate for a day."[77]

Nonetheless the regulation was made effective. Much of the business of the Grand Trunk Railroad was made up of the transit trade from Buffalo to Detroit and this was now severely curtailed.[78] The railroad officials may have complained. Undoubtedly many Canadians cooled in their sympathy toward the Confederacy after the St. Albans raid had made them understand how serious the consequences of a repetition might be. Whatever the motive or the impelling force, in February, 1865, the Canadian Parliament under a suspension of rules rushed through a bill providing for the expulsion of any alien who was suspected of engaging in acts of hostility against a friendly power and for the seizure of any vessels or arms that obviously were to be used for the same purpose.[79] Probably satisfied by this action, the United States government rescinded the passport order on March 8.[80]

Appomattox and the close of the war followed in quick succession. Deserters, draft dodgers, and Confederate refugees had little reason for remaining in the provinces and the only punishment that the former had to fear was the loss of the rights of citizenship—a fear

76. *Buffalo Express*, Feb. 1, 1865.

77. *The Globe* quoted in *Buffalo Express*, Jan. 5, 1865. *The Islander*, June 9, 1865. *Eastport Sentinel*, April 5, 1865. *Montreal Witness*, Jan. 11, 1865. *Detroit Free Press*, Jan. 7, 1865.

78. *Buffalo Express*, Jan. 21, 1865.

79. P.C.: *Jour. of Legislative Assembly, 1865*, 31, 54, 59, 63, 67, 77. P.C.: *Jour. of Legislative Council, 1865*, 76. The act (28 Vic., c. 1) is printed in *Statutes of the Province of Canada*, 8th Parliament, 3d Session (Quebec, 1865), 1–9.

80. *War of the Rebellion: Official Records*, Series III, Vol. IV, 1238.

that was not strong enough to keep them in perpetual exile. The amnesty proclamation of President Johnson issued on May 25, 1865, assured the Confederate partisans that they would not suffer because of the unsuccessful rebellion in which they had been engaged. During the summer the exodus was general and the emigrants left few traces of their residence except an occasional place name like "Skedaddle Ridge" in New Brunswick which fifty years later still marked the site of a temporary colony of Americans.[81] Even persons whose residence antedated the war caught the spirit of the times and joined in the movement back to the land in which they had been born.[82]

The Civil War was more than a mere episode that during four troubled years set in motion some unexpected and temporary exchanges of North American population. The course and outcome of the struggle removed many of the obstacles to population expansion that had arisen out of the slavery controversy. The Republic emerged from the conflict with a new program for the disposal of public lands, a new policy in subsidizing railroad construction toward the Pacific, and a determined resolve to remove the Indian menace from the plains. A westward surge of population was the inevitable consequence of these decisions and the British provinces that were blocked by the Laurentian Shield from a west of their own were destined to be as directly influenced as any eastern state of the Republic.

81. *Buffalo Express,* Aug. 1, 1865. *The Nova Scotian,* July 8, 1865. *The Globe,* May 13, 1865. William F. Ganong, "A Monograph on the Origins of Settlements in the Province of New Brunswick," *R.S.C., 1904,* Sec. ii, 99, 173.

82. *A.R.F.C., 1867,* 141.

CHAPTER VIII

EXPANSION AND DEPRESSION
1865–1880

DURING the decade and a half after 1865 economic conditions in North America fluctuated violently—eight years of swelling prosperity, seven of virtual stagnation. During these fifteen years, population movements, always responsive to the changing prospects of business and agriculture, reflected first the hopes of the period of expansion, then the fears of the succeeding depression.

Transition from war to peace was accomplished without much derangement of New England's industry. Some individual firms that produced only for men in the field were forced into bankruptcy, but in general the falling demand from the army was met, buoyed up, and finally expanded by the increasing needs of a growing country that for four years had postponed all activities except those related to the national emergency. Belated production was not the only circumstance that kept the wheels of industry turning. European harvests were not sufficient to feed the workers of Great Britain, and every bushel of wheat that the American producer could spare brought a welcome cash return that stimulated all the old farming communities and called forth schemes for more ships, more railroads, and more acres under cultivation. This buoyancy was transmitted to the industrial towns. Cotton mills and shoe shops ran machinery day and night in an attempt to fill the orders that poured in, only to learn that their equipment was inadequate and their employees too few. They drew up plans for new factory blocks and hung out the sign: "Help wanted."[1]

The hill farmers of the northern states had not many more sons to send away from home, and Europe with its seemingly inexhaustible reserves of men was too far distant to be of immediate assistance. But between the cities of New England and the villages and farms

1. E. E. Fostor (ed.), *Lamb's Textile Industries of the United States,* II (Boston, 1916), 367. The prosperity and labor demands in a typical mill town in Maine are described in the *Lewiston Weekly Journal,* Oct. 18, 25, Nov. 1, 22, 1866; Jan. 10, March 14, April 4, May 2, 9, 1867.

of the provinces to the north and east the connections were many and intimate. The favorable opportunities available for strong arms and skillful hands were soon known in all the British North American districts from which emigrants had hitherto gone out in search of a better fortune, and now the call had the greater appeal because with the cessation of civil war in the Republic had come a sharp depression in Prince Edward Island, Nova Scotia, and New Brunswick, an economic decline which was the result of an inevitable adjustment that had no compensating features.

In political discussions the residents of these provinces blamed their unsatisfactory condition upon the abrogation by the United States in 1866 of the Reciprocity Treaty of 1854. Without doubt the sudden loss of the open market where the "Maritimers" had found ready sale for the fish, potatoes, and wood products, or the gypsum and coal, that had frequently been taken to the wharf in Boston or New York in a local small sailing vessel was a financial setback of considerable importance.[2] The American tariff barrier could be surmounted only by accepting low prices. But other causes were also at work, factors that were related to great technical changes in agriculture, industry, and transportation which were transforming economic life upon the continent of North America and on the adjacent seas.

The Prince Edward Islanders complained that they could no longer dispose of the oats that their fields yielded in abundance; the customary demand for fish from the West Indies had declined; ships that were constructed could not be sold and there was no employment for them if they remained in the builder's possession. But more disturbing, in view of the local decline in prices, was the operation of the Land Purchase Act, a statute which sought to change the numerous tenants of the large estates that had been established upon the island into freeholders by providing government loans to those who were willing to assume a heavy burden of debt. Too many of them had been willing; they discovered that regular payments due to the government could be just as oppressive as rents owing to a landlord and now when income had declined the danger of losing

2. *Montreal Weekly Witness*, Jan. 25, March 8, 1867; Aug. 14, Sept. 4, 1868.

possession by foreclosure was as threatening as the threat of eviction had ever been. In an island community that offered little field for enterprising youth there was only one way that a young man or young woman could assist hard-pressed parents: that was to go where service was rewarded with liberal wages. The ensuing exodus of young people depleted the households of even the most substantial farmers and tempted many of them to join their children in the foreign country.[3]

The fishermen of Newfoundland and Nova Scotia also learned how American protectionism and technical change could bring many disadvantages to them in their wake. After the wartime suspension the skippers of Gloucester and Boston returned to the banks and the waters of the St. Lawrence with new equipment and revived energy. The older methods that still characterized the provincial fisheries could not meet such competition successfully. The prevailing "credit system," which resulted in all hands being continuously in debt to the owners, coupled with a series of poor catches and the prevailing low prices, discouraged the more energetic. Many transferred themselves for the season to American vessels, where their skill and knowledge were in high repute and the catch had an open market. There was a natural tendency among married men to move the entire family to the States after a few trips of this sort, but the young unmarried men usually returned to spend the winter in their native village unless they were engaged to go out with the American winter fleet. In 1875, out of the seven thousand men sailing in the Gloucester fleet, three thousand had been born in the British provinces.[4]

Nova Scotia also suffered because of the collapse of the export trade in coal upon which such optimistic hopes had been centered. During the last year of the war the development of the mines had

3. *The Islander,* Aug. 9, Nov. 8, 1867; May 22, June 5, 1868; June 18, Aug. 29, Sept. 24, Oct. 29, Nov. 5, 1869. Prince Edward Island, *Report of the Proceedings before the Commissioners Appointed under the Provisions of the Land Purchase Act, 1875.* Reported by P. S. Macgowan (Charlottetown, 1877), 28, 39, 99, 204, 379, 410, 448.

4. *The Citizen* (Halifax), Jan. 30, Aug. 24, 1872; March 14, 28, 1824. *Montreal Weekly Witness,* Oct. 18, 1867. *Yarmouth Tribune,* Dec. 11, 1867; Jan. 5, 1869; Dec. 7, 1870; April 12, 1876. George H. Proctor, *The Fishermen's Memorial and Record Book* (Gloucester, 1873), 119, 120.

been most promising. New England provided a market in which the Nova Scotians enjoyed, under the conditions of the time, a virtual monopoly. Then the advantage was lost as suddenly as it had been gained. With peace, the Pennsylvania mines returned to uninterrupted production, and the consolidation of railroad lines cheapened transportation to such a degree that American coal from the interior could be sold at lower rates than the sea-borne provincial product. As a result many of the Nova Scotia shafts were closed; the workers, many of whom were recent immigrants from the British Isles, passed on to join friends in the United States; and farmers who had supplied the operatives drifted along behind them.[5]

New Brunswick was no better off than its neighbors. A letter from St. John described the situation in the spring of 1868: "Our streets are dull, our shops empty, our factories half employed, our shipyards silent, our tenement houses half deserted."[6] From 1866 on, the departure of mechanics and laborers to seek employment in the States was apparent to all observers and here again the American tariff and new technical developments provided the explanation. The day of sailing vessels was over. Iron and steam were taking the place of wood and sails, and no longer were the craft built from New Brunswick timber in demand in all the commercial ports of the world. Vessels were still built and sold for the slower trades, but deserted yards foreshadowed their impending disappearance from the seas.[7]

In all the British provinces along the Atlantic was heard the complaint already familiar in every New England state—the young people are not content to remain on the parental homestead but they seek the more exciting life of the city or follow the lure of the West.[8] Since the provinces had no great cities to absorb them and no west to tempt them, leaving home meant expatriation, although motives and causes were similar whether the adventurer set out from a rural home in Nova Scotia or in Massachusetts. In both regions an agriculture which could not compete with western lands, once transpor-

5. *N.S.: App. to Jour. H. of A., 1867*, No. 7, 12; *1870*, No. 14.

6. *Montreal Weekly Witness*, March 13, 1868.

7. *Yarmouth Tribune*, Aug. 8, 1866; May 26, 1869. *Montreal Witness*, Sept. 27, 1865; Sept. 8, 1866. *A.R.F.C., 1869*, 209.

8. *The Nova Scotian*, June 8, 1868. *Acadian Recorder* (Halifax), April 11, 1872.

tation to the interior was developed, began to succumb in various ways to its natural handicaps. In coastal New England and in the Maritimes crops declined because small attempt had been made to renew the fertility of the soil. Lack of capital prevented extensive development of existing resources or improvement of less productive lands. Hired help was usually wanted only at haying time or harvest. Families were large and farms were small. Practically every home had at least one son and one daughter whose services were not in demand in the household or the neighborhood. For them, reaching maturity involved emigration.[9] But the movement, when once under way, was not limited merely to farm workers who were superfluous. Their going engendered a spirit of restlessness, and painters, blacksmiths, carpenters, and shoemakers saw apprentices slip away as soon as their terms were over. The dearth of domestic servants in the cities was so annoying (girls from the Maritimes being in particular demand in Boston) that the suggestion that Chinese might be introduced was seriously offered.[10]

The movement outward was not continuous, nor were the Maritimes always affected in the same way at the same time as Quebec and Ontario. The end of the Civil War and the termination of the Reciprocity Treaty started exoduses which alarmed observers in all sections, but return movements and lessening of the emigration "fever" between 1867 and 1870 bred false hopes which seemed to be justified by a fairly general demand for labor all over the new Dominion in 1872. Ontario, Quebec, New Brunswick, and Nova Scotia had, on July 1, 1867, set up the nucleus of a Federal Dominion of Canada whose arms bore the motto *A mari usque ad mare*. This slogan was promptly converted into reality by the addition to the federation of the Northwest Territories of the Hudson's Bay Company, a part of which became the province of Manitoba in 1870. In 1871 the province of British Columbia was added, and in 1873 the province of Prince

9. *The American Canadian* (Boston), March 27, 1865. *Yarmouth Tribune,* Aug. 17, 1870. *The Nova Scotian,* May 25, 1868; April 5, 1869. *N.S.: App. to Jour. H. of A., 1867,* No. 7.

10. *The American Canadian,* Nov. 21, 1874. *Montreal Weekly Witness,* March 13, 1868. *The Citizen,* Sept. 17, 1872. *Acadian Recorder,* April 24, 1873, gives the occupations of those Nova Scotians entering Boston over a three months' period; see also April 22, Sept. 18, Dec. 21, 1872.

Edward Island. Great hopes were entertained for the prosperity of this transcontinental creation. The financial crash of 1873, however, and the depression which followed it ushered in for Canada as a whole a profoundly discouraging twenty-three years of falling prices and shattered hopes.[11] Except for brief interludes, during the same years the United States, thanks to its immense area of continuous good lands (a Middle West instead of a Laurentian Shield), weathered the storm magnificently, growing great in the process. The inevitable result was that, while immigrants still poured into Canada, so many Canadians and newcomers poured out into the United States before the tide turned about 1895 that the new nation seemed destined to be bled white by the process.

The emigration from the Maritimes of young people and of the parents who followed them was not directed toward any one American community nor did they find employment in any single line of economic activity. Fishing, lumbering, manufacturing in the East, agriculture and commerce in the West claimed their services. Wherever Yankees were located, there Canadians from "down East" could be found as neighbors. Their speech, customs, and appearance were alike and there was little to discourage constant association and ultimate amalgamation. Only a strong national patriotism could ward off this end and for the decade following 1865 national patriotism was at a low ebb in the British provinces along the Atlantic.

In contrast, the folkways which sharply distinguished them from other North Americans were exactly the characteristics to which the French Canadians clung. The French language and the Catholic faith were part of the nationalism which they had preserved for over a century against the politically predominant Anglo-Canadians and, although there were those who said that they preferred being Americanized to being Anglicized, few, if any, had the intention of giving up what tradition considered sacred.[12] A well-established routine directed them to New England; the needs of the time, reinforced by

11. *Yarmouth Tribune,* May 4, Dec. 14, 1869; June 8, 15, Nov. 9, 30, 1870. *Acadian Recorder,* April 10, Dec. 21, 1872; April 24, Sept. 2, 22, Nov. 18, Dec. 20, 1873.

12. *L'Echo du Canada. Organne de la population franco-canadienne des Etats-Unis* (Fall River, Mass.), Sept. 5, 1874.

the eloquence of agents sent to woo them, brought them into the operating rooms of the mills. In this industrial world there seemed to exist the possibility of almost unlimited expansion. Every family that had established itself permanently in one of the industrial communities became the nucleus of a growing colony, as the French Canadians gradually displaced the English and Irish laborers who only a short time before had supplanted the native workers in the more skilled activities of the textile trade.[13]

Many preferred the brickyards, where the labor, being seasonal, made possible an extended annual visit to the home seigniories. Active railroad construction in central and southern Maine absorbed a great number of hands during the summer; and logging operations in the Penobscot region provided work in the forest in the winters and on the river during the spring freshets. Digging canals, laying foundations, and building factories and homes were tasks incidental to the rapid expansion of the textile industries and in each of them the hardy French Canadian performed satisfactory service. When the job was over, he went home to await the next call for assistance. The problem of relieving unemployment was not one that worried the capitalists of the time.[14]

Its migratory character was, in fact, the most noticeable feature of the first wave of postwar French-Canadian migration. Within New England they shifted from place to place, and in every town one group replaced another during the first years of their presence.[15]

13. *Courrier de St. Hyacinthe* (St. Hyacinthe, P.Q.), July 2, 29, Oct. 23, 1869. Alexandre Belisle, *Histoire de la presse franco-américaine,* 8. Melvin T. Copeland, *The Cotton Manufacturing Industry of the United States* (Cambridge, 1912), 118, 120. Henry M. Fenner, *History of Fall River, Massachusetts* (Fall River, 1911), 30.

14. Adrien Verrette, *Paroisse Saint Charles-Borromée, Dover, New Hampshire* (n.p., 1933), 163. *Montreal Weekly Witness,* Aug. 7, 1868; June 11, 1869. *Lewiston Weekly Journal,* Feb. 3, 1870, May 22, June 19, 1873. *Courrier de St. Hyacinthe,* April 16, May 29, Aug. 7, 1868; Aug. 6, 27, Oct. 23, 1869. E. Hamon, *Les Canadiens-Français de la Nouvelle Angleterre,* 8, 32, 33.

15. H. A. Dubuque, *Le Guide canadien-français de Fall River et notes historiques sur les canadiens de Fall River* (Fall River, Mass., 1888), 123, 125.

When these nomadic tendencies had worn off and residence became more permanent, most of them felt that at least once a year a visit had to be paid to the family home in the province of Quebec. In many cases there were obligations that could be met most satisfactorily by personal return. Some went to repay the village money-lender who had financed their coming; others returned with the funds to lift the mortgage from the acres that the family hoped to retain as its own; a large proportion had parents whom they supported.[16] Finally, it was said, nineteen out of twenty expected to leave the States permanently when their obligations had been removed or a modest fortune acquired, so that there were many friendly and business contacts which all wanted to maintain because of this hope.[17]

Had employment in the mills been limited to workers of adult age, this hope probably would have been realized in a large percentage of cases. But in time it ceased to be the hope. If the Canadian emigrant brought his family with him, the future had a way of shifting from Quebec to the state in which he was settled.[18] The firstcomers (usually young, single men) had discovered that there was work for their friends. So they sent for these friends. Then they learned that neither age nor sex was a fundamental consideration in the mills; there was work that a child could do and no laws barred even the youngest of them from the factories. So they sent for the neighbor, telling him to bring the family with him.[19] This solicitation was encouraged by the employers, who often preferred to hire a family as a unit. A Worcester, Massachusetts, placement bureau charged a five-dollar family registration fee and among its advertisements were listed an opening for a family of five at a lace factory and one specifying a family of two or three girls or two boys at a linen establishment.[20] Before long all observers commented, often in a facetious

16. *L'Echo du Canada,* July 4, 1874. L'Abbé T. A. Chandonnet, *Notre-Dame-des-Canadiens et les canadiens aux Etats-Unis* (Montreal, 1872), 136, 137.

17. *Le Foyer canadien. Journal de famille* (Worcester, Mass.), June 17, 1873.

18. *L'Echo du Canada,* May 16, 1874.

19. *Ibid.,* July 4, 1874.

20. *Le Foyer canadien,* March 25, 1873.

vein, upon the abundant supply of progeny that the arriving French Canadian brought with him.[21]

Children were the roots that struck deep into the social and economic soil of the American community and planted the transient worker as a permanent immigrant. Instead of boarding in the long, gloomy brick barracks that the corporation had often built for the sake of its combined cheapness and large capacity, the employee and his family pooled their savings to buy a lot and build a cottage.[22] Doctors and lawyers came across the line to serve in these new and prosperous colonies and the far-seeing father began to train his brightest son for one of the professions.[23] French newspapers were established wherever a few hundred subscribers could be secured, and the Canadians usually obtained permission from the bishop to build a church of their own, where priests and language would remind them of the parish from which they had come.[24] By 1873 this new French Canada, although it had no intention of forgetting the old, was well established.

No official statistics were kept at the border, and therefore no immigration records are available to measure either the extent or the fluctuations of the movement. The United States census of 1870 was taken before the influx had reached its crest and that of 1880 after several years of hard times had influenced many of the unemployed French Canadians to find food and shelter in the paternal home. Moreover, neither of these enumerations listed separately "British Americans" of French descent. But in 1873 a special agent, the Reverend P. E. Gendreau, was authorized by the Department of Immigration of the Dominion of Canada to investigate the number and status of Canadian-born residents of the United States with a view to their possible repatriation. His information was derived from esti-

21. "A French Canadian and wife from Canada, by this afternoon's train, brought only nine of their children with them." *Lewiston Weekly Journal,* Dec. 5, 1872.

22. *Ibid.,* April 4, July 18, 1867; June 26, 1873.

23. *Ibid.,* June 27, Dec. 19, 1872; Feb. 13, 1873.

24. H. A. Dubuque, *Les Canadiens-français de Fall River, Mass.* (Fall River, Mass., 1883), 5, 6. The important newspapers are listed in *Compte-Rendu officiel de la XVIIe convention nationale des canadiens-français des Etats-Unis tenue à Nashua, N.H., les 26 et 27 juin, 1888* (Lewiston, Maine, 1890), 79, 80.

mates made by clergymen and editors, fragmentary figures provided by transportation companies, and his own observations. His conclusion was that 800,000 persons, Canadian-born of all languages and blood, were living in the States. Of these approximately 400,000 were French, who were distributed as follows: 200,000 in New England, 150,000 in the "western states," and 50,000 "scattered."[25] Within New England the course of migration was southward. A city like Fall River, where only a few were established in 1865, had become the site of flourishing colonies by 1873, and Worcester, surrounded by many manufacturing villages, was recognized as the "Canadian center" of the country.[26]

Items in contemporary newspapers present some information regarding the ebb and flow of the movement. A short recession in the general advance of business enterprise occurred in the spring and summer of 1867. Many of the plants shut down; others restricted operation to two or three days a week. This situation lessened the usual spring flow of workers; in fact, the movement was reversed, a noticeable northward trek taking place. But by September orders were coming in and all the spindles and looms began to turn with increasing rapidity.[27] This upswing with its accompanying call for help reached a first peak in the spring of 1869. Every bit of information indicates that the exodus attained startling proportions at that time. The demand for hands was so insistent that farms along the St. Lawrence were abandoned, every member of the household departing with no intention of returning in the fall of the year.[28] A second peak was evident from the fall of 1872 to the spring of 1873. Families numbering ten or twelve souls disembarked day after day upon the New England station platforms and agents representing the factories canvassed the Quebec countryside in an effort to enlist workers, young and old, to man the machines that were never idle.

25. *Dom. Can.: Sess. Pap., 1874,* No. 9: "Report of the Minister of Agriculture for the Calendar Year 1873," 66–69.

26. H. A. Dubuque, *Le Guide,* 123. *Le Foyer canadien,* Oct. 21, 1873.

27. *Montreal Weekly Witness,* March 15, 1867. *Lewiston Weekly Journal,* June 13, Sept. 5, 1867.

28. *Montreal Weekly Witness,* March 10, April 2, 16, June 11, 18, July 16, 1869. *Courrier de St. Hyacinthe,* March 19, April 2, 9, 23, 30, May 28, June 4, 1869.

By June, 1873, it was estimated that one-fourth and perhaps one-third of the lands usually tilled in the province were lying uncultivated because of the desertion of farm families and the shortage of laborers.[29]

A large number of these newcomers were destined to experience little but disappointment, for the world depression of the 'seventies was imminent. For a few months the market absorbed the products that came from the mills. But in the summer a crash occurred in the lumber industry, which had overexpanded to meet building needs that did not materialize.[30] A marked decline took place in the railroad construction which had already outstripped the needs of the population of the country.[31] In the early autumn some of the leading banks were forced to close and the textile industries of New England, many of which were closely allied to the embarrassed banks, suffered because of this connection and from the natural falling off in the demand for their goods. Hours and wages were reduced and finally many of the plants were shut down to remain silent for a much longer period than even the most pessimistic had feared.[32]

Thus was inaugurated the depression of the 'seventies. The first notices of unemployment were warning signals which the more prudent readily understood and many traveled back to Quebec knowing that they could live more cheaply during the idle winter before them among friends than among strangers.[33] The stagnation in trade became deeper as month followed month and with the increasing dullness the return migration rose in volume. When the spring of 1874, to which all had looked forward with hope, brought no improvement in prospects, a further impetus was given to the flow which effectively checked the usual spring exodus to the south.[34]

The returned emigrants brought information to which the govern-

29. *Le Foyer canadien*, April 15, May 13, 20, June 10, 17, 1873. *Lewiston Weekly Journal*, Oct. 10, 17, 31, 1872; April 3, 17, 1873.

30. *Montreal Weekly Witness*, July 11, 1873.

31. *The Railroad Gazette*, VI (New York, 1874), 12, 404.

32. *Le Foyer canadien*, Oct. 28, Nov. 4, 11, 1873; May 5, 1874. *Lewiston Weekly Journal*, Nov. 20, Dec. 18, 1873.

33. *Le Foyer canadien*, Nov. 11, 18, Dec. 9, 1873. *Montreal Weekly Witness*, Sept. 5, 1873.

34. *Le Foyer canadien*, June 2, 1874.

ment of the province of Quebec listened attentively. They told of the many who had wanted to accompany them but had been unable because of poverty; others had remained because interested parties were advising them to stay; some hesitated because they had sold their property in the province and did not know where to go.[35] The realization of these facts revived the colonization plans that had been promoted in the 'fifties but which had declined during the 'sixties, and it presented a new argument to those patriots who had been urging the authorities to undertake a comprehensive project for encouraging self-exiled Canadians to come back to the land of their birth.[36] Repatriation was now a timely matter, but it was argued that those who were sought could not be expected to come back and be satisfied with the lands hitherto set aside for colonization in tracts that were distant from roads and markets and notorious for the poor quality of their soil. Attention was also directed to the urgency of the opportunity which the present offered: if ever the expatriates were to be persuaded it must be before their children, American-born, obtained the dominating voice in the family councils.[37]

The hope that success would attend such an effort was brightened by the spirit manifested at a grand celebration staged by French Canadians at Montreal in June, 1874. It was estimated that about ten thousand emigrants came up from the United States to participate in the gathering and demonstrate that their interest and affection had not cooled.[38] At the next session of the legislature three townships of crown lands not far from the American boundary were set aside for a repatriation colony to be known as "La Patrie" and funds were appropriated to advertise the settlement and its advantages among the unemployed and homesick Canadians of New England. Ferdinand Gagnon, editor of *Le Travailleur* of Worcester, Massachusetts, and one of the most influential persons in French-Canadian circles in the United States, was appointed to the office of

35. *L'Echo du Canada,* May 16, 23, 1874. *Acadian Recorder,* May 26, 1874. *Montreal Witness,* June 23, 1874.

36. The difficulties attending colonization are described in the *Montreal Weekly Witness,* Jan. 31, Feb. 21, 1868.

37. *P.Q.: Sess. Pap., 1874–75,* No. 4: "General Report of the Commissioner of Agriculture and Public Works," vii, viii, 120.

38. E. Hamon, *op. cit.,* 50, 52. *Montreal Witness,* June 30, 1874.

American agent. In addresses and by notices in the columns of his paper the information was spread and in April, 1875, the settlement of the first pioneers was begun. In October a census of the colony reported more than a thousand inhabitants, but since the lands were open to Quebec residents as well as to repatriates, only a half of the number had come from the States.[39] The first months were the most prosperous. Not much of a harvest could be reaped in 1875 and that of 1876 was a failure. The popularity of the project naturally declined and although the season of 1877 yielded bountifully, the first enthusiasm had waned and only a few additions were made to the ranks of the settlers. Moreover, by this time the provincial project faced the competition of a Dominion project which had behind it greater resources and the promise of adventure that the West could always offer. Repatriation to Manitoba rather than to Quebec stirred the imagination of the hesitating Canadian American.[40]

Although official effort and public attention were centered upon the special colony, this enterprise was not the only aspect of population development to feel a repercussion from the severe check given by depression to the movement of emigration. Farms that had been abandoned were repeopled and some new life was instilled into the inactive colonization societies. Moreover, for many, residence in the United States had provided an industrial education, and manufacturing plants which had started up in the Dominion after the end of the Reciprocity Treaty and which had from the beginning been crippled by lack of skilled workmen now constantly received applications from spinners and weavers anxious to find employment in Canadian factories where, it was believed, employment would be less subject to the fluctuations that disturbed the course of business in the States. Those who appeared at the factories in Montreal and Hamilton seeking work were not turned away.[41]

39. *Le Travailleur,* Nov. 27, 1874, April 1, 8, 15, 29, May 6, Sept. 9, 30, 1875. *P.Q.: Sess. Pap., 1875,* No. 4: "General Report of the Commissioner of Agriculture and Public Works," 14, 15, 262, 364–367; *1876,* No. 3, 8, 107, 150–153.

40. *Ibid., 1877–78,* No. 4: "General Report of the Commissioner of Agriculture and Public Works," 8, 114–116; *1878–79,* No. 2, 27, 29, 164.

41. *Dom. Can.: Sess. Pap., 1875,* No. 40: "Report of the Minister of Agriculture for the Calendar Year, 1874," iv–vi, 39; *1876,* No. 8: "Report

Just as the emigration of the French-speaking Canadian always aroused more concern than the departure of his English-speaking fellow citizen, so his repatriation was heralded with more enthusiasm than greeted the return of the young man who had left his home in the Maritimes or in Ontario. Yet the onset of the depression produced enough of the latter to attract attention. To Halifax and St. John came disappointed natives of Nova Scotia and New Brunswick bringing gloomy reports of the conditions that they had left;[42] and Toronto and Hamilton were overrun by wandering laborers who, failing to find work, sought shelter in the city jails and depended on charity for their daily support.[43] Others, who were provided with some savings, moved on to the lands bordering upon Georgian Bay, where since 1868 free homestead grants of a hundred acres had been available for anyone who would undertake the laborious task of forest pioneering.[44] Canadians were not the only participants in this movement. Natives of Great Britain who had emigrated to the United States accompanied them, and the presence also of numbers of native Americans demonstrated that a longing to return to allegiance to the British crown was not the only factor involved.[45]

But the return of expatriates to Ontario could not be so extensive as that of the French Canadians to their province because their emigration had been of a different character. During the years that booming industry had attracted the inhabitants of the province of Quebec into New England, the lure of western prairies had proved as tempting to the ambitious farmers of Ontario as it was to their American neighbors in Ohio and Indiana. The fundamental impulse

of the Minister of Agriculture for the Calendar Year, 1875," 35; *1879,* No. 9: "Report of the Minister of Agriculture for the Calendar Year, 1878," 64. *Dom. Can.: App. to Jour. H. of C., 1876,* No. 3: "Report of the Select Committee on the Causes of the Present Depression of the Manufacturing, Mining, Commercial, Lumber and Fishing Interests," 129, 130, 137, 139, 146. *P.O.: Sess. Pap., 1874,* Vol. 8, Part II, No. 3: "Report of the Immigration Department for 1874."

42. *The American Canadian,* Aug. 12, 1874. *The Citizen,* Dec. 22, 1874. *Acadian Recorder,* Sept. 2, 22, Nov. 18, 1873.

43. *Montreal Weekly Witness,* Nov. 21, Dec. 12, 1873.

44. *Dom. Can.: App. to Jour. H. of C., 1877,* XI, 46, 50.

45. *Dom. Can.: Sess. Pap., 1876,* No. 8: "Report of the Minister of Agriculture for the Calendar Year, 1875," 36, 41.

was provided by the natural westward surge of population that followed the close of the Civil War. Throughout the states of the upper Mississippi Valley, farm and harvest hands received wages that were always an attraction to the young men on the more crowded farms to the eastward; and fertile government lands open to homesteading and more accessible lands for sale by the railroads were an inducement to the head of the family who was worried about the future of his children.[46] Kansas and Nebraska were the western states that were settled most rapidly during the course of the first years of this new advance to the westward.[47]

The background of the emigration from Ontario was not unlike that which explains the loss of population suffered by the states of the Old Northwest. Woodless prairies had an appeal to men who had struggled all their lives with trees and stumps, and although they could still secure free lands within their own province, they knew that the clearing of every acre would cost from twelve to fifteen dollars if not done by their own labor.[48] In the face of western competition, wheat and barley, which had hitherto been the staple products, were now being supplanted by cattle and dairy products for which there was a ready sale in Canada as well as in the States, and the smaller amount of labor necessary to carry on this agriculture made it possible for the farmer to remain and make a living after his sons had left.[49] In the more recently settled regions about this time many farm mortgages were revealed to be far out of line with the income that could be made, and the discouraged debtor, seeing no prospect of repaying his creditor, decamped, leaving buildings and fences to decay and fields to revert to wilderness.[50] The provision in the American revenue laws permitting an immigrant to bring in his household

46. For the high wages being paid to farm hands see *The Prairie Farmer* (Chicago), April 25, Aug. 1, 8, 15, 29, 1868; Aug. 16, 1872.

47. *Montreal Weekly Witness,* June 3, 1870. A. E. Sheldon, *Nebraska, the Land and the People,* I (Chicago, 1931), 473.

48. *P.O.: Sess. Pap., 1871–72,* Vol. IV, Part II, No. 56: "Report of the Commissioner of Agriculture and Public Works." On the cost of clearing land see the *Montreal Weekly Witness,* Feb. 23, 1872.

49. *Ibid.,* Nov. 11, 1870. Fred Landon, "Some Effects of the American Civil War on Canadian Agriculture," *Agricultural History,* VII (1933), 163–170.

50. *Montreal Weekly Witness,* April 1, 1870.

goods and one team of horses free of duty encouraged the movement of small farmers across the border.[51]

Kansas and Nebraska were not the only destinations. Missouri and Minnesota and the eastern districts of the Territory of Dakota received many settlers from Ontario.[52] Population also flowed over into Michigan where the building of roads in the more northern section of the state opened new counties that could be reached from the border in a few days of travel by wagon.[53] Settlement, however, meant more than the taking up of lands. Railroads and commerce accompanied, indeed often preceded, the advance of population. Village mechanics went along with their rural friends and the opportunities offered by the expanding railway network on the prairies attracted many engineers, clerks, trainmen, and telegraphers who had received their training on the Great Western and Grand Trunk lines in Canada.[54] In Chicago a colony of fifteen thousand Canadians was employed in the trades, machine shops, and commercial establishments, especially those related to the grain interests which had close connections with the shippers of Montreal.[55]

The only explanation that comforted patriotic Canadians who were concerned over the loss of man power that resulted from this exodus was the statement that the westward trend was inevitable and the Dominion had no West. But this did not satisfy all. Those who knew more about geography and resources maintained that there was a West that was deficient only in accessibility and they argued that if communications were open between Lake Superior and the Red River, a new empire of prairies and mountains would be available to the enterprising and adventurous, a field of achievement that could mean as much to Canadians as the trans-Mississippi empire did to the Americans.[56] This thesis had been one of the powerful underlying elements in the federation of the British North American colonies which made its start in 1867, and it endowed the new Do-

---

51. *A.R.F.C., 1867*, 160. *Montreal Weekly Witness*, Feb. 23, 1872.

52. *A.R.F.C., 1867*, 141.

53. *Joint Documents of the State of Michigan for the Year 1870*, I (Lansing, 1870), No. 2: "Biennial Message of the Governor, Jan. 4, 1871," 3, 4.

54. *Montreal Weekly Witness*, March 8, 1867.

55. *Ibid.*, Jan. 3, 1873.   56. *Ibid.*, Dec. 13, 1867.

minion with a sense of mission which helped to carry it through the difficult early years.

The barrier of low, rocky terrain, muskeg swamps, lakes, and tortuous rivers that nature had placed between Georgian Bay and the Manitoba Basin was not the only hindrance that blocked approach to this empire. It was still the domain of fur trader, Indian, and half-breed and the Hudson's Bay Company still enjoyed most of the rights of government that its seventeenth-century charter had conferred. But the twelve thousand inhabitants were restless under its rule and apprehensive about the impact upon them of the expanding Eastern regions, and the six years between 1865 and 1871 were troubled times, marked by revolt and by filibustering expeditions that had their origin in the frontier outposts below the forty-ninth parallel.[57] Unless some satisfactory political arrangement could be made that would ensure to the inhabitants all the benefits of union with the confederation, the rising desire for annexation to the United States might easily develop into a more formidable revolt that would heighten the tension already existing between Great Britain and the United States and make more likely the war that some men hoped for and some men dreaded.[58]

The emergency was met in 1868 when the company sold most of their rights to the British government for transfer to Canada, and the situation was further cleared when, in 1870, delegates from the province of British Columbia agreed to enter the Dominion upon the promise of a transcontinental railroad that would bind it to the other parts of the new state. The way was now open for the planting of that mid-continental settlement which, it had always been understood, was a necessity if the East and the West were to be linked in population as well as government.[59] Liberal land inducements were offered—a 160-acre homestead grant for ten dollars, and preëmption rights to another quarter section at the end of three years of

57. Alexander Begg, *History of the Northwest,* I (Toronto, 1894), 373–460. G. F. G. Stanley, *The Birth of Western Canada* (New York, 1936).

58. *Senate Executive Documents,* 41st Congress, 2d Session, Doc. No. 33: "Affairs in the Red River."

59. F. W. Howay, *British Columbia from the Earliest Times to the Present,* II, 277–298.

residence on the payment of a dollar an acre.[60] Settlement under the new regime began in 1871 and the Americans who were already swarming into the Red River Valley on their side of the line and rapidly occupying the narrow wooded strip that bordered the stream were ready to take possession of the corresponding opportunities within the new province of Manitoba.[61]

Canadians were in no mood to allow the peopling of the province to fall into the hands of Americans and in 1871 the sons of the Dominion started to move into their own West by an "all-Canadian" route. This line of approach, which followed in general the century-old canoe trail of the *voyageurs* from Lake Superior to Lake Winnipeg, had been constructed in 1870 by an engineer in the Department of Public Works, S. J. Dawson, to facilitate the advance of the military expedition that was dispatched to quell the uprising in Manitoba of the half-breed Louis Riel. Waterways had been cleared of obstructions and small steamers had been placed on the lakes and rivers; corduroy roads had been built at all the portages and at convenient stations buildings for the accommodation of travelers had been provided. Three hundred and ten miles of navigable water and twelve portages constituted the "Dawson Route" between Port Arthur and Winnipeg.[62]

Although to follow the all-Canadian Dawson route was a patriotic venture, it was neither so convenient nor so comfortable for the emigrant from the eastern provinces who was bound for the Red River as an American route which became available the same year. The Northern Pacific Railroad pushing westward from Duluth reached the Red River at Moorhead, where connection was made with the small steamers that brought Winnipeg within two days' journey.[63]

60. "Recent Progress in Manitoba," *Chamber's Journal*, Series 4, Vol. 17 (London, 1880), 65–67. A. S. Morton and C. Martin, *History of Prairie Settlement and "Dominion Lands" Policy.*

61. *History of the Red River Valley*, I, 73, 76, 80; II, 581. A. H. Moehlman, "The Red River of the North," *Geographical Review*, XXV, 79–91.

62. *The Weekly Manitoban* (Winnipeg), Feb. 12, 1872. *Manitoba Gazette* (Winnipeg), May 13, 1874. *Montreal Witness*, May 23, July 2, 1874. *Dom. Can.: Sess. Pap., 1875*, No. 7, "General Report of the Minister of Public Works," 181–185.

63. W. W. Folwell, *History of Minnesota*, III (St. Paul, 1921), 61. Har-

The advantages of this route were so obvious that it at once became the established course, and the only remaining inconvenience was removed in 1872 when the Secretary of the Treasury decreed that Canadians in transit might pass with team and household effects through American territory without payment of duty upon giving bond to be forfeited in case the through journey were not actually completed.[64] So great was the tide of humanity that flowed into the valley on both sides of the line that by 1873 plans were ready for a northward branch of the railroad that would connect with a Canadian project that was to be built southward from Winnipeg.[65]

Not for six years did this plan become a reality. The panic of 1873, so clearly the product of overexpansion of railroads, put an end to their construction and for the time being halted the westward movement. The panic year was followed by the grasshopper scourge of 1874 and reports from both the Canadian and American Wests told of a retreating frontier, destitution, and public relief instead of alluring stories of fertile fields and golden opportunities.[66] Immigration, which was the lifeblood of the new communities, came to an end and the dullness that fell upon manufacturing enterprise in the East was equaled by the stagnation that halted the business of railroads and turned many prospective cities of the West into towns dead and deserted.

Thereafter western settlement, if it were to flourish, had to be subsidized, and the interest that the government of the Dominion took in the vital task of establishing a loyal colony on the Red River initiated a scheme of repatriation broader than that sponsored by the province of Quebec. To begin with, many of the old white and half-breed settlers were French-speaking parishioners of a vigorous Roman Catholic diocese. Now two agents were appointed to travel through the Canadian-American settlements, one in the West, the other in New England. The latter was authorized to offer attractive

old E. Briggs, "Pioneer River Transportation in Dakota," *North Dakota Historical Quarterly*, III (Bismarck, N.D., 1929), 159–181.

64. *Montreal Weekly Witness*, Feb. 23, 1872.

65. *A.R.F.C., 1871*, 650.

66. *Centennial Edition of the Fourth Annual Report of the State Board of Agriculture to the Legislature of the State of Kansas for the Year Ending Nov. 30, 1875*, 24.

terms: an advance of a large part of the railroad fare, travel in conducted parties, and assistance in the acquisition of farms.[67] With the encouragement of repatriation societies and of the publicity given by the paper *Le Travailleur*, beginning in 1875 and continuing until the end of the decade, every year saw the introduction of several hundred French Canadians from the manufacturing cities of New England and the addition of an uncounted number of repatriates from the more scattered settlements in the central and western states.[68]

About 1876 the tide of migration had again started toward the West. The painful process of bankruptcy proceedings had restored financial health to the railroads and they were ready to undertake reasonable and needed additions to their lines. Cheaper transportation lowered the cost at which American grain could be delivered in the European ports and a widened market was opened to farm exports. To take up lands was once more a promising venture and year by year the number of homesteaders and pioneers who set out for the prairies increased. Perhaps most important of all, stubborn pioneers were tediously acquiring the new and often strange techniques of seed, cultivation, and harvest which the high, dry midlands required, and millers were both working out the special machinery necessary to handle the hard grain and persuading consumers to receive a new and wonderful kind of flour. The valley of the Red River then gradually won its way into favor and for a second time Canadians and Americans mingled on the way to their destination and exchanged nationality with a surprising unconcern.[69]

For some time a steady drift of population had been carrying the half-breeds and pioneers of Manitoba out to the valley of the Saskatchewan, and the farms along the Red River which they were

67. *Dom. Can.: Jour. H. of C., 1875,* App. No. 4: "First Report of the Select Committee on Immigration and Colonization," 6. *Dom. Can.: Sess. Pap., 1880,* No. 10: "Report of the Minister of Agriculture for the Calendar Year, 1879," 76, 77.

68. *Ibid., 1876,* No. 8: "Report of the Minister of Agriculture for the Calendar Year, 1875," 179–180; *1878,* No. 9: "Report of the Minister of Agriculture for the Calendar Year, 1877," 61–63, 75–76. *Le Travailleur,* April 4, May 9, 1878; May 22, 1879.

69. *History of the Red River Valley,* I, 90; II, 581, 824.

willing to sell were attractive locations for incoming settlers who were comfortably provided with funds.[70] This helped to make Manitoba become a particular destination for emigrating farmers from Ontario, and the railroad from Duluth to the Red River was well patronized by migrants from one part of the Dominion to another. To facilitate this movement, the Canadian Department of Immigration stationed a representative at Duluth to act as official bondsman, to assist the travelers in the transfer of their belongings from steamboat to railroad, and undoubtedly to protect them from the American "so much per head" agents who were reported to lie in wait for the incoming prosperous Canadian and persuade him to buy Minnesota or Dakota lands.[71] By 1877 the journey to Winnipeg had become easier, although the all-rail route was not completed. A branch north from the main line to the West led up to Crookston, Minnesota, and there a stub line a few miles in length connected with Fisher's Landing on the Red Lake River, not far from the point where it flowed into the Red River. This was the new terminus of the Winnipeg steamboats and here an immigrant-receiving house provided accommodations for four or five hundred passengers while they awaited the departure of the river boats.[72]

The agents of whose activities the sponsors of Manitoba colonization stood in fear were successful in persuading some of the Canadians to interrupt their journey to look at the lands that they had to offer. What they saw and the cordiality which they met on every hand were factors that often brought the trip to an end within the United States. Approximately 5 per cent of those who entered at Duluth bound for Manitoba failed to appear at the border and they were listed as "lost" in transit.[73] Their number, however, was small

70. *Dom. Can.: Jour. H. of C., 1876,* App. No. 8: "Report of the Select Committee on Immigration and Colonization," 29.

71. *The Weekly Manitoban,* Feb. 12, 1872. *Montreal Witness,* March 12, 1879. *Dom. Can.: Sess. Pap., 1879,* No. 9: "Report of the Minister of Agriculture for the Calendar Year, 1878," xxxii; *1880,* No. 10: "Report of the Minister of Agriculture for the Calendar Year, 1879," 53.

72. *Ibid., 1878,* No. 9: "Report of the Minister of Agriculture for the Calendar Year, 1877," 52.

73. *Dom. Can.: Jour. H. of C., 1879,* App. No. 1: "Report of the Select Standing Committee on Emigration and Colonization," 20, 67, 84.

in comparison with those who deliberately chose Dakota and Minnesota before leaving home, and in the American part of the valley many compact colonies from the provinces in the East bore testimony that a favorable farm site predominated over patriotism when it came to choosing the spot where family fortunes should be reestablished.[74]

While expansion and depression were determining the population relations between provinces and states in the East and central West, the Pacific coast was as usual responding to circumstances peculiar to itself. Shortly after 1865 all excitement died out of the gold fields of British Columbia. The more restless, disappointed, or venturesome moved away to prospect in the mountains of Montana and later in the unknown valleys of the new territory of Alaska.[75] During the decade of the 'seventies the population of miners remained almost stationary and few farmers came in to provide for their needs.[76] The grain of Washington and Oregon was imported too easily to encourage local agricultural settlement and all business felt the dullness of the time. Many of the men connected with commercial enterprises went back to California, which had entered upon its second period of development, the era of exploitation of agricultural resources and the opening of lumbering activities. The Puget Sound region also, in spite of rather violent fluctuations in its needs for labor in the forests, drew off a goodly number of persons from quiescent British Columbia.[77]

The new surge of prosperity that in the summer of 1879 restored confidence to all phases of economic life in both the United States and Canada was foreshadowed and then spectacularly accompanied by North Americans on the march. The tragedy for Canada was that continental forces shepherded so many Canadians into the United States. Again the smaller, but ambitious, farmer of Ontario

74. *History of the Red River Valley*, II, 863.

75. *A.R.F.C., 1879*, 308.

76. The number of miners in the province during each year between 1858 and 1879 is tabulated in *B.C.: Sess. Pap., 1880*, 233.

77. *Dom. Can.: Jour. H. of C., 1876*, App. No. 7: "Report of the Select Committee Appointed to Consider the Agricultural Interests of the Dominion," 2. *Puget Sound Weekly Courier* (Olympia, W.T.), March 13, July 31, 1875; June 16, 1876; Aug. 16, 1878; Feb. 20, 1880.

set out with his sons in search of new lands and promising opportunities in Michigan and the West.[78] In the Maritime Provinces, as in New England, lumbering and shipbuilding remained stagnant and artisans as well as farmers joined in an exodus that aroused extensive comment in the contemporary press and public documents. Patriots tried to explain the movement as the departure of former exiles who had been at home awaiting the first encouraging sign, but the events of the next decade were to prove that the permanent emigration which they most feared was again under way.[79]

By the spring of 1879 only one development was necessary to restore to population movements the lively activity that they had exhibited a decade before. That change came in the summer of the year when, as a startling surprise—so sudden was the improvement—orders began to pour into all the factory offices. Again a call was sent up to the villages and seigniories of Quebec and this time it was a truly cordial invitation. For the events of recent years had removed the last prejudices that manufacturers had felt against the French-Canadian worker. When English and Irish laborers engaged in a strike, the French Canadian remained at his work if he possibly could, and he had no hesitation about taking the place of the dissatisfied employee who walked out on his job.[80] He, and his children even more, had become Americanized to a considerable degree. They had grown accustomed to, almost dependent on, ways of living and articles of consumption which they could not find at home in Quebec, and return to the old province was no longer the dominating motive in their lives. Their dependability had endeared them to local merchants as well as to employers of labor. Now, when workers were once more in demand, in so far as French Canadians could provide the desired numbers the jobs in the mills and factories of New England were theirs.[81]

78. *A.R.F.C.*, *1879*, 298, 315, 327, 328, 380, 395.

79. *Acadian Recorder*, Oct. 12, 1878; June 12, Oct. 9, 1879. *Yarmouth Tribune*, June 4, Oct. 22, 1879. *Dom. Can.: Sess. Pap.*, *1880*, No. 10: "Report of the Minister of Agriculture for the Calendar Year, 1879," 118.

80. *La République: Journal hebdomadaire* (Fall River, Mass.), April 15, 1876. *A.R.F.C.*, *1879*, 298. State of Massachusetts, *Report of the Bureau of Statistics of Labor*, XI (Boston, 1880), 59; XIII (1882), 64.

81. *Ibid.*, 81, 89, 90.

CHAPTER IX

FROM THE PROVINCES TO THE
PRAIRIE STATES
1880–1896

THE statement made earlier,[1] that the twenty-three years after the panic of 1873 were profoundly depressing for Canada because of the immense outflow of population to the United States, might appropriately be amplified here before turning again to the actual annals of the migrations.[2] It can be said in general that during the 'sixties and 'seventies, while many native Canadians did leave their country, the exodus was predominantly one of immigrants to Canada. During the decade of 1851–1861 the immigrant population had increased by about 200,000 persons,[3] but during the next decade it actually decreased by over 91,000, although 179,000 more newcomers had announced their intention of remaining, and from 1871 to 1881 it increased by only 11,409 in the face of 342,000 similar declarations. During these last two decades, on the other hand, the main tendency of native Canadian migrants was to move outward to fill up the more thinly occupied areas in Canada. This was accompanied by a relatively minor, if increasing, willingness to leave Canada for the United States.

This minor tendency expanded to major proportions between

1. See above, p. 164.

2. The information for this and the succeeding paragraph is drawn from *Seventh Census of Canada, 1931,* I (Ottawa, 1936), Part II, chapter i (1), "The growth of population in Canada," 99–132, and tables, 348–372. This summary volume repeats, much more elaborately, the procedure of the first volume of the first Dominion census (1871), by providing historical treatment. This, combined with close periodical statistical analysis of population change, makes it an invaluable aid to understanding the pattern of the growth and distribution of the Canadian peoples in North America as a whole.

3. A number practically equivalent to the declared intending settlers of the decade. From 1851 to 1901 about half the immigrants to Canada were declared intending settlers and half declared in transit to the United States. About one out of three intending settlers actually stayed in Canada; *ibid.,* 121.

1881 and 1901. The rate of increase in native population abruptly fell well below the rate of natural increase, being only 12.6 per cent for 1881–1891, and 11.5 per cent for 1891–1901. Canada was very clearly losing native Canadians on a large scale. Including natives and established and recent immigrants, Canadian emigration to the United States from 1881 to 1891 exceeded one million persons. By 1896 the rate of total population increase had about reached the vanishing point, and had it not been for the great increase in the westward and northward migrations in Canada after 1901 "the population would have been all but stationary in another twenty years."[4]

By comparing Canadian and American population changes from 1851 to 1891, and by inquiring into the waxing and waning of Canadian counties in east and west,[5] it is possible to indicate in general what had been happening within Canada. As early as 1851 there could be detected in eastern Canada clear signs that some counties had become "overpopulated"; that is, had reached their maximum density in terms of the unwillingness of some inhabitants to accept a lower standard of living. A few of these counties actually began to decline in population, while many others failed to hold their natural increase. This trend had relatively little to do with the rise of cities and it deepened with the years. The inevitable outcome was an expansion into contiguous more thinly inhabited areas, within Canada if possible, but in the United States if not. Quebec felt the pressure first, in the decade of 1851–1861, and her "surplus" moved outward, as we have seen, within and without Canada to all points of the compass. Ontario was next, 1861–1871, and when her marginal lands to the north had taken what they could, most of her "surplus" went south or west into the United States, although the Canadian West beyond the Lakes and the Laurentian Shield was beginning to attract some. By the time, 1881–1891, that signs of "surplus" population were emphatically confirmed in the Maritimes, although the United States was still the principal destination, the transcontinental Canadian Pacific Railway was luring increasing numbers of eastern Canadians from all three regions into their new West. It is clearly necessary to think of these years (1861–1896) as a period when substan-

4. *Ibid.*, 104.   5. *Ibid.*, 352–354.

tial parts of the Canadian population, native and immigrant, formed "an aggregate of persons temporarily established at points of distribution,"[6] whence they were constantly moving in order to maintain or to improve their accustomed standards of living, often with necessarily little regard for political allegiance. In spite of the greater accessibility and often superior inducements of life in the Republic, more than half of the Canadian migrants of the period managed to find new homes in the Dominion. Meanwhile, however, the Canadian-born population of the United States grew as follows:[7]

1851	147,711	1881	717,157
1861	249,970	1891	980,938
1871	493,464	1901	1,179,922

The generalizations above, while they are statistically sound and while they accurately reflect a thoroughly disquieting period in Canadian history, are also so sweeping and impersonal as to carry us rather far from the immediate motives to which the North American migrants felt they were responding and also from what contemporary observers thought about these movements. The drama becomes more intimate and realistic if we turn from ingenious statistical reconstructions to describe again how the people were acting from year to year and from region to region.

The activity that became so evident during the summer of 1879 in all the industrial communities in the United States was not the only evidence that depressing business conditions had come to an end. Optimism had also returned to the prairie states and territories. For two or three years past, the number of settlers taking up land had increased from season to season. Now the movement to the West swelled to unprecedented proportions and along with the farmers came mechanics and tradesmen and professional speculators who plotted towns and mapped railroads and promised a fortune to all who could provide some of the funds with which to inaugurate any one of the enterprises that their fertile minds had invented. A new western "boom" was under way.

Every section of the United States west of the Mississippi and many of the less developed regions to the eastward felt the impulses

6. *Ibid.*, 99.   7. *Ibid.*, 131.

awakened by the belief that a new era was at hand. The foreign demand for American wheat was so insistent that to say that the prairies would feed the world was only to repeat a truism. At first the rush seemed to be nothing but a stampede to occupy every acre on which grain would grow. From the states that had been settled a generation before, young men went out to repeat the pioneering experiences of their fathers; and families in which children were plentiful made a profitable exchange when they sold their farms and bought extensive stretches of railroad lands or homesteaded along the Missouri and beyond.

Ontario was one of those older settled areas and the exodus that took place from the townships north of Lake Erie was not unlike that which was evident to the south. To leave Ontario usually meant to leave Canada and although everyone deplored the expatriation, a few penetrating observers viewed the situation with equanimity. It was all part of the continental westward march; and that the son of an Ontario or Quebec farmer should set out from his paternal home was no more of a reflection upon the society and politics of the Dominion than that the departure of the young people of the eastern United States was an indication that something was wrong with the Republic. Someday the westward tide would sweep across the Canadian prairies. The less the movement was interfered with the better it would be for all concerned. Like all its predecessors it would come to an end with time.[8]

Nevertheless, more immediate explanations were offered and the scores of American land agents that swarmed over the province were cited as an obvious cause of the emigration.[9] Undoubtedly they did induce some to go. Many of the potential emigrants were already favorably inclined to a change, but needed direct personal persuasion. Yet in most cases agents were effective only in turning a movement already under way in a particular direction. All the American land-grant railroads had representatives in Canada who not only could argue the advantages of settlement near a line of communication, but could also offer special inducements in the matter of rates

8. *The Globe,* July 17, Nov. 23, Dec. 4, 1880.
9. *Southern Manitoba Times* (West Lynne, Man.), March 19, 1881. *U.S. Consular Reports, 1882–83,* 30.

on household goods and equipment to those who bought their lands. The Canadian railroads, realizing that a part of the traffic would fall to them, coöperated in the distribution of pamphlets, handbills, and newspapers.[10] It was charged that in some cases ticket agents received a higher commission percentage on passages sold to one of the western states than on passages to Manitoba.[11] American consular officers in Canada were the special target of patriotic criticism. Official duties consumed only a part of their time and many of them served as agents for land and railroad companies, their position giving weight to the arguments they presented.[12] So strong was the resentment against all these inciters to emigration that an attempt was made in the Canadian Parliament to secure legislation that would curb their activities.[13]

But the real incitement to emigration was not found in advertisement and propaganda. It lay deeper, in the fundamental changes then affecting the agriculture of the province. The farms in the old settled parts were small. Usually the future of only one child could be provided for. The other children had traditionally moved away, striking off into the backlands of the community or into the new townships that were opened up to the west and north.[14] But now the limit of desirable agricultural settlement within Ontario seemed to have been reached and the present phase of the migration was different only in that the young people were obliged to go farther from home, crossing the international boundary on the way. There was nothing revolutionary about this; but there was a new and disturbing note in the growing tendency toward consolidation of farms, a process that inevitably squeezed out the more mobile, the more adventurous, or the less fortunate family in the vicinity.[15]

Consolidation was, in fact, the reflection of the growing prosperity enjoyed by some of the more successful farmers who wanted to

10. *Dom. Can.: Jour. H. of C. Sess. 1880–81*, App. No. 1, 23, 32, 39, 111. *Dom. Can.: App. to Jour. H. of C. Sess. 1892*, No. 2, 158. *Dom. Can.: Sess. Pap., 1891*, No. 6, 158; *1892*, No. 7, 185.
11. *Dom. Can.: Jour. H. of C. Sess. 1880–81*, App. No. 1, 42.
12. *Ibid. 1887*, App. No. 4, 33.
13. *Dom. Can.: Debates H. of C. Sess. 1881*, X, 1303.
14. *Dom. Can.: Jour. H. of C. Sess. 1889*, App. No. 4, 52, 81.
15. *Ibid. 1880–81*, App. No. 1, 68.

add to their acres and thereby advance into the ranks of the country gentlemen.[16] It was also closely related to changing market conditions which made the fattening of livestock or skillful dairying more remunerative than the mixed farming that had hitherto prevailed. Imported western wheat forced down the price of grain and the farmers of Ontario, many of whom were renters or mortgagors, and all of whom were paying high taxes and high wages for harvest help, learned that it was unwise to continue the competition. On the other hand, stock raising paid well and the demand that came from the growing metropolitan centers of eastern Canada and the United States for cheese and butter encouraged a shift in land use. Consequently, some farmers were willing to buy land and others were willing to sell.[17] As in every period of transition, discontent and discouragement were present among the less successful, and the sovereign device of trying one's luck elsewhere swelled the number of sellers.[18]

During the decade of the 'eighties the emigration expanded. Canadian officials and American officials differed as to its numerical totals.[19] To secure any exact enumeration was, in fact, impossible. Many farmers crossed the border on exploring expeditions and then returned to guide their families to the new home.[20] Others crossed only once, having disposed of furniture and equipment before departure; they were considered ordinary travelers, or designated "gripsack emigrants" by those who recognized their nature.[21] The American consuls who issued the certificates that allowed bona fide settlers to

16. *Ibid.*, 26, 34.

17. *Emerson International* (Man.), April 6, 1882. *Montreal Weekly Witness*, June 30, 1880; July 19, 1882; July 21, 1886. *P.O.: Sess. Pap., 1882*, XIV, No. 6, 34, 35; *1884*, XVI, No. 83, vi. *Dom. Can.: Sess. Pap., 1880–81*, No. 12, 19; *1887*, No. 12, 25; *1888*, No. 4, 42. *Commercial Relations of the United States with Foreign Countries, 1886–87*, 524 (hereafter *C.R.U.S. F.C.*).

18. *Canadian American* (Chicago), June 11, 1885. *C.R.U.S.F.C., 1885 and 1886*, I, 848.

19. Regarding the great difference of opinion as to the number of Canadians emigrating by the Sarnia–Port Huron route, see *Dom. Can.: Sess. Pap., 1885*, No. 8, Annex: "Report on the Alleged Exodus on the Western Frontier."

20. *C.R.U.S.F.C., 1884 and 1885*, I, 610.

21. *Ibid., 1885 and 1886*, I, 851. *Western British American* (Chicago), March 3, 1888.

bring in household effects and some livestock free of duty ventured no estimates of the total, but merely reported that the movement was large and that, judging by those whom they saw, the typical emigrant was a farmer of the "better class," well provided with children and with sufficient means to buy cheaper and more fertile lands in a newer part of the continent.[22]

The trend, however, was unmistakable. The United States census of 1890 reveals the presence of Canadian-born residents in all of the states that had been growing from the influx of settlers. Michigan, in particular, had drawn many from Ontario. The wooded landscape that was so similar in soil and terrain to that which they had known in their province, cheap rates and accessibility, and the opportunity of working in the lumber camps and buying cut-over lands at from twenty-five cents to two dollars an acre were all factors that had led to their presence. The counties that bordered Lake Huron had been increasing in population very rapidly[23] and the growth of the Canadian stock, although the increase in number of Canadian-born did not quite equal the recorded rate of local growth, clearly kept pace with it if it is remembered that any children added to the Canadian family were listed in the column of American natives.

Throughout the states that lay beyond the Great Lakes, infiltration had also been taking place. There were no great colonies of Canadians, no large groups that dominated a county or a number of counties in the way in which German and Scandinavian immigrants in the same period took over parts of the Mississippi Valley and created a New Sweden or a New Germany. An analysis of the census figures reveals a very even distribution of Canadians in the agricultural areas. There was some variation in the percentage of Canadian-born from county to county, but in most cases the shading off was gradual, the exceptions being found in areas where communities of French Canadians had been established. As in all migra-

22. *C.R.U.S.F.C., 1882 and 1883,* II, 154; *1885 and 1886,* I, 848; *1887 and 1888,* 22. *U.S. Consular Reports:* House Misc. Doc. No. 232, 51st Congress, 1st Session, Oct., 1889, 235; House Misc. Doc. No. 18, 52d Congress, 1st Session, July, 1891, 434.

23. *Dom. Can.: Jour. H. of C. Sess. 1880–81,* App. No. 1, 68, 77; *Dom. Can.: Sess. Pap., 1880–81,* No. 12, xli; *1892,* No. 7, 187; *1893,* No. 13, Part VI, 101. *C.R.U.S.F.C., 1884 and 1885,* I, 615.

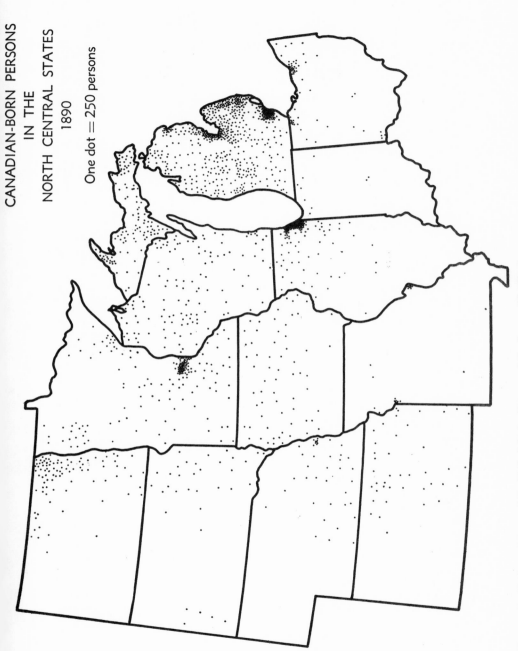

CANADIAN-BORN PERSONS
IN THE
NORTH CENTRAL STATES
1890

One dot = 250 persons

Prepared with the assistance of the United States Bureau of the Census, Washington

tion movements, family and neighborhood ties caused an occasional concentration of the Canadian stock. But it was no more usual than in the case of Pennsylvanians and New Yorkers; and all the circumstances of origin and destination confirm the judgment that the influx from across the border was only one phase of the prevailing continental westward flow.

One exception demands consideration, not only because it was an exception but because it illustrates significantly how closely related the settlement of adjacent areas located on opposite sides of the line happened to be. In 1890 the northern and eastern districts of North Dakota and the northwestern districts of Minnesota reported the presence of thousands of Canadians, in totals that amounted to a distinct concentration and a very high percentage in the general population.[24]

During the preceding decade much had been said and written about the "Dakota boom" and the "Manitoba boom." But both were, in fact, only part of a more comprehensive development: the "Red River Valley boom." In addition, both represented the violent ups and downs of a great adventure in North American agriculture. Easterners swarmed into the Red River Valley expecting to farm as they had farmed at home, only to learn by years of painful experience that they had many new problems to solve. They needed heavier plows; they had to learn something about dry farming; and they had to experiment in the field with Canadian, American, and foreign wheats to find varieties that would ripen quickly or else end up their hard year's work with musty, frostbitten, partially ripened grain. Every prospect of treeless land, deep black soil, and gently rolling prairie had been incredibly inviting, but the destruction which the excessively cold winters of the mid-continent wrought upon fall-sown grain, the delicate balance between excessively hot summers and early-encroaching frosts, and the hazards of rust and smut and grasshoppers broke the spirits of thousands before hard spring

24. *Montreal Weekly Witness,* May 25, 1881. *Canadian American,* Feb. 16, March 3, 30, April 13, June 8, 1883. In 1890 the percentages of Canadian-born in the total population of the four northeasternmost counties of North Dakota were: Pembina, 38.2; Cavalier, 37.8; Walsh, 20.3; Grand, 14.5. In the adjoining counties on the Minnesota side of the Red River the percentages were: Kittson, 13.6; Marshall, 5.8; Polk, 11.6.

wheat began the triumphant march which was to carry it to its most perfect development more than a generation later far to the north in the Peace River Valley.

In 1879 a railroad connected Winnipeg with the main line of the Northern Pacific and travelers and trade were no longer dependent upon the primitive Red River carts or the uncertain steamboat traffic upon the river.[25] After a series of false starts during the 'seventies, the Dominion government in 1880 put the full weight of its material and other encouragement behind an adventurous group of Canadian, Canadian-American, and American railway builders and financiers who formed the Canadian Pacific Railway Company. In spite of the embittered gibes and open hostility of J. J. Hill, the Canadian head of the rival Northern Pacific, W. C. Van Horne, the American construction boss of the Canadian line, had managed by 1885 to drive it not only across the forbidding Laurentian Shield from the Ottawa Valley to Winnipeg but also through the Rocky Mountain ranges to the shores of the Pacific. Roseate expectations of the possibilities that would fall to the lot of those pioneers who were established when the last railroad links were connected turned the attention of many land seekers to the Red River Valley and the railroad and land companies were not slow in strengthening the interest and facilitating the process of settlement.

To these inducements had been added the motive of patriotism. There were many Canadians in the old provinces and in the States about 1880 who were willing to move and to whom political allegiance had considerable importance. Now that the Dominion had a West of its own which in a few years would be as accessible as any part of the Mississippi Valley, the attraction of Manitoba was doubled.[26] The Immigration and Land departments of the Dominion and of the new province strengthened the sentiment by means of their advertisements and through the activities of their representatives.[27] The influx started in 1879, increased in the succeeding years, and culminated in 1882 when the rush was characterized by a feverish excitement that indicated that not only homeseekers but specu-

25. Robert England, *The Colonization of Western Canada* (London, 1936), 55.

26. *Emerson International,* Jan. 9, 1879.

27. *Dom. Can.: Jour. H. of C. Sess. 1880–81,* App. No. 1, 61.

lators were on hand. Trains were crowded, hotels were full, and everywhere villages and towns were rising on the prairie. Winnipeg prospered the most and there the crash came first.[28] Ignorance of prairie agriculture and inflated anticipation of a still distant future reaped their toll. In 1883 the labor market was flooded with unemployed workers and paper fortunes were lost by the score. But the taking up of land in the adjacent agricultural regions did not cease and although its volume decreased, settlement did not come to an end.[29]

The "Manitoba boom" added an impetus to that already under way in the adjoining Territory of Dakota. Both directly and indirectly, the American landowners profited from the human current that was flowing in such a strong volume along the borders. The railroad route from Ontario still passed through the United States, and at every junction point along the way the travelers were subjected to solicitation on the part of American agents. When success attended these efforts, the Canadians, it was said, were "kidnaped."[30] So strong was the danger made out to be that the Canadian land companies stationed their own representatives in St. Paul to give information to bewildered passengers and to guard them from the wiles of competitors.[31] Here and there in the course of the journey some of the migrants dropped off to remain in the United States, and only those who traveled on the specially chartered trains that ran through from Toronto to Manitoba were considered to be entirely safe.[32]

But crossing the border from Minnesota into Manitoba did not mean that the prospect was forever lost to Dakota. Some of the passengers were deliberately following a roundabout route because of certain advantages that it brought. The customs examination at Detroit was considered very searching. On the other hand, the

28. *Ibid. 1887,* App. No. 4, 20. *Southern Manitoba Times,* April 2, 1881; Feb. 3, June 23, July 11, Nov. 17, 1882. *Emerson International,* April 29, 1880; March 9, 1882.

29. *Montreal Weekly Witness,* May 16, 1883. Robert England, *op. cit.,* 56, 57.

30. *Dom. Can.: Jour. H. of C. Sess. 1880–81,* App. No. 1, 21. *The Globe,* July 20, 1880.

31. *Dom. Can.: Jour. H. of C. Sess. 1880–81,* App. No. 1, 43.

32. *Ibid. 1880–81,* App. No. 1, 21; *1885,* App. No. 3, 82, 83.

American inspectors stationed at Pembina, Dakota, were less thorough and less inclined to exact a duty upon every article that was liable. Goods and stock were shipped through the United States in bond, but as soon as the boundary was crossed at Emerson, Manitoba, the freight could be unloaded, the team could be hitched to the wagon, and the family and their belongings might proceed across the river and, turning south, pass back into the United States through Pembina, where only a superficial examination was made. One observer maintained that 25 per cent of the arrivals at Emerson were really bound for Dakota.[33]

These were not the only apparent settlers that the province lost. Pioneers were proverbially restless and inclined to shift their residence in the hope that some hardship or grievance could be eliminated by a change of even a few miles.[34] The hardships of Manitoba were those that were common to all prairie beginnings. But some of them were felt more acutely because the effective economic base of the settlement was in a foreign country. Lumber was an expensive essential and, since it was usually lumber from the Minnesota mills, its price was increased by the tariff the importers had to pay. Farm machinery was a necessity, but the Manitoba farmer was charged 20 to 30 per cent more for his implements because of the duty levied upon them as they crossed the boundary from the Chicago factories.[35] Only the adoption of free trade would have removed these disadvantages, but the depression of the 'seventies had bred high protectionism in Canada, the so-called "National Policy" of 1878.

Other circumstances were effective in persuading new arrivals that their lot could be made more fortunate by a short journey over the boundary. The plan used in the distribution of land in Manitoba reserved alternate "blocks" for future occupation. Settlement, therefore, could not be immediately continuous, but was broken by patches of open prairie that were depressing to the spirits and caused inconvenience in travel.[36] Moreover, large areas had been granted to per-

33. *Ibid. 1880–81,* App. No. 1, 26, 27.
34. *The Globe,* Aug. 7, 1880.
35. *Emerson International,* Dec. 16, 1880. *Montreal Weekly Witness,* May 25, 1881.
36. P. H. Bryce, "The Immigrant Settler," *The Annals of the American Academy of Political and Social Science,* CVII (Philadelphia, May, 1923),

sons and corporations who held land on speculation, thereby inten-
sifying the patchwork nature of the communities.[37] In the province
there were no herd laws such as those which in Dakota and Minnesota protected the crops and the young trees of the pioneer from
droves of wandering cattle. Safety was assured only when an expensive fencing of the fields had been accomplished.[38] Titles in some
districts were uncertain and if investigation proved that a settler
was consciously or unconsciously a "squatter," he had no right of
preëmption to the land that he had improved.[39] These were some of
the conditions cited by contemporaries in explanation of the continual southward drift of people whose original intention was to remain under the British flag. Every departure meant more than the
loss of an individual or a family. For although some of these conditions were soon remedied, the openly voiced grumbling of the first
arrivals deterred others from going into the province and their removal to Dakota tended to draw neighbors and relatives into that
territory.[40]

Among those who engaged in a second migration were many homesteaders. The Canadian laws were in many respects more liberal than
the homestead regulations of the United States but both were alike
in that a citizen was allowed to exercise his right only once. From
the point of view of the government this was a very reasonable restriction, but the settler saw in it a barrier to what he considered a
legitimate profit. A large percentage of those coming into the province, particularly in the boom year of 1882, brought some capital.
They had no desire to take up unimproved lands and begin with
breaking the unexpectedly tough prairie sod. Prairie pioneering was
a skilled trade in which they had had no training and for which they
had no desire. They were eager to do business with the homesteader

35–45. For a systematic analysis of Western Canadian settlement, see A. S.
Morton and C. Martin, *History of Prairie Settlement and "Dominion Lands"
Policy.*

37. *The Globe,* June 16, Nov. 20, 22, 23, 1880. J. B. Hedges, *The Federal
Railway Land Subsidy Policy of Canada* (Cambridge, Mass., 1934), and
*Building the Canadian West: The Land and Colonization Policies of the
Canadian Pacific Railway* (New York, 1939).

38. *Emerson International,* July 17, 24, 1879.

39. *Ibid.,* Jan. 6, 1881.

40. *Ibid.,* May 6, 1880; July 27, 1882. *The Globe,* Nov. 23, 1880.

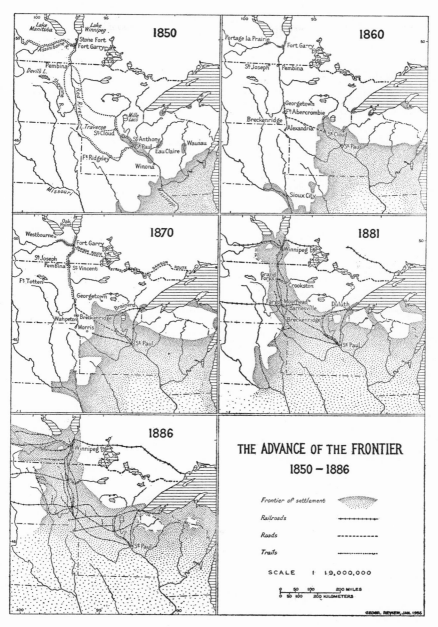

THE ADVANCE OF THE FRONTIER

1850 – 1886

Frontier of settlement
Railroads
Roads
Trails

SCALE 1: 19,000,000

0 50 100   200 MILES
0 50 100   200 KILOMETERS

Reproduced through the courtesy of Professor A. H. Moehlman and of the Geographical Review published by the American Geographical Society of New York.

who had "proved his right" and was willing to sell. The latter was then in a position to homestead again (very often in the company of his sons who were also eligible), and with the funds from the sale of the first improvement capital would be available with which to acquire implements and stock and make of the second experience a far more successful venture. To go through with this procedure would be impossible if he remained in Canada, but there was nothing to prevent him from accepting the buyer's bid, traveling across the line into Dakota and there, after declaring his intention of becoming an American citizen, homesteading again.[41]

This was a solution that was applied in the other direction as well. Among the immigrants into Manitoba were American farmers and their sons who came from Nebraska and Kansas where they had sold their holdings at from twenty to thirty dollars an acre and now acquired Canadian government land to the full extent of their homestead rights and often bought additional railroad land grants at three dollars an acre. Some Americans who had never homesteaded chose Manitoba instead of Dakota because in the former three years instead of five was the required period of occupation, and young men aged eighteen instead of twenty-one could enter upon residence.[42]

The immigration of American citizens into Manitoba was not large in proportion to the magnitude of the migration that was carrying tens of thousands of settlers into the states of Minnesota and the territories that lay to the west of them. Some of these American immigrants were persons of Canadian birth who had been naturalized in the United States and now, disappointed in their condition and prospects, or having acquired a modest fortune, were desirous of returning to their first allegiance. Some were Canadians of French stock who were brought in by means of the subsidized repatriation efforts that were still being carried on in a rather dilatory way.[43] The Dominion authorities recognized the desirability of making efforts to encourage the return of their former citizens from the States

41. *Dom. Can.: Jour. H. of C. Sess. 1880–81,* App. No. 1, 29; *1887,* App. No. 4, 25. *Emerson International,* June 8, 15, 1882.

42. *Dom. Can.: App. to Jour. H. of C. Sess. 1894,* No. 4, 204. *Emerson International,* April 20, 1882.

43. *Dom. Can.: App. to Jour. H. of C. Sess. 1884,* No. 1, 110. *Dom. Can.: Jour. H. of C. Sess. 1885,* App. No. 3, 17–18. *Le Travailleur,* Feb. 2, 1880; April 8, 1881; April 1, 1884; April 8, 1887.

and they also understood the value of the pioneering qualities possessed by the Yankee who had had a frontier training. Accordingly, agents were commissioned to travel about in parts of the United States in which the current of westward migration had its origin. These representatives visited prospective migrants, delivered lectures, and distributed literature, using, in fact, the methods that their American rivals had found so successful in Ontario. Activities were gradually broadened and personnel increased. At Portland, Rochester, Chicago, Duluth, and other strategic points immigration offices were opened. At one time six agents were operating in Michigan alone, a state which was considered an unusually promising field, partly because of its large Canadian-born population and partly because of discouraging local agricultural conditions.[44] The efforts swelled mightily in 1893 when the World's Fair brought a large number of the residents of the Middle West to Chicago. At first the authorities of the fair refused to allow any advertising of opportunities offered by a foreign country, but finally the rules were relaxed and five men were stationed at the Canadian exhibit to answer the inquiries of visitors.[45] The historian of the settlement of Saskatchewan records that the first American emigration to that province grew out of this demonstration of what the prairies of the northwest had to offer.[46]

But the day of Saskatchewan had not yet come. No such province was, in fact, in existence. The region to the west of Manitoba was organized as the Northwest Territories and Indian tribes and half-breed traders made up the majority of the inhabitants. The steamers on the north branch of the Saskatchewan River constituted the principal line of communication toward the mountains and a few settlements had grown up about the trading posts along its course.[47] Each of these places looked into the future with anticipations of great growth; and their hopes were not unfounded, because the original

44. *Dom. Can.: Jour. H. of C. Sess. 1893*, App. No. 1, 143, 144. *Dom. Can.: Sess. Pap., 1888*, No. 4, 129; *1893*, No. 13, 99.

45. *Dom. Can.: App. to Jour. H. of C. Sess. 1894*, No. 4, 196, 197.

46. E. H. Oliver, "The Settlement of Saskatchewan to 1914," *R.S.C., 1926*, Sec. ii, 63–89.

47. The classic description of the Saskatchewan country at this period is Rev. William Newton, *Twenty Years on the Saskatchewan, N.W. Canada* (London, 1897).

route surveyed for the Canadian Pacific Railway followed the valley of the river. There was some immigration, principally on the part of the younger members of the old families settled in Manitoba, but the possibilities of an early agricultural boom were soon dissipated.[48] For the route of the railway was abruptly changed and, instead of swinging in a half circle through the more fertile northern park lands, it cut directly toward the west from Winnipeg, passing through the less inviting dry plains area that projected northward across the forty-ninth parallel from the United States.[49] For upwards of twenty years the valley of the North Saskatchewan was neglected. Lands remained unsurveyed, no publicity was given to the region, and the few settlers that did stray in found no provision made for the education of their children.[50]

The change in the route of the railroad shifted the current of migration to the south, nearer the international boundary, where its proximity to the American states might lead to the expectation that citizens of the United States would appear to pioneer on the lands now opened up. They did come, but not in large numbers. A provision in the charter of the Canadian Pacific which prohibited connection with the lines in the neighboring Republic was not removed for several years and an all-rail journey could be made only through Winnipeg.[51] In 1885 the rising of the frontier half-breeds, once more under the leadership of Louis Riel, brought the Canadian Northwest to the notice of all newspaper readers, but this relatively mild incident was exaggerated into a lurid story of Indian massacres in the traditional frontier style and a campaign for settlers that had been planned for that year had to be abandoned.[52] Canadians who had volunteered for service in putting down the rebellion were rewarded by generous gifts of land in the region and in 1886 a considerable

48. *Saskatchewan Herald* (Battleford), Aug. 11, 29, 1879; May 13, 1882.

49. H. A. Innis, *A History of the Canadian Pacific Railway* (London, 1923), 102, 103.

50. *Saskatchewan Herald*, July 28, 1879; Feb. 25, 1882; June 9, 1883; Aug. 23, Nov. 28, 1884; March 3, 1888; Jan. 5, 1889. *Manitoba Free Press* (Winnipeg), July 25, 1905.

51. *C.R.U.S.F.C., 1888 and 1889*, 292.

52. *Canadian American*, April 23, 1885. *Le Travailleur*, May 1, 1885. *Dom. Can.: Sess. Pap., 1886*, No. 10, 139. *U.S. Consular Reports:* House Ex. Doc. No. 157, 49th Congress, 2d Session, 602.

number of them came west to occupy their grants.[53] Occasionally an American family drove over the border in a covered wagon and some exiled Canadians repatriated themselves by joining the settlers who came from the old provinces.[54] But the movement was not yet characteristically an international one because the typical American land seeker could still find what he wanted on his own side of the line.

There were, however, two kinds of Americans who were not typical of the mass, and in the 1880's they arrived as a kind of vanguard for the great crowds that in a little over a decade were to swarm into the new Northwest. They were representatives of two elements in the army of American pioneers which had been far in advance within their own country, and their early appearance in western Canada is another evidence of the continental character of the spread of the expanding population. By 1890, ranchers and Mormons had moved over the line.

The history of the American ranching industry is marked by a persistent drift toward the northwest. Cattlemen and their herds followed the retreating buffalo along the natural grazing pastures that skirted the Rockies and finally reached the valley of the Bow, the principal tributary of the south branch of the Saskatchewan. Here, in the "land of the Chinook," mild winters made year-round grazing possible, and the attention of British capitalists was directed to the attractive profits to be found in the raising of stock. In the early 'eighties the region now included in the southern part of Alberta was dotted with ranch houses and the plains were alive with cattle. Proprietors were usually Englishmen or Canadians, but the cowboys as well as the herds were immigrants from Montana, and the cow towns on the American side of the line were both the base of supplies and the marketing points.[55] For a quarter of a century the

53. *Dom. Can.: Sess. Pap., 1887,* No. 12, 124.

54. Norman F. Black, *History of Saskatchewan and the Old North West* (Regina, 1913), 418. *Dom. Can.: Sess. Pap., 1889,* No. 6, 133; *1893,* No. 13, 89, 90.

55. John R. Craig, *Ranching with Lords and Commons* (Toronto, 1903), 9–11, 22, 83, 88, 253, 293. M. A. Leeson (ed.), *History of Montana, 1739–1885* (Chicago, 1885), 436. Alva J. Noyes, *In the Land of the Chinook or the Story of Blaine County* (Helena, 1917), 26. C. M. MacInnes, *In the Shadow of the Rockies,* passim.

rancher ruled the border country until he was crowded out, as he had been crowded out elsewhere, by the inrush of settlers.

That the farmer would ever come to this region, or stay if he arrived, was doubted by many observers. Rainfall was scanty and it was questionable whether agriculture could ever be carried on with success. This condition was no deterrent to the Mormons of Utah, however, for they were skilled in dry farming and in the late 'eighties and early 'nineties they were looking about for promising fields for occupation. A general dispersion was taking place from the old settlements around Salt Lake where large families and restricted opportunities made some emigration necessary. Several new Mormon communities were founded in various western states and territories; but the hostile attitude then being exhibited toward adherents of the faith by the citizens and authorities of the United States induced many of them to seek homes outside the confines of the Republic. Some went to Mexico and others explored Canada.[56]

To the latter the advantages of the area directly north of the boundary were evident—an agreeable climate, enough water for irrigation, a market among ranchmen, easy access from Utah. In 1887 the first group of Mormons came northward through Montana, and in the succeeding years they were joined by one party after another until by 1905 they numbered six thousand. Cardston, Alberta (named in honor of a daughter and a son-in-law of Brigham Young who were members of the pioneer group), became the center of a prosperous agricultural section because the men from Utah understood irrigation and because in sugar beets they found a product for which the soil was suitable and the market encouraging. Salt Lake City remained the ecclesiastical and social capital for this colony; to it they made religious pilgrimages and the young people traveled south to be married in its tabernacle. Moving back and forth, they undoubtedly did much to advertise the new country and, without question, their successful beginnings prompted the later extensive irrigation enterprises that became the basis of agricultural life in southern Alberta.[57]

56. *Puget Sound Weekly Courier,* May 28, 1880.

57. There is a brief history of the Mormon settlement in the *Manitoba Free Press,* Nov. 18, 1905. See also: *Seattle Weekly Post-Intelligencer,* May 30, 1889; *Manitoba Free Press,* Jan. 26, 1907; James Mavor, "Report on the

The Canadian Pacific was completed to the coast in 1885. The Northern Pacific, following a route three hundred miles to the south, had passed down the valley of the Columbia River, reached Portland in 1883 and, through a branch line that had already been built, established connections with Puget Sound. The appearance of these two new arteries of commerce inaugurated a new era in the history of the Pacific Northwest. But they came too late to influence materially the course of settlement during this period. That was already determined.

Another "gold rush" in 1879–1880 had illustrated the north-south tendency in the population movements along the coast. In the autumn of 1878 gold was discovered among the headwaters of the Skagit River, a stream rising in British Columbia west of the Cascade Range and a few miles above the forty-ninth parallel, which, after looping toward the north, flowed southwestwardly through the Territory of Washington into Puget Sound.[58] During the winter former miners and farmers from all points on the coast gathered at Seattle and Victoria, shouldered their packs, and struck off up the valley or across country to the new "diggings."[59] Reports from the mines varied and arguments with regard to routes and jurisdiction were frequent; but by the summer of 1880 information from "the Skagit" was eclipsed by the knowledge that prosperity had returned to the coast, and the parties of men hunting for gold became but a trickle compared with the flood of humanity that was flowing toward the shores of Puget Sound.

The return of prosperity was doubly welcome because in the Pacific Northwest, on both sides of the line, the last years of the decade of the 'seventies had been a period of inactivity and pessimism. British Columbia and Washington Territory were full of men waiting

North West of Canada with Special Reference to Agricultural Production," *United Kingdom, House of Commons Sessional Papers, 1905,* LIV, 13, 18; J. D. Rogers, *A Historical Geography of the British Colonies,* V, Part III (Oxford, 1911), 241.

58. There is a description of the Skagit River region in the *Seattle Weekly Post-Intelligencer,* May 29, 1884. On the subject of American mining penetration into British Columbia, consult W. J. Trimble, *The Mining Advance into the Inland Empire* (Madison, Wis., 1914).

59. *Puget Sound Weekly Courier,* Nov. 7, 1879; March 26, April 16, June 4, 1880. *The Weekly Intelligencer,* April 26, Nov. 29, 1879; Feb. 28, 1880.

for work to begin on the westernmost lines of the Northern and the Canadian Pacific and the postponement of construction had kept all business in a state of continued stagnation.[60] Oregon and Washington were also affected in other ways. There was little market for timber and for several years lumbering operations had been at a standstill and mills were closed. Farming on cut-over lands had few attractions and the unemployed had little incentive to take up agriculture.[61] But the revived economic activity that in 1879 had appeared in all the industrial centers of the East spread to California during the course of the following winter and the ensuing demand for timber in railroad and city construction at once raised the price, started the lumber mills on Puget Sound sawing the supply of logs on hand, and sent gangs of choppers out into the woods.[62] By June, 1880, there were no more workless men and the reports of the three following years tell of a condition never before witnessed—railroads, building contractors, and timber operators constantly calling for workers and the supply never meeting the demand.[63]

In response there began an influx from California, the intensification of a population movement that had already been under way. So long as there was only one railroad across the continent, Sacramento and San Francisco were the destinations of emigrants from the East who had fixed upon the Pacific coast as their future residence. But not all found what they had hoped for in California, and these, along with others who after a few years of farming or mining there wanted to move on to more promising fields, trekked toward the north into western Oregon or in increasing numbers followed up the Columbia River to engage in the production of wheat on the plateau of eastern Washington.[64] Every European nation and every state and province that had sent its people into the Pacific West was represented in this expansion of population. Another wave of migrants

60. *Ibid.,* Sept. 13, Dec. 6, 1879.

61. *Ibid.,* June 21, July 4, 1879; June 12, 1880.

62. *Ibid.,* Nov. 22, 1879; June 19, Sept. 15, Nov. 6, 1880.

63. *Ibid.,* May 14, June 11, 1881. *The Seattle Weekly Post-Intelligencer,* March 24, June 16, Nov. 24, 1882; Jan. 5, Aug. 2, 1883.

64. *Puget Sound Weekly Courier,* June 13, 1879; Aug. 30, 1880. *The Weekly Intelligencer,* June 14, Aug. 2, 1879; Sept. 15, Nov. 6, 1880; Feb. 5, 1881. *The Seattle Weekly Post-Intelligencer,* May 5, 1882; April 19, 1883; March 6, May 15, 1884. *Canadian American,* March 22, 1883.

went up to Puget Sound by steamer and, in the light of the fact that logging and lumbering were the activities most in need of workers, men from Maine and New Brunswick were largely represented among the arrivals.[65] In 1882 a "Canadian Society" was organized by residents of Washington and Oregon who had been born in the Dominion.[66]

In the recovery from the "hard times" British Columbia lagged behind its American neighbors. But in 1881 construction on the western end of the Canadian Pacific began and there was abundant employment for carpenters and laborers, bridge builders and mechanics. Many of them came by steamer from the American ports and they had no difficulty in finding work.[67] In their company appeared land seekers from the western states who were less fortunate. The areas available for agricultural settlement were scattered and the facilities for providing information about them were not well organized. Accordingly a large proportion of the intending farmers who arrived remained only a short time and, disappointed in their prospects, took the boat for Seattle to become farmers again within the United States.[68]

The entire Pacific coast experienced a recession in all activity during the years 1884 and 1885. The depression continued a few months into 1886 and then a returning prosperity, unprecedented even in a land of booms, acted like a magnet to draw coastal Americans into British Columbia and midland Canadians into the states from California northward.[69] The completion of the Canadian Pacific in 1885 led to a temporary flooding of the labor market in the province.[70] Within a few months, however, the surplus had been

65. *Puget Sound Weekly Courier,* Feb. 20, 1880. *The Seattle Weekly Post-Intelligencer,* May 10, 1883. *Dom. Can.: Jour. H. of C. Sess. 1890,* App. No. 6, 69.

66. *The Seattle Weekly Post-Intelligencer,* Sept. 22, 1882.

67. *The Weekly Intelligencer,* April 2, 9, 1881. *The Seattle Post-Intelligencer,* Sept. 1, 1882.

68. *Ibid.,* March 30, 1883. *B.C.: Sess. Pap., 1884,* 301.

69. *The Seattle Weekly Post-Intelligencer,* June 26, July 31, 1884; Jan. 6, 1887. *Southern Manitoba Times,* May 31, 1885. *B.C.: Sess. Pap., 1885,* 304.

70. *Dom. Can.: Sess. Pap., 1886,* No. 10, 131. *B.C.: Sess. Pap., 1886,* 490, 617.

drained off and, until the severe collapse of 1893 introduced a prolonged period during which all expansion lagged, every year saw an increase in population, important elements among the newcomers being made up of merchants from Puget Sound and California, capitalists from Michigan and Wisconsin who were interested in investing in timberlands, and men skilled in the building trades.[71] For the farmer, opportunities in the United States were more encouraging and the excitement described as the "orange-grove mania" launched a number of Canadians into the fruitgrowing districts of California.[72]

After through service had been provided upon the Canadian Pacific Railway, a new factor influencing population relations made its appearance. Many Europeans arriving at Quebec and Montreal, following the tendency of the time, set off for British Columbia with the intention of locating in that part of the Dominion, but not finding at once the opportunity for which they had hoped they continued by steamer for Seattle, Portland, or San Francisco.[73] This circling was rather less remarkable than the use of the Canadian line by passengers from the eastern United States bound for the Pacific states. The Canadian Pacific was not subject to any of the rulings of the Interstate Commerce Commission of the United States and it refused to enter into any rate agreements with American railroads. As a result it offered passage across the continent more cheaply than any of its competitors, and it advertised widely the convenient boat connections at Vancouver that would carry travelers at once to their American destinations.[74] An official estimate made in 1890 stated that about 75 per cent of those arriving in British Columbia via the railroad were through passengers of American origin.[75]

So confusing was the situation that to classify those crossing the border in either direction as emigrants or immigrants was an impos-

71. Dom. Can.: Sess. Pap., 1888, No. 4, 77, 79, 82; 1889, No. 5, 62, 65; 1890, No. 6, 118; 1891, No. 6, 141, 142; 1892, No. 7, 139, 140. B.C.: Sess. Pap., 1889, 288.

72. Dom. Can.: Sess. Pap., 1888, No. 4, 82. Canadian American, Jan. 5, 1888. Montreal Weekly Witness, Feb. 9, March 2, 1887.

73. Dom. Can.: Sess. Pap., 1889, No. 5, 46.

74. The Seattle Weekly Post-Intelligencer, Aug. 26, Oct. 7, Nov. 12, 1886; April 21, July 14, 1887.

75. Dom. Can.: Sess. Pap., 1890, No. 6, 113.

sibility and the effort was not made. In so far as the United States government was interested in any migration of this nature, its concern was directed toward one special group—the Chinese. Before the American act of 1882 prohibited the immigration of the Orientals, Victoria was the leading center in the Northwest for the distribution of Chinese laborers.[76] The passage of the law did not put an end to the activity. So great was the demand for workers that every person, irrespective of race, could find employment, and whoever would engage in human smuggling could ask a liberal reward for his services. The island-dotted waters of Puget Sound were ideal for carrying on the traffic. Many of the small trading sloops and fishing craft that sailed in and out made the most of the opportunity because the risk of detection was small and when the cargo was once landed on American soil no questions were asked.[77] In the autumn of 1885, during the temporary business recession, anti-Chinese riots were general along the coast.[78] The Dominion passed a law prohibiting their importation and many employers refused to hire them. Thereafter the influx was small. Many of those who were already in British Columbia moved eastward and scattered in the older provinces.[79] A stricter border administration prevented easy entrance into the United States, and, except for those who drifted into Washington by working along the old placer-mining camps on the banks of the rivers that crossed the boundary (camps that were deserted by all except Chinese), the movement was largely at an end.[80]

The emigration from the provinces to the prairie states and beyond was not composed entirely of farmers and their families in search of land. Some of the emigrants wanted to get away from the land and they sought the rising West where every town might become a city and where business was expanding to include a new empire. Like the old agricultural sections in the United States, Ontario had produced a class of young people who were not satisfied with the routine of rural life. Some had received a higher education and

76. *Montreal Weekly Witness*, Nov. 16, 1881. *The Weekly Intelligencer*, July 31, 1880; May 14, 1881. *The Seattle Weekly Post-Intelligencer*, May 19, June 2, 30, 1882.

77. *Ibid.*, Sept. 27, 1883; Nov. 13, Dec. 4, 25, 1884.

78. *Ibid.*, Sept.–Nov., 1885.   79. *Ibid.*, July 30, 1885; Aug. 9, 1888.

80. *Ibid.*, Feb. 4, 1886; July 26, 1888.

found little call for their services; some had prepared for professions which were already crowded; some were experienced in trades or commerce but lived in communities where no opportunities for advancement were at hand.[81] For all such the growing cities in the neighboring States possessed an almost irresistible appeal. The young men of Ontario, it was explained, "look upon Chicago as the Mecca of their ambition; . . . the average young Canadian holds this city as the goal of his fortunes."[82] Reports from the city told of hundreds of Canadians employed in the printing establishments, of the men from the provinces who were connected with every banking institution, of young medical graduates who were starting practice, and of enterprising merchants who were opening stores. The many social organizations composed of Chicago residents who wished not to forget their Dominion birth testify to the presence of many energetic young people.[83]

Chicago was only one city from which such reports might come. Particularly in railroad centers men from Ontario were numerous. The Grand Trunk and Great Western railways of Canada were considered very efficient "training schools," and those who had learned railroading upon these lines always claimed that they had no difficulty in securing positions upon the expanding railway systems of the United States. In the business departments, mechanical shops, and telegraph offices Canadians were particularly evident, many of them occupying positions of the highest authority.[84] Transportation had, in fact, always been an important feature of Canadian economic life, and so long as the Great Lakes continued to carry a part of the commerce of the Middle West, sailors of Canadian nationality were numerous among the crews of vessels that were registered at Cleveland, Chicago, and Port Huron.[85]

81. *Dom. Can.: Jour. H. of C. Sess. 1889*, App. No. 4, 52, 81. *Dom. Can.: Debates H. of C. 1891*, XXXIII, 5227. *Montreal Weekly Witness*, March 12, 1879.

82. *Canadian American*, April 17, 1884.

83. *Ibid.*, Feb. 8, March 27, April 10, 1884; Feb. 5, Aug. 6, May 14, 1886; Nov. 25, 1887. *Western British American*, Feb. 4, 1888.

84. *Canadian American*, March 16, May 4, 1883; April 10, 1884; March 5, 12, May 15, 1885; Jan. 22, Feb. 19, July 2, 30, 1886. J. J. Hill is probably the most conspicuous example.

85. *Dom. Can.: Jour. H. of C. Sess. 1890*, App. No. 4, 9. *Dom. Can.: Sess. Pap., 1882*, No. 11, 215.

The history of the personnel of every economic activity in the United States might include a chapter on the Canadian-born. In two fields they were so numerous as to warrant special mention: lumbering and mining. Many of the woodsmen were not emigrants in the true sense of the word. Those who went to Michigan should on the whole be classified rather as seasonal workers.[86] When cutting was about to begin in the pinewoods special trains were made up at various Canadian points to collect the laborers.[87] How many of them remained in the United States it was impossible for the railroad officials to state, because those that came back usually returned in the spring after the opening of navigation and traveled by steamer instead of by rail.[88] But there certainly was a residue left at every sawmill town and to take up cut-over land was a recognized way of becoming established in agriculture.[89] Those who set out to work at more distant points were naturally more inclined to remain, and at every lumber district in the West—in Wisconsin, Minnesota, Colorado, Montana, Idaho, and on the Pacific slope—Canadians were found in the woods, in sawmills and planing mills, and in the merchandising of timber products.[90]

Miners were not so numerous because mineral industries were not yet an important feature of Canadian economic life except in that part of the province of Nova Scotia known as Cape Breton. Here coal deposits had been worked for a century with varying success as a business venture, the determining factor being the demand from the American market. During the 1880's that demand lagged and many of the pits were closed, forcing the miners either to attempt to make a living from the barren and rocky countryside or to depart for some place where their technical skill could be put to use.[91] Those that emigrated sought the new western mining regions in preference to the old ones in the East, and in Montana, Idaho, and Colorado,

86. *Dom. Can.: Jour. H. of C. Sess. 1880–81,* App. No. 1, 17, 25, 76.

87. *Dom. Can.: Sess. Pap., 1880–81,* No. 12, xxxix.

88. *Dom. Can.: App. to Jour. H. of C. Sess. 1884,* No. 1, 3.

89. *Dom. Can.: Sess. Pap., 1893,* No. 13, 101.

90. *Canadian American,* March 16, 30, 1883; May 1, 1884; Jan. 14, 1887. *Dom. Can.: Sess. Pap., 1888,* No. 4, 130. *Acadian Recorder,* March 30, 1880.

91. *The Morning Chronicle* (Halifax), Sept. 26, Oct. 16, 1879. *Montreal Weekly Witness,* April 12, 1882.

Canadians were engaged in the varied branches of mining and smelting.[92]

The plight of the Cape Breton miner did not receive the attention that he might have expected because all of his provincial neighbors had some complaints to air. That the fishermen of the Maritime Provinces were suffering was clear, and that their condition was affected by Dominion politics was just as evident. Since early in the nineteenth century, many of them had preferred to spend some seasons at least on the American vessels that sailed out of Gloucester, claiming that conditions on board ship in the matter of provisions and equipment were more satisfactory and the wages higher and more promptly paid.[93] Every spring about five hundred Nova Scotians set out for the Massachusetts port, returning at the expense of the fishing masters when the crew was disbanded.[94] This practice was sharply stimulated when, on July 1, 1885, the fishing articles of the Treaty of Washington of 1871 lapsed. By that agreement, in return for the privileges that the United States enjoyed in the British waters off the provinces, fish shipped from Nova Scotia and New Brunswick had been allowed to enter American ports duty-free. But beginning in 1886 (to avoid confusion the agreement was extended by special arrangement until the end of the season of 1885) the American tariff wall shut the Canadian fishermen out of their best market. With no future agreement in sight, all prospects were discouraging and prudence suggested that it would be well for the fisherman to attach himself permanently to the Gloucester fleet. He migrated again, this time with his family, and his departure was cited in the arguments of the political partisans as evidence that the interests of the Maritime Provinces were being sacrificed for the sake of general Canadian policies that benefited them not at all.[95]

Along with the decline of fishing went the decline of shipping.

92. *Canadian American,* Aug. 21, 1884; April 30, 1886. *Dom. Can.: Sess. Pap., 1888,* No. 4, 137, 138.

93. *Canadian American,* April 10, 1884; Dec. 16, 1887. *Yarmouth Times* (N.S.), March 14, Aug. 1, 1883.

94. *Dom. Can.: Sess. Pap., 1882,* No. 11, 230.

95. *Acadian Recorder,* June 27, 1885; Jan. 4, 1886. *Montreal Weekly Witness,* July 8, 1885; March 9, 1887. J. M. Callahan, *American Foreign Policy in Canadian Relations* (New York, 1937), 345, 361–370.

This could not be so convincingly ascribed to politics. Life at sea was proving to be less attractive to the younger generation than it had been to their fathers who had had fewer opportunities for adventure on land. A captain now found it a difficult matter to secure sufficient hands.[96] But even had this difficulty been overcome, the Maritime shipbuilders and operators could not have hoped for a return of prosperous times. The day of the wooden ocean carrier had passed, and, in the expression of a journalist, the future fortunes of the commercial families were shelved as "high and dry" as the vessels that they discarded.[97] Shipbuilding, which had once been one of the most important activities in the provinces, now came to an almost complete standstill and in the city of St. John the streets in which the carpenters had lived were left almost deserted by the departure of the workmen.[98]

The emigration of fishermen and shipwrights was small in comparison with the exodus of young people of all classes, but particularly the sons and daughters of the farmers. They complained of no special grievance but the dullness of rural life and the feeling of hopelessness regarding the future that prevailed during the decade.[99] The local atmosphere was in striking contrast with the opportunities that the neighboring New England states could offer. What Chicago was to Ontario, Boston was to the Maritime Provinces—the goal of ambitious youth.[100] Everyone could point to the five natives of New Brunswick and Nova Scotia who occupied chairs in the faculty of Harvard University.[101] Steamship rates to the city were low, and if the young woman did not at once secure a position as a domestic servant or the young man find an opening as a mechanic or tradesman, a score of other cities were within a short distance.[102] The news-

96. *Yarmouth Tribune*, Oct. 4, 1882.   97. *Ibid.*, Oct. 26, 1881.

98. *The Morning Chronicle*, Oct. 18, 1879. C.R.U.S.F.C., *1886 and 1887*, 539.

99. *Acadian Recorder*, June 12, Oct. 9, 1879. Dom. Can.: *Debates H. of C. Sess. 1891*, XXXIII, 5255.

100. "Boston Is the Promised Land of Canadians," *The Prince Edward Island Magazine*, I (Charlottetown, P.E.I., 1899–1900), 82.

101. *The British American Citizen* (Boston), Dec. 28, 1889.

102. *Reports from the Consuls of the United States, 1880–81* (Washington, 1881), 59. Dom. Can.: *Jour. H. of C. Sess. 1890*, App. No. 5, 71. Note the advertisement for "one thousand Protestant girls for general housework" in *The British American Citizen*, Jan. 18, 1890.

paper accounts of the exodus are monotonous reading when repeated year after year. Some editors questioned the validity of the reports and explained the heavy passenger lists as being made up of tourists who had enjoyed a vacation in the quiet provinces or emigrants of a previous period who had been on a visit to the old home.[103] But the state censuses of Massachusetts and Rhode Island of the year 1895, which record the provincial origin of the Canadian-born, indicate their presence in every community where maritime skills or commercial capacities were likely to be in special demand.[104]

Perhaps as startling as the proportions of the emigration was the philosophical attitude of the parents who saw their children depart. "They will do better away" was the common remark in Prince Edward Island.[105] The emigration of family groups was not so common in eastern Canada and when it occurred it was usually directed to the western states where agriculture was the attraction.[106] The loss of so many of the young people naturally created some problems. There was a lack of domestic servants and an acute shortage in farm laborers that caused the provincial governments to renew efforts, not to stop the emigration (which now had come to be taken for granted), but to turn a larger part of the European immigration into North America in the direction of Nova Scotia and New Brunswick.[107] By advertisements and in some cases by financial assistance these efforts enjoyed some success, but they were discontinued because so many of the new arrivals caught the prevailing spirit and moved on to the United States before they had acquired any permanent interests in the provinces. Not until the early 1890's was there any stoppage of the outward movement of the residents, either native or foreign-born.[108]

103. *Acadian Recorder,* March 22, 1880; March 30, May 15, June 13, 1882; Sept. 18, 1883; Jan. 14, 1886; April 4, 1887; April 5, 1888. *The Globe,* June 19, 1880. *The Morning Chronicle,* Oct. 9, 1879.

104. *Census of the Commonwealth of Massachusetts,* 1895, II (Boston, 1897), 581–715. *Census of Rhode Island, 1895* (Providence, 1898), 262–263.

105. *Montreal Weekly Witness,* Nov. 22, 1882.

106. *Dom. Can.: Jour. H. of C. Sess. 1890,* App. No. 5, 71. *Acadian Recorder,* June 13, 1882.

107. *Dom. Can.: Debates H. of C. Sess. 1891,* XXXIII, 5234.

108. *British American Citizen,* Oct. 25, 1890.

From the Eastern Townships of Quebec the accounts read the same: enterprising Anglo-Canadian youth, so soon as they were able to shift for themselves, set out for the cities in their own province and the United States or for the "Far West."[109] Little attention, however, was paid to this, for it had come to seem an entirely natural phenomenon. It was among their French neighbors who had taken up land in the Townships and among the habitants in the parishes to the north that emigration became a matter for concern. Not that it was anything new; but in its extent the movement was unparalleled, and the characteristic tendency to settle permanently in the industrial sections of New England indicated that migration was no longer a seasonal search for work, but a transfer of family and property into a new home.

The reports of high and increasing wages and the activity of labor solicitors would not in themselves have caused a response of such unusual magnitude.[110] The habitant was in debt. The preceding hard years (1873–1880), during which fewer sons had added to the household income by an annual visit to southern brickyards and factories, had left many families involved in obligations from which they could be freed only by concerted and vigorous action.[111] During the decade of the 'eighties the situation did not greatly improve. The Dominion tariff of 1879 increased the price of the implements that the farmer used and in the purchase of which he often went into debt; and in 1890 the McKinley Tariff in the United States, by putting a duty on agricultural imports, shut off the most accessible market, the great urban communities not far below the line.[112] Measured by their production, the habitant's home acres were few; winter idleness was inevitable because there was little employment outside the home for adults or children; the great demand from the States was for year-round, not seasonal, workers. Therefore, encouraged by the low rates that the railroads offered, he closed the house, took wife and family, and left, abandoning his fields until such time as he could

109. *Montreal Weekly Witness,* June 14, 1882.
110. For labor solicitation see *L'Indépendent* (Fall River), April 23, 1866; *Le Travailleur,* Nov. 23, 1881.
111. *Le Courrier de Worcester,* June 3, 1880. P.Q.: *Sess. Pap., 1890,* XXIV, No. 2, 281.
112. P.Q.: *Sess. Pap., 1891,* XXV, No. 2, 156–157.

return and pay off the mortgage and square accounts with the village merchants.[113]

Inevitably there were families that did not come back. The children who grew up in the new environment were only one tie that made their elders stationary. A new environment surrounded the parents as well. It was no longer entirely Yankee. Industry was American, but society could be French, for there were French parishes and parochial schools, and French clubs.[114] The excitement that attended the uprising of Louis Riel, although the event took place far off upon the Canadian prairies, did much to reawaken nationalistic sentiments among the expatriates.[115] But it was a new kind of nationalism, one that was strongly tinged with Americanism. It was the feeling of a minority struggling to secure recognition and organizing to obtain its share of political preferment. During 1886 naturalization became a much agitated question in the French-American communities, with the leaders of local opinion strongly favoring the step.[116] This logically hastened a process that was already under way: the securing of real property—houses and lots; and in Rhode Island, where the French element was strong, naturalization fostered such purchases to a remarkable extent because that state required that a naturalized citizen must be the possessor of some property in order to vote, whereas the native-born was exempt.[117] Permanency encouraged the coming of doctors, lawyers, and teachers from Quebec, where all professions were crowded, and they, in turn, made life more congenial for those who had once been considered exiles.[118]

113. *Le Courrier de Worcester,* April 1, May 20, 1880. *Le Travailleur,* Nov. 12, 1880.

114. *Ibid.,* Nov. 23, 1881; Oct. 2, 1885; Oct. 18, 1888. *L'Indépendent,* July 23, Oct. 8, 1886. *P.Q.: Sess. Pap., 1889,* XXII, 282.

115. *L'Indépendent,* Dec. 11, 1885; Nov. 19, 1886.

116. *Ibid.,* Oct. 8, 15, 22, 29, Nov. 5, 1886. *Le Travailleur,* Aug. 6, 1886. "Naturalization without assimilation" was the expression of the ideal. *Compte-Rendu de la seizième convention nationale des canadiens-français des Etats-Unis tenue à Rutland, Vt., le 22 et le 23 juin, 1886* (Plattsburg, 1886), 13.

117. *Courrier de Worcester,* Aug. 16, 1883. *L'Indépendent,* April 16, 30, Oct. 22, 1886.

118. *Courrier de Worcester,* Nov. 3, 1882. *L'Indépendent,* Feb. 5, 1886. *P.Q.: Sess. Pap., 1881–82,* XV, No. 5, 131; *1884–85,* XVIII, No. 5, App. No. 1, 152.

Until the family was rooted by the possession of real estate, there was much coming and going in all the French communities. Some went back to reoccupy the farms that had not been sold; others to take up lands in the Quebec colonization areas. Even in the years when the immigration into New England was greatest, return travelers were so numerous as to arouse comment. A constant replacement in personnel was evident in the mills, those who were going ceding their places to those that came.[119] It was a realization of the existence of this return instinct that caused the province of Quebec to persist in its schemes for repatriation in spite of the insignificant results that had come out of the earlier ventures. Agents were sent out to organize clubs that would return as a group and free grants were made available along the colonization roads north of the St. Lawrence.[120] The French-Canadian newspapers in the States, however, fought all schemes that would deprive them of subscribers, arguing that people who were now, after hard struggles, comfortably settled should hesitate before making another and uncertain beginning.[121] But prosperity was the principal deterrent. The emigrants did not want to be repatriated and a mass return movement was never successfully organized.[122]

Between 1879 and 1893 the influx varied in keeping with the trends exhibited by the figures of general immigration. The years 1880, 1881, and 1882 witnessed a southward exodus that attracted widespread attention.[123] Again in the latter part of 1885 and 1886, after a short period of closed mills, strikes, and lower wages, the

119. *Courrier de Worcester*, April 13, 20, June 23, 1882. *L'Indépendent*, April 16, Oct. 22, 1886. *Le Travailleur*, June 16, 1882. *Dom. Can.: Sess. Pap., 1894*, No. 13, Part III, 117. *P.Q.: Sess. Pap., 1886*, XVIII, No. 2, 3, 87, 96, 119.

120. *L'Indépendent*, Aug. 20, Sept. 10, 1886. *U.S. Consular Reports:* House Ex. Doc. No. 157, 49th Congress, 2d Session, 571–572. *P.Q.: Sess. Pap., 1883*, XVI, No. 2, App. No. VII, 117, 119.

121. *L'Indépendent*, Nov. 19, 1886. *Le Travailleur*, Sept. 12, 1890.

122. *Ibid.*, Nov. 5, 1889. *P.Q.: Sess. Pap., 1891*, XXV, No. 2, 161. A. Desrosiers and Abbé Fournet, *La Race française en Amérique*, 221. A. Labelle, *Considérations générales sur l'agriculture, la colonisation, le repatriement et l'immigration* (Quebec, 1888), 17.

123. *Courrier de Worcester*, April 1, May 6, 20, 1880; May 19, 1881; April 20, 1882. *Le Travailleur*, March 26, May 11, 14, 1880; April 22, May 6, 1881; Jan. 10, 1882.

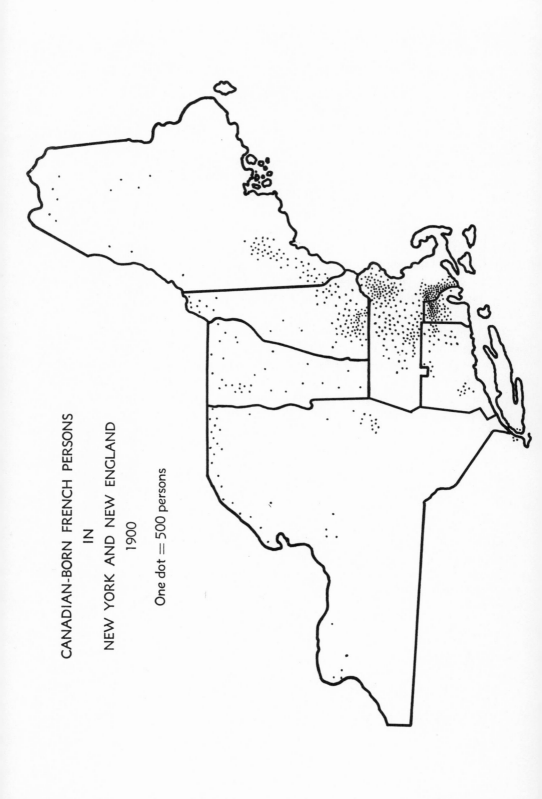

CANADIAN-BORN FRENCH PERSONS

IN

NEW YORK AND NEW ENGLAND

1900

One dot = 500 persons

current was strong.[124] In 1890 and 1891, an exodus reported to be without parallel in the history of French-Canadian emigration took place.[125] The check did not come until the year 1893, when the sudden closing up of factories started a backflow that would have been considered unbelievable a short time before.[126]

New England was not the only destination of emigrants from Quebec. The Hudson Valley still provided employment for thousands, and in the woods of Michigan crews of French loggers hired along the St. Lawrence made an annual appearance.[127] Detroit and Bay City became considerable centers of French population and society, and it was estimated that more than 25,000 had made their homes in Chicago.[128] In fact, in all the western states where the English-speaking Canadians were numerous, the French were also on hand. In the buoyant season of 1880 they came to the upper peninsula of Michigan in such crowds that a newspaper declared: "About half the population of Canada has arrived here during the month past."[129] They worked in the lumber mills and mines from the Mississippi to the Rockies and planted large colonies in Minnesota, Nebraska, and Dakota. Former fur-trading centers like St. Paul continued to draw in relatives of the old *voyageur* families and new settlements were formed to attract land seekers from both Canada and New England.[130] The most flourishing of these colonies was that founded dur-

124. *Dom. Can.: Sess. Pap., 1884,* No. 14, 125; *1885,* No. 8, 86. *L'Indé-pendent,* Oct. 9, Nov. 27, Dec. 4, 24, 1885; Jan. 1, March 26, April 2, 9, 16, May 21, 1886. *Le Travailleur,* March 10, 1885; May 21, 1886; April 29, 1887.

125. *P.Q.: Sess. Pap., 1891,* XXV, No. 2, 154. *Le Travailleur,* Sept. 12, 1890.

126. *Montreal Weekly Witness,* Aug. 16, 23, 1893.

127. *Le Travailleur,* June 21, 1881. *Montreal Weekly Witness,* Dec. 28, 1881. *Dom. Can.: Sess. Pap., 1882,* No. 11, 215. *Dom. Can.: App. to Jour. H. of C. Sess. 1884,* No. 1, 3. E. Hamon, *Les Canadiens-Français de la Nou-velle Angleterre,* 12, 452.

128. *Le Travailleur,* June 5, Dec. 18, 1888; Dec. 13, 1889. *Canadian American,* Nov. 4, 1887.

129. *The Mining Journal* (Marquette, Mich.), July 3, 1880. See also Rev. Antoine Ivan Rezak, *History of the Diocese of Sault Ste. Marie and Mar-quette,* II (Houghton, Mich., 1906), 205, 207, 220, 225, 230, 368, 420.

130. N. E. Dionne, *Etats-Unis, Manitoba et Nord-Ouest. Notes de voyage* (Quebec, 1882), 90, 135, 142. *Le Travailleur,* Nov. 11, 1879; Nov. 16, 1888;

ing the depression of the 1870's by some residents of Minneapolis and St. Paul in the vicinity of Crookston, Minnesota. Being located on the edge of the Red River Valley, they profited from the inrush of settlers in the early 'eighties and in 1883 it was estimated that over eight thousand persons of French-Canadian birth or descent had located in the colony or had taken up residence in the town.[131]

So strong and persistent was the drift of population during these years from all parts of Canada into the United States that little attention was paid to the reverse movement. Nevertheless there was a steady immigration, the results being revealed by the census figures showing the distribution of American-born in the Dominion in 1891. Some of these were the children of Canadians who had returned after a residence in the Republic. Some were bona fide immigrants who had come in, particularly to the large cities, to act as representatives of the business enterprises in the United States that were extending operations across the line. Many of them were skilled factory operatives who had deliberately chosen Canada as a promising field where they might profit from their experience and training.

The "National Policy," or high protectionism of the Canadian Conservative party, was the agency that had drawn these Americans over the border. During the depression years sentiment for a protective tariff grew steadily, and it culminated in 1878 in the creation of a customs structure to which this patriotic title was applied. The hope had been held out that by creating opportunities for employment at home the necessity for emigration would be removed. Such was not the outcome.[132] The Canadians did not cease to emigrate, but the loss in population was not quite as great as would otherwise have been the case because of a moderate increase in industrial employment. Some of the skills that could not be found in the Dominion

Aug. 9, 1889; July 11, 1890. *P.Q.: Sess. Pap., 1886,* XIX, No. 29, 27. *Dom. Can.: App. to Jour. H. of C. Sess. 1884,* No. 1, 3, 101. *Dom. Can.: Sess. Pap., 1890,* No. 6, 166. The wide distribution of the French-Canadian emigrants is illustrated by the lists of names published in E. Z. Massicotte, "L'Emigration aux Etats-Unis il y a 40 ans et plus," *Bulletin des recherches historiques,* XXXIX, 21–27, 86–88, 179–181, 228–231, 381–383, 427–429, 507–509, 560–562, 697, 711–712.

131. *Description de la colonie canadienne du comté de Polk* (Crookston, Minn., 1883), 5, 6, 8, 16, 18. *Le Travailleur,* July 14, 1882.

132. *Reports from the Consuls of the United States, 1880–81,* 556.

were available among enterprising artisans in the United States, who, provided with some funds, were choosing Canadian localities in which to begin as independent operatives. Larger concerns were incorporated by both Canadian and American capitalists to manufacture for the newly protected Canadian market, and many of these enterprises could not get under way until workers and managers had been secured from factories in the States. The reports of the immigration inspectors, from New Brunswick to Ontario, make constant mention of the entrance of mechanics and weavers in response to this need.[133]

The modest industrial expansion of this period in Canada came to an end with the decade of the 'eighties. The report for 1890 revealed that there was no longer any demand for more hands and that some of the Canadian mills were shutting down.[134] But at the same time there were evidences that in Ontario the movement of emigration had also run its course.[135] The attractions of the western prairies were being dimmed by news that disillusioned the most credulous. Drought and frost, declining prices coupled with high taxes and high interest rates, crop shortages and crop failures, scanty supplies of timber and fuel, and dry wells were experiences that were never forgotten by the pioneers of Dakota. Other western states were little better off and the westward movement of people first halted and then receded. Discouraged homesteaders went back to Iowa, Indiana, and Ontario. By 1890 a withdrawal of the frontier had started.[136] The wheels of industry were kept turning by some temporary and fortunate demands, but they could not be kept going very long after the stimulus of an expanding West had been removed. In the spring of

133. *P.O.: Sess. Pap., 1882*, XIV, No. 6, 34; *1882–83*, XV, No. 6, 37. *Dom. Can.: Sess. Pap., 1882*, XV, No. 10, 82; *1883*, No. 14, 127; *1886*, No. 10, 34, 97; *1889*, No. 5, 29, 77; *1890*, No. 6, 57. *U.S. Consular Reports 1882*, 427; *1882–83*, 43, 218; *1884*, 106; House Ex. Doc. 157, 49th Congress, 2d Session, 604. *C.R.U.S.F.C., 1886 and 1887*, 520. H. Marshall, F. A. Southard, and K. W. Taylor, *Canadian-American Industry* (New Haven, 1936), 12–15.

134. *Dom. Can.: Sess. Pap., 1891*, No. 6, 31.

135. *Dom. Can.: Jour. H. of C. Sess. 1890*, No. 6, App. No. 5.

136. *Ibid.*, 69. *Dom. Can.: App. to Jour. H. of C. Sess. 1891*, No. 5, 118, 119, 130. *Dom. Can.: Sess. Pap., 1889*, No. 5, 97, 113; *1890*, No. 6, 133; *1891*, No. 6, 130, 131, 151, 158, 159, 160, 170.

1893 the depression already present in agriculture reached the factories, the warehouses, and the banks. The stagnation of the 'seventies had come back and with its appearance Canadians and Americans remained where they were, content to let dreams of new homes and new fortunes await the return of more hopeful days.

CHAPTER X

FROM THE STATES TO THE PRAIRIE PROVINCES
1896–1914

To Sir Wilfrid Laurier, Prime Minister of Canada from 1896 to 1911, was ascribed the sentiment that, just as the nineteenth century had belonged to the United States, the twentieth would be that of Canada.[1] During the first decade of the century every aspect of economic life in the Dominion corroborated the confident optimism of the Premier. Work was plentiful and capital was abundant. Every year saw the completion of hundreds of miles of railroad and the breaking of thousands of acres of land. Mounting figures of wheat exportation indicated that Canada was a land of plenty, and the rising curve of immigration statistics proved that to Europeans it was as much a land of promise as the United States. From 1896 until 1913, with only a slight break in 1907 and 1908, the prosperity continued. Bumper crops in the West and high prices in the markets of the world were the fundamental reasons for this good fortune; and the influx of hundreds of thousands of farmers who left the American states to take advantage of the opportunities offered by the prairie provinces makes the period an important chapter in the history of Canadian-American population relations.

This was all in sharp contrast with the depression that had prevailed in the middle of the 'nineties. Agriculture as well as industry had then been in a state of stagnation and people had remained where they were unless the most real necessity forced a change. The Canadian government recalled its salaried immigration agents from the States and the reports that it received from other representatives brought the information that, although many Americans were revealing an interest in the free lands of Canada, difficulty in disposing of property and the burden of indebtedness that could not be liquidated rendered migration impossible.[2]

1. *Manitoba Free Press*, July 4, 1906.
2. *Dom. Can.: Sess. Pap., 1895*, No. 13, xi; Part III, 4, 74; *1896*, No. 13, Part IV, 47.

A gradual improvement in trade and rise in prices for most commodities set in during 1896. The same year was marked by the adoption of a more intense Dominion immigration policy. These two forces, operating together, combined to bring almost a million Americans over the international line into the great wheat belt that extended westward from the Red River to the foothills of the Canadian Rockies during the succeeding fifteen years. The movement, in its direction, at least, was natural. The farmer was only following the northward extension of the prairie land of the middle western states that had been put under the plow twenty years before. Within the United States the great prairies merged into the great plains, where bitter experience had taught that only a new agricultural technique could produce grain. But a little north of the forty-ninth parallel the prairie belt curves to the west and before reaching the Rockies turns to the southwest. When viewed upon a map of North America it forms a gigantic question mark, the upper loop being filled by a bulge of the American high plains extending beyond the boundary to form the semiarid lands of southern Alberta.[3] That this northern prairie curve was fertile had long been known; that it could produce wheat in spite of early frosts had to be demonstrated. But by 1900 this was done and a few years later Americans were reading with amazement that northwest Canada possessed a potential wheat area four times as large as that of the United States. It was inevitable that in a world demanding more and more wheat these acres should be peopled by Canadians, Americans, or Europeans.[4]

The new governmental policy made it more certain that Americans should have an active part in the process. In 1896 Clifford Sifton became Minister of the Interior. He set out to advertise the new agricultural empire throughout the upper Mississippi Valley, knowing well that in these states were to be found farmers and farmers' sons

3. A map of the soil quality can be found in J. G. Bartholomew, *An Atlas of Economic Geography* (London, 1914), 41, 42. See also W. A. Mackintosh, *Prairie Settlement, The Geographical Setting* (Toronto, 1934), 22, 23.

4. *C.R.U.S.F.C., 1903,* I, 125; *1904,* 439, 440. *M. C. and T. Reports,* Nov., 1905, 9. *The Nation* (New York), July 2, 1903, Vol. 77, 6. For close analysis of prairie settlement, consult A. S. Morton and C. Martin, *History of Prairie Settlement and "Dominion Lands" Policy;* J. B. Hedges, *The Federal Railway Land Subsidy Policy of Canada;* and his *Building the Canadian West.*

gathered like bees ready to swarm, and appreciating to the fullest the pioneering virtues that they could offer. Publicity and persuasion were only the beginning of the program. Special rates on railroads, barracks for waiting settlers, and a general watchfulness over their subsequent well-being were other elements.[5] Among the offices opened was one in Omaha. During 1896 the agent stationed there was successful in sending only one settler who was willing to venture into what his neighbors described as a "frozen country." In 1897 the same office persuaded ninety to go.[6] Meanwhile, another method was inaugurated. Capitalists in the United States were induced to buy wide stretches of land at bargain prices and the companies that they formed then adopted their own advertising and selling procedure, entering into the campaign with the vigor of experienced real-estate promoters. It was common for a company of this nature to pay its local representative a dollar for every acre that he sold, thereby encouraging persistent work.[7]

The publicity efforts of the Immigration Department expanded with the years. From the beginning advertisements were inserted in local newspapers and agricultural journals, and in 1902 they appeared in about seven thousand periodicals. At state and county fairs and at larger expositions, such as those at Buffalo in 1901 and at St. Louis in 1903, exhibits of the agricultural products of the northwestern provinces aroused interest and provided lists of prospects. Printed information was forwarded to inquirers and distributed by the bureaus that were opened in the most promising localities. Salaried general agents were sent to the border and middle western states and a great number of commissioned representatives were appointed who received three dollars for every man, two dollars for every woman, and one dollar for every child whom they persuaded to emigrate to Canada.[8] The government did not, however,

5. *Manitoba Free Press,* Oct. 22, 1906. *Canadian American,* June 4, 1898. John W. Dafoe, "Western Canada: Its Resources and Possibilities," *The American Monthly Review of Reviews,* Vol. 35, 697–710. John W. Dafoe, *Clifford Sifton in Relation to His Times* (Toronto, 1931), 131–141.

6. *Canadian American,* July 15, 1911.

7. *Ibid.,* Feb. 10, 1906. *Manitoba Free Press,* Nov. 27, 1907. *C.R.U.S.F.C.,* *1903,* I, 125.

8. *Dom. Can.: Sess. Pap., 1898,* No. 13, 27; *1900,* No. 13, Part II, 178;

provide any free transportation. The railroads of the western provinces granted a special rate of one cent a mile from the international boundary to his destination to anyone who was certified by some immigration agent as a bona fide land seeker and if he returned for his family the same concession was made to them.[9]

The private land companies were more generous. They also advertised widely, both in their individual capacities and as members of a joint organization known as the Western Canada Immigration Association. Excursions for invited guests, who in the course of two or three weeks visited the most rapidly developing areas and the most scenic spots, were numerous and effective. The guests were usually professional journalists of established reputation who were connected with periodicals of wide circulation, some of them the "muckraking" periodicals that were reaching dissatisfied workers and farmers at that time. The glowing descriptions of new farms, new towns, and new railroads were often successful in arousing a curiosity that could be satisfied only by a personal visit, and if the interested person were considered one whose judgment enjoyed great respect among his neighbors, a land company did not hesitate to pay his expenses on a tour of observation.[10]

A generation earlier, when Canadians had been leaving for the western states in numbers that aroused concern, many patriotic observers maintained that propaganda was the only cause and urged that steps be taken to curb the operations of land companies and their agents. Now it was the turn of Americans to feel the same way and make the same suggestions. In the United States, however, the opposition was a little more practical, because there were rival organizations that were conducting their own campaigns: railroads that still had millions of acres of their original grants unsettled, logging companies in Michigan and Wisconsin that possessed tracts from which the timber had been cut and which they now wanted to dispose of to farmers, states that had unoccupied school and swamplands.[11] Their counterpropaganda of detrimental reports regarding

1902, Part II, 144. *M. C. and T. Reports*, Jan., 1905, 306. A typical advertisement is printed in *The Prairie Farmer*, Feb. 2, 1905.

9. *Manitoba Free Press*, March 9, 1906.

10. *Dom. Can.: Sess. Pap., 1898*, No. 13, Part IV, 168. *M. C. and T. Reports*, Nov., 1905, 5. *Manitoba Free Press*, Jan. 6, 1905; April 11, 1907.

11. *Dom. Can.: Sess. Pap., 1902*, No. 25, Part II, 145, 153, 175; *1903*,

the western provinces was not, however, successful. It was discounted by those who had friends among the settlers, from whom they were receiving encouraging letters, and it was often answered by the presence of the prosperous emigrant himself who had returned to pass a winter in his old home and conduct a party of his neighbors back with him. In some places the American rivals succeeded in persuading the directors of fairs to prohibit the showing of Canadian exhibits, and numerous state and regional immigration societies were formed in the United States to use the same methods of advertisement and publicity that the Dominion officials had found so successful.[12]

Propaganda, however, was not the basic cause of the migration across the line, and propaganda could not bring it to an end. Expanding population forced an emigration from the farms of the Middle West and opportunity directed the course of the current toward Canada. The farmer with several sons growing into manhood was anxious regarding their future. His own career had probably been fortunate. The homestead on which he had pioneered had by 1912 become a valuable farm which could be sold for from seventy-five to a hundred dollars an acre. But that had been the experience of all his neighbors as well; and the lands that belonged to him were surrounded by lands that could command the same price. To buy every son a farm large enough to support a family was out of the question. Some sons entered the professions and others were attracted by the lure of the city which the moralists of the time so zealously deplored. But in the well-filled households there were still many sons left over, each of whom had the ambition of becoming the owner of a hundred and sixty acres of good wheatland which he could cultivate in the ways that he had learned at home.[13]

That was not a new problem in rural America. But the father and

No. 25, Part II, 160; *1905,* No. 25, Part II, 32, 41; *1906–07,* No. 25, Part II, 79.

12. *Ibid. 1904,* No. 25, Part II, 138, 139; *1905,* No. 25, Part II, 33, 39; *1906–07,* No. 25, Part II, 79, 80. *The Globe,* Dec. 14, 1909; June 13, 1912. *Manitoba Free Press,* Sept. 26, 1905; Jan. 16, 1906; Nov. 27, 1907; March 30, 1908.

13. *C.R.U.S.F.C., 1903,* I, 125. *The Literary Digest* (New York), Dec. 28, 1912, XLV, 1217–1219. *Dom. Can.: Sess. Pap., 1899,* No. 13, Part II, 284. *Manitoba Free Press,* April 25, 1905.

grandfather had solved it by "moving west" and with slight variations continuing the agriculture that they already knew. Free land had not disappeared by 1900, but the acres that were available as homestead grants, instead of black prairie, were of soil that had to be irrigated or farmed by a new routine that conserved the moisture. In the states in the Pacific Northwest and in California and the Southwest, land was also available either from the government or at prices that were low. But here also methods had to be changed.[14] In the wheat provinces of Canada, however, little modification was necessary. Crops were the same and, except for a shorter growing season and different seed and planting, conditions were about the same as at home. The prudent father, therefore, sold his farm and with the proceeds bought lands several times the extent of the farm he had given up, constructed the necessary buildings, and often had cash left over for a reserve. Thereafter the future of the sons was assured.[15]

Canada also offered opportunity to less prosperous Americans. Some of these had been unable to recover from the poor crops and low prices of the 1890's, and a new start in a new country seemed more hopeful than a continued struggle with mortgages and high taxes or high rents. To the tenant class, also, many advertisements were directed; and the argument that the man who was paying ten dollars an acre rent could purchase in Canada land at ten dollars an acre that would yield him an income of ten dollars per acre was irresistible. The "hired men" also looked to the Northwest with hopes.[16] The labor history of the Canadian prairie region during the ten years following 1900 was a record of widening demand and rising wages. Farmers offered year-round employment at a rate which made it possible for the worker to accumulate in a short time sufficient capital to enable him to purchase a hundred and sixty acres of his own. In the States, the most that he could expect was to save enough to buy the equipment necessary for a renter. The pioneer settler whose resources were slender could find a job for himself and his team upon the railroad projects that were gradually being woven

14. *The Prairie Farmer,* Jan. 11, 1909.

15. *D. C. and T. Reports,* Oct. 18, 1910, No. 90, 235.

16. *The Canadian,* II (New York, July 1905), 29. *Manitoba Free Press,* Nov. 4, 1905. *Dom. Can.: Sess. Pap., 1898,* No. 13, Part IV, 108, 109.

together into a comprehensive network of transportation. Harvest hands were always in seasonal demand and it was not unusual for a laborer who had worked his way with the harvest up the prairie belt and across the line to remain in the provinces when he learned at first hand that a few years of steady service would assure him the position of an independent landowner.[17]

But tenants and laborers were not the class that the agents of the Dominion were seeking from the United States. A growing flood of immigration from Europe was pouring into the ocean ports on the St. Lawrence. These newcomers had muscle, energy, and ambition. Many of them were absorbed in the prosperous cities and towns of Quebec and Ontario; many were routed through to Winnipeg and beyond. Here as servants and laborers they could take an active part in the great forward movement of development. But the Europeans usually lacked capital and they had had no North American experience, two factors that were almost as indispensable as labor for establishing new farms. It was these two essentials that the authorities recruited chiefly in the middle western states.[18]

The pioneering qualities of the American were well known. He was accustomed to prairie farming; an unbroken expanse of grass was not a terrifying scene. He struck out boldly and confidently, knowing how to turn the sod and plant the wheat. The European, unless he came from the eastern European steppes, and to some extent even the American and Canadian from the old farming sections to the east, hesitated to leave the vicinity of the railroad and his beginnings in agriculture were timid and uncertain. Provide an Englishman and an American with the same amount of capital, so the saying went, and the former will prove himself an amateur and secure only a scanty return, whereas the latter will enjoy success. The settlers from the United States usually had their land under crop by the second year and had established churches and schools for the community. The American was thought of as an immigrant in a sense different from the meaning of the word when it was applied to other arrivals.[19]

17. *Canadian American,* Aug. 7, 1909. *The Globe,* Aug. 21, 1909. *Manitoba Free Press,* March 10, 1906. *Dom. Can.: Sess. Pap., 1900,* No. 13, Part II, 80, 141; *1903,* No. 25, Part II, 126; *1904,* No. 25, Part I, 11; *1912,* No. 25, Part I, 13.

18. *The Literary Digest,* Dec. 28, 1912, XLV, 1217–1219.

19. *The Prairie Farmer,* April 15, 1909. *Manitoba Free Press,* July 17,

In like manner, the capital brought in by the farmer from below the line was in a form that made it possible to put it to work at once. In addition to the sums which he used to pay for land, he was generally provided with a cash reserve that in some years was estimated to average as much as a thousand dollars a family. This was good for local business, but in the long run it was not so significant as the working equipment that came in as "settlers' goods." The horses, cattle, and implements of one family often filled a car and sometimes two. What the value of this property was could at no time be stated with any certainty. Customs officials were generous in their interpretation of tariff regulations when goods were brought in by bona fide settlers. Two thousand dollars a family was the estimate made by an American consul in 1909, and in that year a magazine writer declared that the immigration of Americans during the preceding six years represented an investment of a billion dollars.[20]

During the early years of the great influx, homesteads had undoubtedly the largest drawing power. Free lands alternated with purchase lands, and the observant settler who was provided with some means could buy a desirable section or more, not far from the hundred and sixty acres that he was developing under the provisions of the homestead regulations. Rapid occupation quickly removed the most promising opportunities and although new areas were opened for entry, the process did not keep pace with the advance of settlement. Homesteaders who were delinquent in fulfilling the requirements were at once turned out. Other pioneers were ready to step in and continue improvement.[21] But in spite of the decline in the availability of free land, the immigration movement increased and many of the arrivals deliberately chose to buy without wasting any time in a search for what was difficult to find. As early as 1905 it was

1905. Agnes C. Laut, "The Last Trek to the Last Frontier," *Century Magazine* (New York), new series, Vol. 56, 99–112. *C.R.U.S.F.C., 1903*, I, 124–125. *M. C. and T. Reports*, Nov., 1905, 5. *Dom. Can.: Sess. Pap., 1902*, No. 25, Part II, 133.

20. *Ibid., 1899*, No. 13, Part II, 259; *C.R.U.S.F.C., 1909*, 435. *M. C. and T. Reports*, Nov., 1905, 5. *The Globe*, June 11, 1909. Agnes C. Laut, *op. cit.*, 99–116.

21. *Dom. Can.: Sess. Pap., 1899*, No. 13, Part II, 258; *1906*, No. 25, Part I, 13; *1906–07*, No. 25, Part II, 81; *1907–08*, No. 25, Part I, 11; *1912*, No. 25, Part II, 93. *C.R.U.S.F.C., 1903*, I, 124, 125; *1909*, 435.

recognized that homesteaders who came from the United States were generally from the less prosperous parts of the Republic. The wealthier American immigrants bought from the railroad corporations or from some resident who, coming early, had invested in a larger tract than he could cultivate and was now willing to dispose of part of his holdings at a substantial profit. The financial success of these early arrivals, many of whom multiplied their original capital several times, encouraged the emigration of others who learned what their fortune had been. The successful one often went back to the States, but he left several Americans in his place.[22]

Except for some fluctuation in numbers, the succeeding years of immigration revealed few new features. The statistics of the movement were incomplete at best and left unanswered many questions as to origin and condition which would provide an enlightening commentary on the nature of the migration. However, information derived from many sources indicated that among the first arrivals from the States were many who were Canadian by birth or the children of Canadians who, a generation earlier, had been carried by the trend of the time into the Mississippi Valley. Professor George Bryce, who knew the situation well, estimated that one-half of the entrants to western Canada were of Canadian stock.[23] It was natural to ascribe this return to the old allegiance to a deep-seated patriotism that could not forget the Dominion. Undoubtedly sentiment was a factor in many cases, but it was only one of several. The early agents that were sent out to advertise the Northwest concentrated their first efforts in communities where ex-Canadians were numerous and met an encouraging response. The drawing power of the new lands was felt first in the state of North Dakota and in the adjacent parts of Minnesota, an area in which many expatriate Canadians had taken up lands.[24] They were a border people and the sweep of

22. *Manitoba Free Press*, April 8, 1905; May 15, 1907. John W. Dafoe, "Western Canada," *The Literary Digest*, Dec. 28, 1912, 1217–1219. *M. C. and T. Reports*, Nov., 1905, 5–6.

23. *Canadian American*, June 30, 1906. *The Globe*, Dec. 22, 1909. *M. C. and T. Reports*, Nov., 1905, 4–5. Castell Hopkins (ed.), *The Canadian Annual Review of Public Affairs, 1902*, 333.

24. *Dom. Can.: Sess. Pap., 1898*, No. 13, Part IV, 111. *C.R.U.S.F.C., 1903*, I, 125.

the westward movement merely carried them once more over the international line.

This broader explanation of the high proportion of returning Canadian stock is strengthened by the fact that during the first five years of the century the states of the upper Mississippi Valley contributed to the migration in proportions that were directly related to their nearness to the Northwest. Thereafter more remote states began to send increasing numbers. By 1907 it was realized that in the Middle West the people who could be most easily moved had already departed for Canada or elsewhere, and solicitation was thereupon intensified in New England, where presumably many homesick Canadians might be found, and in New York, Pennsylvania, and Ohio, where farm prices were also high and where a "back to the land" movement was evident among industrial workers.[25] Somewhat surprising was the interest in the Canadian provinces which was manifested in the Pacific states. The office of the agent in Spokane was crowded with inquirers and in 1910 Washington was the border state that sent the largest number to Canada. But this was in no sense abnormal. It was merely a continuation of the northward flow of population that had been the underlying characteristic of the settlement of the country to the west of the Rocky Mountains.[26]

The location of Americans in the Northwest was closely associated with the opening of rail communications. Manitoba did not receive many at this time. Its boom had occurred twenty years before and, although there were sections within its boundaries as yet unpeopled, the brightest opportunities were offered by the territory bordering it on the west, which, in 1905, was divided into the two provinces of Saskatchewan and Alberta. Almost up to the opening of this period the Canadian Pacific had been the only line of importance, and west of Manitoba it passed through a region in which stockmen had staked out ranches wherever water and grass could be found.[27] In 1894 the "Soo Line," running northwestwardly from St. Paul, after cutting

25. *Manitoba Free Press*, June 27, 1907. A. S. Hard, "The Foreign Invasion of Canada," *The Fortnightly Review*, Dec., 1902, Vol. 72, 1055. *C.R. U.S.F.C., 1909*, 414.

26. *Canadian American*, April 10, 1909. *Dom. Can.: Sess. Pap., 1897*, No. 13, Part IV, 154. *D. C. and T. Reports*, June 24, No. 147, 1319.

27. W. A. Mackintosh, *Prairie Settlement*, 46, 48–52, 53, 54, 59.

diagonally through North Dakota, crossed the boundary at Portal and established connections with the Canadian Pacific. This route became the great highway of middle western migration. During the season, night after night, trains left St. Paul with from three to five hundred settlers aboard, whose immediate destination was Moose Jaw and the neighboring Regina in Saskatchewan. Thence they spread to the north and west.[28]

The rancher could not maintain himself in the face of this influx. His experience in the states to the south was repeated: the cattleman was compelled to surrender when he began to be surrounded by homesteaders. Any land that was suitable for agriculture was taken up by farmers and many of the large ranching enterprises went out of business. In Saskatchewan some retreated to the broken country known as the Cypress Hills and in Alberta others were crowded up into the foothills of the Rockies. There were still numbers of huge estates known as "ranches" and many of the settlers who came from Montana and Wyoming made the raising of stock their principal concern. But the open range had passed.[29]

In the most southern part of Alberta two conditions operated to force the American from the Mississippi Valley to pass farther on. This area was the northward projection of the great plains and in much of it only the construction of extensive systems of irrigation would make possible the production of grain. The second deterrent was the presence of the Mormons—not that they were unpleasant or inhospitable neighbors, but the community feeling was strong among them, so strong that when land in the vicinity appeared upon the market some adherent of the faith was willing to pay a price a little in advance of the prevailing rate in order to assure the maintenance of the original character of the community. The close connection that the colony retained with their original home and the success that attended their ventures in sugar-beet raising resulted in a steady,

28. *Manitoba Free Press,* April 25, July 17, 25, Nov. 11, 1905. *The Globe,* March 18, 1909; March 29, 1910. *Dom. Can.: Sess. Pap., 1902,* No. 25, Part I, 109; *1906,* No. 25, Part I, 14, 17.

29. *Manitoba Free Press,* March 5, July 19, 1905; Feb. 18, 1907. *Dom. Can.: Sess. Pap., 1902,* No. 25, Part I, 22; *1906,* No. 25, Part I, 19, 23, Part II, 70. *The Prince Edward Island Magazine,* V, 309. A map of the ranching areas can be found in W. A. Mackintosh, *Prairie Settlement,* 130.

although not large, annual influx from Utah. In 1912 it was estimated that their numbers totaled over twenty thousand.[30]

These immigrants, being acquainted with canal engineering and the science of cultivating the soil under artificial conditions, used irrigation whenever it was considered desirable. The example was not lost upon the government or the private owners of the semiarid districts. Early in the century several companies and syndicates were organized to secure the title to extensive tracts and to construct the necessary canals. They had no difficulty in securing settlers, many of them being laborers who had originally come in to work upon the projects, but who, becoming interested, returned to the States and brought back their families to a permanent home.[31] The largest private landholder, the Canadian Pacific Railway, was somewhat slow in getting started on such enterprises, but when it did, it undertook a development that was in keeping with its resources and prestige. In 1903 the surveying of a three-million-acre tract began and by 1905 the first irrigated farms were available. Although the land sold at thirty dollars an acre and was subject to an annual water fee of fifty cents, applicants were numerous from the central and Pacific states where irrigation was no mystery. Not until hard times came in 1913 did they complain about the terms to which they had agreed.[32]

Until the completion of these schemes, the majority of the arrivals from the United States located either to the north of Regina or along the branch of the Canadian Pacific from Calgary to Edmonton. This line, opened in 1891, attracted many from 1902 on, and by 1906 all land set aside for homestead occupation that was within a reasonable distance of the railroad had been taken up.[33] By this time the arrangement of the settled areas in the two new provinces had assumed

30. *Canadian American*, April 8, 1905. *The Globe*, March 25, 1912. *Dom. Can.: Sess. Pap., 1899*, No. 13, Part II, 262; *1900*, No. 13, Part I, 17, Part II, 154; *1901*, No. 25, Part II, 145; *1904*, No. 25, Part II, 111.

31. *Ibid., 1895*, No. 13, xx; *1897*, No. 13, xxvii; *1900*, No. 13, Part I, 17, 27; *1906*, No. 25, xxvii; *1906–07*, No. 25, xxix, xxx, Part I, 72; *1912*, No. 25, Part I, 36.

32. *Canadian American*, Oct. 14, 1911. *Manitoba Free Press*, Jan. 13, April 4, Dec. 22, 1906. *Dom. Can.: Sess. Pap., 1914*, No. 25, Part VII, 4. *D. C. and T. Reports*, June 7, 1912, No. 134, 981.

33. *Dom. Can.: Sess. Pap., 1902*, No. 25, Part II, 109; *1906*, Part I, 14. *C.R.U.S.F.C., 1903*, I, 124, 125.

a form that suggested a hollow square: the north and south belt through central Saskatchewan extending from the border to the Saskatchewan River at Prince Albert; the east and west block that filled in the region between the Canadian Pacific Railway and the boundary; and the western area from Calgary to Edmonton.[34] The north, alone, was open—the valley of the North Saskatchewan River where transportation was still about as primitive as in the days before the railroad had reached the great prairies. But the Grand Trunk Pacific was already building from Saskatoon to Edmonton, and in 1907 the tide of immigration began to flow along this new course. The connections were more directly with the east than with the south, however, and Europeans and Canadians, rather than Americans, were the pioneers.[35]

Every traveler through Edmonton heard of an agricultural empire still farther to the north. This was the Peace River district, an area as large as Texas, where the Northwest's staple, wheat, could be grown with every prospect of success. As early as 1907, some adventurous Americans had gone up and found the lands to their satisfaction. The long wagon journey and the slow river steamers which formed the only transportation system were a distinct drawback and tardiness in surveying and in establishing land offices slowed up the progress of development. Nevertheless settlement continued and numbers increased until an ambitious project brought a railroad to the edge of the district in 1912. The result was the "rush" of 1913, a movement that foreshadowed what would have happened had not the prairie depression of that year introduced caution into public and private enterprise alike.[36]

Important though the railroad was in determining the course and outline of settlement, some of the immigrants dispensed with it altogether. There was one more chapter to be written in the epic of the covered wagon. For the residents of the border states who were, per-

34. W. A. Mackintosh, *Prairie Settlement*, 62–64.

35. *Dom. Can.: Sess. Pap., 1906–07*, No. 25, Part II, 93, 94, 98; *1907–08*, No. 25, Part II, 94, 95, 100.

36. *Canadian American*, Feb. 3, 1912. *Manitoba Free Press*, Oct. 10, 1906; June 8, 1907; May 8, 1908. *Dom. Can.: Sess. Pap., 1907–08*, No. 25, Part II, 95; *1912*, No. 25, Part I, 29; *1915*, No. 25, Part I, 22, 23. C. A. Dawson and R. W. Murchie, *The Settlement of the Peace River Country* (Toronto, 1934), 22, 23, 27.

haps, within a hundred miles of their Canadian destination, traveling by road involved less trouble and consumed little more time than the loading and unloading of a carful of household effects and implements, and it eliminated the worry and care that attended the transportation of livestock by rail. It was also less expensive. Others more remote from Canada also considered the traditional pioneer way of moving feasible. It was the customary manner in which the Mormons traveled from Utah to Alberta;[37] and when emigration from Nebraska and Iowa assumed large proportions, wagon trains, often including a hundred vehicles, set out from the rendezvous at the haymarket in South Omaha and followed the old trail along the Missouri River to Fort Benton, in Montana, and thence, striking off to the north, finally reached their destination after an overland journey of eight hundred or a thousand miles.[38] Smaller companies of relatives and neighbors started from many localities and the questions and comments that they provoked en route provided constant advertisement of the new lands to the northwest.[39] In estimating the immigration in any year, the authorities added 20 to 25 per cent to the number who entered through the customs stations at the railroad crossings in order to account for those who simply drove across the line with family and property.[40]

Although many traveled in groups, group settlement was not typical. The American pioneer was still an individual. The exceptions were the Mormons, already mentioned, and residents of the United States of foreign birth or descent who were bound together by the common tie of language and often of religion.[41] Western Canada had always been more friendly toward communities of this nature than the United States, in which social minorities of European

37. *Dom. Can.: Sess. Pap., 1899,* No. 13, Part II, 230; *1900,* No. 13, Part II, 114; *1903,* No. 25, Part II, 99. Donald W. Buchanan, "The Mormons in Canada," *Canadian Geographical Journal,* II (Montreal, 1931), 259.

38. *Manitoba Free Press,* April 8, 1905. *Dom. Can.: Sess. Pap., 1901,* No. 25, Part II, 164.

39. *Manitoba Free Press,* July 25, 1905.

40. *Dom. Can.: Sess. Pap., 1902,* No. 25, Part II, 109. *M. C. and T. Reports,* Nov., 1905, 6.

41. Donald W. Buchanan, *op. cit.,* 262. W. A. Mackintosh, *Prairie Settlement,* 83, 84.

nationalities were almost as unwelcome as if they were political minorities. Accordingly, when a colony of immigrants in the United
States had reached the stage in development at which it began to
feel symptoms of overpopulation, instead of looking about in the
western states for a promising spot to which a subcolony of young
people and newcomers might be sent, many of them turned their attention to the much advertised provinces. Conversely, land promoters
and the immigration agents realized that if a party of settlers of this
nature were once planted, large numbers would follow, and they were
therefore active in spreading among them information regarding the
advantages that Canada could offer. Any history of this phase of the
movement would be a catalogue of colonization projects of various
origins, various nationalities, and various destinations. The group
settlements in western Manitoba, Saskatchewan, and Alberta were
arranged in no pattern, but were scattered in a way that proves that
no coördinated program was behind their coming. Although there
migrated from the United States groups of Austrians, Russians,
Dutch, Belgians, and Jews, Germans from Michigan and Swedes and
Norwegians from Minnesota and North Dakota predominated.[42]
The coming of several hundreds of Negroes from the cotton states
in 1908 and again in 1911, to locate in a half dozen townships west
of Edmonton, was an event that aroused considerable publicity and
some apprehension at the time.[43]

The immigrants from the United States were not all from the
rural sections, but the movement was predominantly agricultural
and the preponderance of farmers among the arrivals was a striking
feature that impressed all observers. Many of those who came with
no intention of taking up lands were nevertheless in some way connected with the agricultural expansion. Experienced real-estate
operators closed their offices in the States and hung up their signs
in the new boom country. Professional grain men from Minneapolis

42. A map showing racial origins of the settlers in the Canadian northwest
in 1905 can be found in the report by James Mavor in *United Kingdom,
House of Commons Sessional Papers, 1905,* Vol. 54. Map IV; see also C. A.
Dawson, *Group Settlement: Ethnic Communities in Western Canada* (Toronto, 1935).

43. *Canadian American,* June 6, 1908; March 4, April 1, 1911. *Manitoba
Free Press,* March 17, April 20, 1908. *The Globe,* March 23, April 4, May
27, 1911.

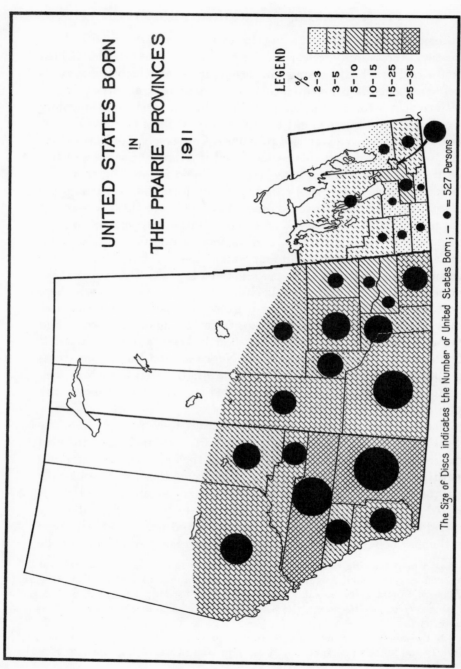

UNITED STATES BORN
IN
THE PRAIRIE PROVINCES
1911

LEGEND
%
2—3
3—5
5—10
10—15
15—25
25—35

The Size of Discs indicates the Number of United States Born; — ● = 527 Persons

Prepared by the Dominion Bureau of Statistics, Ottawa

established commission houses in Winnipeg and appointed buyers in every railroad town. The market for farm implements was ever widening and the manufacturers of the United States sent representatives to serve as salesmen and distributors of their products. Commercial opportunities existed in every community, so that the young man in Indiana or Nebraska who found all lines of business crowded with competitors, if he could muster any capital, need only choose where he would open up shop in Canada. Every year hundreds of new schoolhouses were built and hundreds of additional teachers were needed to meet the demand.[44]

Prairie settlement was such an amazing phenomenon, both in numbers and in the extent of the country occupied, that it has overshadowed some other Canadian developments of the period that were just as significant in their own areas and which also drew upon the great reservoir of man power available in the States. The advance of population into Saskatchewan and Alberta was paralleled by a contemporary movement into Montana, Idaho, Oregon, and Washington. Irrigation and dry farming were the words that encouraged the taking up of lands that lay in the areas of scanty rainfall, and fruit raising was the attraction that drew others into the sheltered mountain valleys. Among these migrants were the usual proportion who soon experienced pioneer dissatisfaction and felt the restless urge to move on and try again. Immigration agents persuaded some of them to take the short journey over the forty-ninth parallel into Alberta; and reports concerning the prosperity that was visiting British Columbia were arguments in favor of continuing on toward the Pacific.[45]

Periods of prosperity and rushes of people were nothing new in the history of British Columbia. But between 1896 and 1913 activity was in evidence, not in a single line of economic enterprise, but in all. Mining and lumbering, which were old industries in the province, felt a renewed impulse and fishing, salmon canning, and agriculture rose to new importance.[46] To some extent the activity was but the response to the demands created by the settlement of the treeless

44. *Canadian American*, May 14, 1910. *Manitoba Free Press*, Sept. 14, 1905; Jan. 8, 1906. *D. C. and T. Reports*, Aug. 15, 1911, No. 190, 710.

45. Alva J. Noyes, *In the Land of the Chinook*, 25, 26.

46. *B.C.: Sess. Pap., 1902,* 5.

prairies. The construction of hundreds of thousands of homes and farm buildings kept the sawmills on the coast busy, and British Columbia fruit and vegetables were sold in the markets as far east as Winnipeg. To develop new timberlands more railroads were necessary and branch lines were built up into the valleys to reach the more remote forests.[47] At the same time a semi-leisured class of people came in to take up residence in the vicinity of the cities of Vancouver and Victoria. Among them were retired farmers from the Canadian and American West who, after a lifetime of pioneering, were now able to dispose of their holdings on advantageous terms and locate in a more balmy climate for their declining years. Urban growth was no less notable than the busy scenes witnessed in every mining, lumbering, and railroad camp.[48]

Capital and labor were necessary for the continuation of this activity on an increasing scale; large amounts of both came from the United States. Fortunes had been made on the American side of the line when the same development had been going on in Oregon and Washington, and investors were eager to repeat the process. They provided the funds for the opening up of copper and gold properties; they bought timber preserves that were measured in hundreds of square miles; they built lumber mills and financed the working of coal deposits. British capital was usually invested before it could reach the most remote of the Canadian provinces, and American banking houses, financial syndicates, and private individuals seized many of the opportunities as they arose.[49]

There had always been a large supply of floating labor that moved up and down the Pacific coast as the need for workers shifted from place to place. Now the summons of British Columbia became insistent, and until 1913, except during certain winter seasons when the

47. *Manitoba Free Press*, Oct. 28, March 3, June 17, 1905; Jan. 1, 12, 1907. *B.C.: Sess. Pap., 1902*, 5; *1914*, D71. W. A. Carrothers, "The Forest Industries of British Columbia," in A. R. M. Lower, *The North American Assault on the Canadian Forest*.

48. *The Globe*, Jan. 10, April 6, 1912. *Manitoba Free Press*, April 8, Sept. 2, 1905. *B.C.: Sess. Pap., 1906*, F79.

49. *Manitoba Free Press*, July 24, Sept. 23, 1907; May 1, 1908. Agnes C. Laut, *op. cit.*, 99–116. *C.R.U.S.F.C., 1900*, I, 428. *D. C. and T. Reports*, Sept. 27, 1910, No. 72, 940. Marshall, Southard, and Taylor, *Canadian-American Industry*, 6, 55–56, 89, 91, 92, 102, 111, 121.

employment in fishing and construction slackened, every man who applied ready for work was soon drawing a day's wage. The capitalists who invested their fortunes in the mills and mines usually sent over American managers to conduct the operations and they, in turn, encouraged the coming of skilled laborers with whose methods and temperament they were acquainted.[50] In addition to these immigrants who had deliberately chosen British Columbia for a home, the province also received from Alberta an overflow of Americans who had not found everything in the prairie districts to their liking.

Mines and mills were not all that British Columbia had to offer. Agriculture was also entering upon an encouraging period of development. An ideal home market existed in the cities and in the camps and villages where thousands of men were dependent upon food that was raised by others. The farmer who could locate some alluvial acres near these enterprises was assured of a profitable cash return for all that he produced. Expansion was hindered only by the difficulty of securing help, for men preferred the highly paid although seasonal work in the industries to the routine of year-round farm life. Only the assistance of Indians and Orientals made possible the gathering of the harvests. The average farmer was not much interested in expansion. He was generally a person from the prairie states or provinces, a man with some savings who had given up the responsibility and uncertainty of a hundred and sixty acres of wheat for twenty acres of fruit, vegetables, and poultry, and who had exchanged hot summers and cold winters for the more equable temperature of the Pacific valleys. Fruit raising on a large scale and for the export trade was growing in popularity in the southern parts of the province, however, and trained growers passed over the high-priced fruit lands in Washington to plant more extensive orchards in British Columbia.[51]

50. *Manitoba Free Press,* Jan. 1, 1907. *B.C.: Sess. Pap., 1900,* 40. *C.R. U.S.F.C., 1901,* I, 320. *D. C. and T. Reports,* July 6, 1910, No. 2, 25; July 20, 1911, No. 168, 293–294; Nov. 25, 1911, No. 277, 1018. H. A. Innis, *Settlement and the Mining Frontier* (Toronto, 1936), 270–320.

51. *Manitoba Free Press,* Jan. 12, 1907. *M. C. and T. Reports,* March, 1903, 452. *B.C.: Sess. Pap., 1902,* 11, 40, 82, 517–519; *1905,* 83, 84; *1906,* F79.

One other part of the Dominion was attracting the attention of investors and settlers—the wilderness to the northeast and northwest of Lake Superior. The Canadian Pacific Railway had been built, not to open up the resources of this almost unknown territory, but to reach the western prairies. Its development awaited the time when prospectors reported the presence of minerals and the province of Ontario became interested in the use of its lands. This time came shortly before 1900. The fabulous wealth coming out of the copper and iron ranges in Minnesota stimulated the search for similar deposits in areas of like geological formation in Ontario, and the search was rewarded to such an extent that American capital considered it worth while to undertake mining operations. The construction of a railroad northward from Sault Ste. Marie to connect with the main line of the Canadian Pacific made the region directly accessible from Michigan and Wisconsin, and people from these states, both as investors and as laborers, had a hand in the development.[52]

New Ontario was the name given to the district, an area that extended westward from the Ottawa River to Port Arthur and Fort William. There was no uniformity in conditions and there was no concerted effort to bring in people. Nevertheless they came, to farm as well as to mine. The Algoma Central Railroad had been given a grant of land on condition that a thousand settlers be located along the line each year for ten years; and in 1905 a Bureau of Colonization was set up by the province of Ontario. The advertisements issued by these two agencies succeeded in starting an inflow of population: French Canadians from the mines of Michigan, and Scandinavians from the woods of northern Wisconsin and Minnesota. But getting a farm established in a region of such difficult pioneering was bound to be slow and no fortune could be made in places where supplies were expensive and harvest labor scarce. Not until 1912 did it seem that the response to the opportunities would be at all general and then the great wave of Canadian prosperity had almost run its course.[53]

52. A. J. Herbertson and O. J. R. Howarth (eds.), *The Oxford Survey of the British Empire: America* (Oxford, 1914), 112. *C.R.U.S.F.C., 1906,* 62. *Dom. Can.: Sess. Pap., 1906,* No. 25, Part II, 79. H. A. Innis, *Settlement and the Mining Frontier,* 321–371.

53. *Canadian American,* June 15, 1912. *Dom. Can.: Sess. Pap., 1901,* No.

Beyond New Ontario lay the Rainy River district, stretching from Lake Superior to the Lake of the Woods. This was a second border section that felt the impulses arising out of the early twentieth-century boom. The building of a railroad from Port Arthur to Winnipeg that followed the old canoe route from the Great Lakes to the Northwest was projected as a link in a new transcontinental system. While construction was in progress, there was need of much labor, and the future of the new towns and of the scattered agricultural areas along the route was so encouraging that, in anticipation of a rise in values, farmers and tradesmen moved in from the United States and laborers on the railroad sent for their families. The year 1905 marked the completion of the line and thereupon much of the activity came to an end. An unprecedented number of immigrants arrived in that year, but thereafter settlement lagged, for the region offered no opportunities that were not present elsewhere and usually with more promise.[54]

Although the province of Ontario was not successful in any program of attracting experienced pioneers from the United States to settle its frontiers, nevertheless immigrants from the Republic did come. The history of population expansion in North America reveals that in the last stages of every great westward surge of settlement a reverse movement set in. This was made up of prudent buyers who realized that the departure of farmers had depressed the price of lands below their true value and that the purchase of a farm that was near city markets would be a wise investment. During 1911 and 1912, residents of Ohio, Indiana, and Illinois turned their attention to bargains available in the western counties of Ontario. Families who sold their lands in the middle western states at from $125 to $150 per acre bought farms just as fertile, not far from the city of Detroit but on the Canadian side of the river, at prices that ranged

25, Part II, 172; *1906*, No. 25, 90; *P.O.: Sess. Pap., 1896*, XXVIII, No. 6, 19; *1901*, XXXIII, No. 29, 8, 11, 12. *M. C. and T. Reports*, July, 1900, 390. *D. C. and T. Reports*, Sept. 7, 1912, No. 211, 1223. A. R. M. Lower, *Settlement and the Forest Frontier in Eastern Canada* (Toronto, 1936), 58–75 and *passim*.

54. *Dom. Can.: Sess. Pap., 1899*, No. 13, Part II, 290; *1900*, No. 13, Part II, 188, 197; *1902*, No. 25, Part II, 171; *1903*, No. 25, Part II, 154; *1905*, No. 25, Part II, 60. *M. C. and T. Reports*, June, 1901, 164.

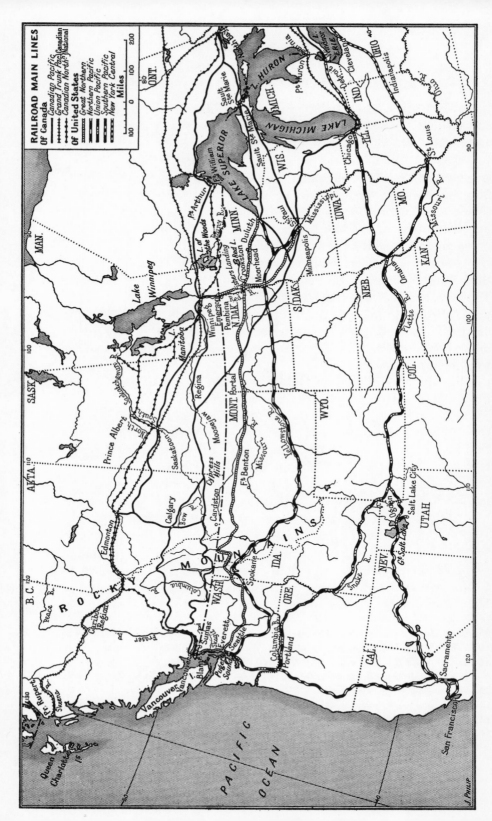

RAILROAD MAIN LINES

Of Canada
- •••••• Canadian Pacific
- ++++++ Grand Trunk Pacific|Canadian
- ········ Canadian North'l National

Of United States
- |||||| Great Northern
- •••••• Northern Pacific
- |||||| Union Pacific
- •••••• Southern Pacific
- ········ New York Central

Miles

Transportation and Settlement in the Western Canadian-American Region, 1861–1914

J. Philip.

from $60 to $85 per acre. Real-estate operators saw the possibilities and, taking options upon available lands, advertised them in the neighboring states.[55]

Not much publicity appeared regarding this movement or regarding another that was taking place at the same time. For reasons of good will as well as because of the tariff, American manufacturers considered it wise to build branches of their establishments within the Dominion. At the beginning of 1910 an estimate placed the number of factories operated by Americans within Canada at two hundred. Every factory of this nature meant American foremen and superintendents, and occasionally skilled workers, who often entered for a temporary stay which tended to become permanent.[56]

The migrations of men, capital, and skill that were noticeable along the international boundary from Quebec to British Columbia occasionally aroused worried comment in the American press. Domestic land companies and railroads entered upon advertising campaigns and adopted policies that were intended to counteract the attractions of the neighboring country. Several of the states that were painfully aware of the loss subsidized bureaus of immigration whose duty was not only to invite outsiders into the state but also to persuade the residents to remain.[57] The American Federal government took no direct steps to stem the tide, but some of its land policies undoubtedly had the effect of cutting down the number by shifting part of the current and inducing some prospective emigrants to hesitate. The opening for settlement of certain lands that had hitherto been set aside for Indian reservations in South Dakota and Nebraska reduced the flow of immigrants into western Canada in 1905; and the Kincaid Law of the same year which offered homesteads of 640 acres in the "dry belt" on the same terms as the traditional 160 acres elsewhere was thought to have exerted a similar

55. *The Globe*, July 10, 1912. *D. C. and T. Reports*, July 15, 1911, No. 164, 230, 231; Jan. 3, 1912, No. 2, 42. *Dom. Can.: Sess. Pap., 1901*, No. 25, Part II, 173. B. Hudgins, "Tobacco Growing in Southwestern Ontario," *Economic Geography*, XIV (July, 1938), 223–233.

56. *Canadian American*, Jan. 13, 1906; Jan. 22, 1910. *C.R.U.S.F.C., 1906*, 35, 42, 60, 70; *1909*, 494. Marshall, Southard, and Taylor, *op. cit.*, 29–87.

57. *Manitoba Free Press*, Jan. 16, 1906. *Dom. Can.: Sess. Pap., 1905*, No. 25, Part II, 31, 32; *1906–07*, No. 25, Part II, 79; *1914*, No. 25, Part II, 105, 112.

influence. The irrigation and reclamation plans that were being pushed so enthusiastically in the years from 1905 to 1912 would, it was believed, when completed, turn the course of American westward migration back into American channels.[58]

Those who were worried could find some consolation in the fact that the flow of people was not entirely away from the United States. From the Maritime Provinces there was still a steady migration of young people to the commercial cities of New England and beyond which was so persistent that farms and shops complained of the difficulty of securing the necessary help, and the provincial governments were induced to renew their efforts to secure the location of immigrants from Europe within their boundaries.[59] Quebec, also, sent its annual contingents down to the textile centers from the French villages that seemed to be always stocked with young people; and although some workers returned to settle upon lands in the province of their birth, the balance was decidedly in favor of the States. Moreover the emigration of well-to-do Ontario farmers to the United States had not entirely come to an end.[60]

Any program that the Federal government of the United States might have undertaken would have been unnecessary after 1913. That date rather than 1914 marked the end of the boom and an accompanying slump in migration. British Columbia was the first region to feel the recession. There had always been some who were concerned over the unsatisfactory character of its development. Many of the local farmers failed in the new type of agriculture that they undertook to practice. Not all could shift successfully from the cultivation of grain to the raising of fruit and vegetables, and after a few years of failure the temptation to enter the mills and the mines could no longer be resisted. Others who did not actually fail in agriculture did not like the isolation of farms, often rather inaccessible, and they also joined the industrial ranks. So long as the export de-

58. *The Globe,* July 10, 1912. *Dom. Can.: Sess. Pap., 1905,* Part I, 33; Part II, 51; *1906,* No. 25, Part II, 74; *1906–07,* No. 25, Part II, 79, 94.

59. *C.R.U.S.F.C., 1904,* 463; *1908,* II, 48; *1909,* 444. *M. C. and T. Reports,* Oct., 1906, 54; May, 1907, 83. *D. C. and T. Reports,* Aug. 11, 1910, No. 33, 451; Nov. 19, 1913, No. 271, 924, 925.

60. *C.R.U.S.F.C., 1903,* II, 106; *1909,* 466, 494. *D. C. and T. Reports,* Sept. 7, 1912, No. 211, 1223.

mand for lumber continued, the presence of these men caused no difficulties. But building operations could not go on forever at the pace
that had continued for a decade, and when the demand from the
prairies abruptly declined, mills shut down, camps were closed, and
railroad construction came to an end.[61]

Nature, which had given rain and sunshine in abundance for several years, did not continue to favor the prairies. In South Dakota
some seasons had already been producing crops so short that they
could be characterized as failures. Farmers there who wanted to
better their condition by emigration to Canada could not find purchasers and therefore lacked the money to finance the change. In
western Canada the summer of 1912 was a disappointment and early
frosts destroyed the hopes that remained when autumn had begun.
During 1913 a financial stringency was apparent; there was less
buying and employment. In the summer it became evident that the
movement of European immigration was declining in volume. The
whole world was feeling a severe economic contraction. The first part
of the year 1914 was marked by poor business and an oversupply of
men seeking work.[62] Whether this was the beginning of a prolonged
agricultural depression, or merely a pause in what was destined to
be a steady progress, was a question which was repeatedly asked. It
was, however, never answered. Before the summer of 1914 was over
the British Empire was at war, and for the next four years, indeed
for several years thereafter, the course and the aftermath of that
conflict determined the nature of the population relations that
existed between the Dominion and the neighboring Republic.

61. *B.C.: Sess. Pap., 1902,* 518; *1903,* J31; *1914,* D57, D69, D71. *Dom.
Can.: Sess. Pap., 1915,* No. 25, Part I, 27. *D. C. and T. Reports,* March 26,
1912, No. 72, 1245; Oct. 22, 1913, No. 247, 415.

62. *The Globe,* Jan. 1, Nov. 20, 1912. *Dom. Can.: Sess. Pap., 1913,* No.
25, Part I, 38; *1914,* No. 25, Part II, 108; *1915,* No. 25, xxxv, Part I, 14.

CHAPTER XI

WAR AND ITS AFTERMATHS
1914–1938

BETWEEN 1914 and 1933 the United States and Canada passed
through a rapid sequence of violent experiences out of which emerged
their first systematic efforts to curb the free interchange of their
peoples. The demands of the war of 1914–1918, which had engaged
Canada actively from its beginning and the United States from
April, 1917, evoked tremendous increases in the productivity of
North America. Not only did both countries expand their agriculture to unforeseen heights, but they also built up industrial apparatus of such magnitude as considerably to alter their economic, social,
and political organizations, domestically and internationally. In
four years the United States was transformed from a debtor into a
creditor nation and Canada rose cometlike to take and hold her place
as the fifth among the trading nations of the world.

Vulnerable because so much of her prosperity depended on her
ability to sell her products abroad, Canada felt the effects of the
immediate postwar depression longer than did the United States, but
from 1923 to 1929 both countries "boomed" dizzily until they top-
pled over the edge of a depression whose bottom was not reached
until 1933. In that depression, when bread lines scarred the cities,
and drought and falling prices set farmers drifting across the continent, each country began to repatriate the immigrants from the
other who had become public charges, to discourage the entry of immigrants who would be competitors for the seriously reduced opportunities for employment, and in many other ways to cut down the
old free migration to and fro across the boundary. Such border regions as those along the Detroit and Niagara rivers, where residents
of both countries had frequently lived on one side of the boundary
and worked on the other, and where there were Americans who had
chosen to live in Canada because alcoholic beverages were obtainable
there, underwent serious and prolonged disruptions while working
out a *modus vivendi*. The streams of Canadians and Americans bent
on transferring residence from one country to the other dwindled to

comparative trickles, and only the enormous seasonal waves of tourist interchange served as reminders of the earlier, easier days.[1]

The same years gradually brought home to some Canadians, at least, an underlying fact which had been somewhat obscured in the past by the surges and excitements of the North American migrations and by the waves of immigration from Europe. This was that North America north of the Rio Grande contained at any given moment what amounted approximately to a single structure of opportunities for making a living. The inhabitants of older settled regions and newcomers from abroad had never ceased moving outward, north and south and east and west, to occupy good new lands, as transportation reached them and provided outlets to markets, or to seize upon other opportunities. The migrants themselves had paid next to no heed to territorial sovereignty, so that the combined populations of the United States and Canada had always presented a picture of one body of North Americans making the best livings they could from what the whole continent offered at any one time.

The logical consequence of all this, however, once almost the last cheap good lands in western Canada were gobbled up between 1895 and 1914, was that a general readjustment began to take place as restless Americans and Canadians looked about them with an eye to improving their condition. Distinct movements inward became noticeable. All sorts of old and new factors could now be clearly seen operating in a relative way—cheapness and goodness and accessibility of farms and fisheries, forests and mines; the pulling power of cities and metropolitan areas; the effects of protective tariffs on markets and on the location of industries; and the appetite for labor of industrial enterprises. No one in the United States paid much attention to these circumstances as they operated on American and Canadian residents of Canada except a few anxious labor leaders

1. During the depression year 1931–1932, according to the relatively unsatisfactory border records, some 10,500,000 Canadian visits of business or pleasure were made to the United States and about twice as many American visits to Canada, or, at least 30,000,000 border crossings in all. "If we add in our 345,000 permanent American-born we might almost say that every tenth person the ordinary active Canadian meets as he goes about his business is or has been an American." R. H. Coats, "Movements of Population," in R. G. Trotter *et al.* (eds.), *Conference on Canadian-American Affairs* (Boston, 1937), 120.

along the border, but Canadians, alarmed by a great exodus to the United States, began to realize that their Dominion could retain only as many North Americans as were at any particular time satisfied that they were better off there than south of the international boundary.

Statisticians set to work on the population movements after 1867 and were able to show that neither country's records of border crossings were at all adequate to explain what the decennial censuses so clearly suggested; that is, that Canada's population relative to North America's represented her share of the total in terms of the profitable economic opportunity which she could provide.[2] In fact, a few observers were prepared to maintain that Canada's share of the total population of North America in 1931 would have come to be approximately the same by natural increase and immigration even if no efforts had been made by public authorities to attract immigrants since the founding of the Dominion in 1867.

The situation can be sharply summarized statistically. Whereas it had been estimated that over 2,000,000 Americans had entered Canada with the purpose of settlement during the thirty years before the census of 1931, the Canadian census takers could find only 344,374 American-born residents in that year, an increase for the same period of only about 217,000. A year earlier the American census takers had revealed another aspect of the obvious exodus from Canada in the fact that there were 1,286,389 Canadian-born residents of the United States, an increase of about 106,000 since 1901. These figures took no account of foreign-born North Americans who had moved to and fro between the two countries, nor were the records of all kinds of migrants which were kept by border officials of much

2. Interesting examples of this statistical inquiry are R. Wilson, "Migration Movements in Canada, 1868–1925," *Canadian Historical Review*, XIII, 156–182; A. R. M. Lower, "The Growth of Canada's Population in Recent Years," *ibid.*, 431–435; W. B. Hurd, "Population Movements in Canada, 1921–31, and Their Implications," *Proceedings of the Canadian Political Science Association*, VI (1934), 220–237; W. B. Hurd and J. C. Cameron, "Population Movements in Canada, 1921–1931—Some Further Considerations," *Canadian Journal of Economics and Political Science*, I, 222–245; W. B. Hurd, *Racial Origins and Nativity of the Canadian People*, reprinted from *Seventh Census of Canada, 1931*, XII (Ottawa, 1937); R. G. Trotter *et al.*, *op. cit.*, 106–132.

help in measuring the exodus.[3] Obviously thousands of North Americans, native and foreign-born, had found it inconvenient to inform the border officials of their intentions. Many long stretches of the international boundary, with countless road crossings, had so few control offices that, as in Montana and Idaho in 1913–1914: "It would be such a hardship and inconvenience for them [migrant farmers] to enter by rail through one of our established ports of entry that they can hardly be blamed for entering as they do, by driving across the boundary with all their equipment and effects along the overland trails"; or in the state of Washington: "Thousands have walked across the border. Several hundred aliens have been arrested and returned to the border ports of Blaine and Sumas for examination. Hundreds of others have undoubtedly crossed the border during the night-time, thus evading our officers."[4] Native North Americans and immigrants from other countries were behaving true to type and they continued to do so remarkably freely until a sort of economic equilibrium between the two countries was established in the late 1920's.

From the figures which are available[5] it appears that more Americans were continuing to go to Canada than Canadians to the United States down to and including 1914, in spite of the disastrously deflationary effects on western Canada, and notably on British Columbia, of the world credit contraction of 1912–1914. Crops were poor or unremunerative in 1912, 1913, and 1914; railway and other construction was at a standstill; forest and mine operations contracted sharply; and where real-estate booms had been youngest and most vigorous, as in Vancouver, their collapse was most abject. Appar-

3. The following recent statistical reconstructions give the general picture by decades: 1901–1911, immigration to Canada, 1,847,651, estimated emigration, 865,889; 1911–1921, immigration, 1,728,921, estimated emigration (including military losses), 1,297,740; 1921–1931, immigration, 1,509,136, estimated emigration, 1,245,555. The emigration was chiefly to the United States. The net gain of population (two-thirds by natural increase), 1901–1931, was 5,005,471, or about 93 per cent. *Canada Year Book, 1936* (Ottawa, 1936), 107.

4. *Annual Report of the U.S. Commissioner General of Immigration.* Fiscal year ending June 30, 1914 (Washington, 1915), 296, 306.

5. For example, see J. C. Hopkins (ed.), *The Canadian Annual Review, 1920* (Toronto, 1921), 241.

ently because both countries were adversely affected, distressed American farmers from Atlantic to Pacific still calculated that one of the best ways to escape debt troubles at home was to clear out with their remaining capital and equipment to make a fresh start in the Canadian West, even though they met distressed Canadians on their way to the United States.[6] In those days, too, agricultural machinery had not yet rendered superfluous the annual harvesters' excursions on which so many farmers and farmers' sons from older settled regions went to spy out new lands. Probably it is best to think of the two and a half years before the war of 1914 as a very trying period during which transient labor and men whose property margin was wiped out tended to scurry for shelter to the broader economic wings of the United States, at the same time that experienced farmers in that country who had been through economic fluctuations before still saw manifest gains to be made by moving to western Canada.

The war years, 1914–1918, were marked by a great variety of often conflicting influences on North American migrations. For a few months after August, 1914, the economic dislocation was serious and bewildering to peoples accustomed to peace. In addition, on the one hand Canada contained thousands of immigrants whom the war had converted into "enemy aliens," many of whom as reservists of European armies either sought refuge in the United States from Canadian action or went there so as to be able to return home; whereas on the other hand the United States contained thousands of recent male emigrants from the British Isles and other adventurous or unemployed men, who hurried to Canada to enlist in the armed forces.[7] Then again, up to the United States' entry into the war in April, 1917, that country provided a convenient, easy refuge for

6. *Royal Commission on the Natural Resources, Trade and Legislation of Certain Portions of His Majesty's Dominions* (Cd. 8458, Feb., 1917), Part I, *passim. Farmer's Advocate and Home Journal* (Winnipeg), Feb. 10, 1915.

7. The early Canadian contingents contained very high percentages of British-born. There was a great deal of loose comment on the possibility of solidly American battalions and even brigades (see for instance *The Times* [London], Oct. 28, 1914; Feb. 8, 1915; Dec. 11, 1915), which for various reasons proved to be impracticable. Large numbers of Americans did enlist in Canada, but owing to such complications as their change of citizenship the exact totals are not obtainable. Unofficial estimates varied widely.

Canadians who did not want to enlist or to be called "slackers" for not doing so. In 1917, however, ironically enough for the diffident in both countries, the United States instituted conscription from the beginning of its active participation, thus anticipating the Canadian conscription of that year. Ultimately, early in 1918, the two countries reached an official agreement on methods by which they attempted to control and distribute their man power.[8]

Meanwhile, a world at war was consuming food products at rates which sent prices soaring and made farmers rich. The United States and Canada responded to these demands by expanding their acreages and their flocks and herds with full confidence that everything they produced would command a market. Yet the farmers of both countries were confronted by a serious and novel problem. The war had shut off practically completely the hitherto sustained flow of labor from across the Atlantic, and the opportunity of enlistment in the Canadian Army, followed as it was by conscription in both countries, had dried up much of the available North American reservoir of farm hands. In spite of vast adventures in large-scale farming in the United States, Canada continued to attract a substantial, if dwindling, stream of propertied farmers from all along the northern fringe of states, and until the United States entered the war, she systematically, if expensively, recruited farm labor there as well. Only a war agriculture could have stood this competitive strain, however, and by the end of the war agricultural intermigration had fallen to small proportions, except for the seasonal movements of American harvesters following the ripening grain or sugar beets northward, or Canadian hay cutters and potato pickers going south to meet the season before it reached their own fields.

These were years when considerable numbers of fortunate "wheat-miners," in Canada as well as in the American Northwest, found it possible to sell out at a profit and trek southward to swell the popu-

8. *Annual Report of the U.S. Commissioner General of Immigration.* Fiscal year ending June 30, 1918 (Washington), 17. *The Globe,* April 16, 1917, estimated the recent exodus from Canada as "of large proportions, averaging some weeks fully one thousand per day," and the total during the past two years as "probably over 200,000." Its issue of April 24, 1917, contained particulars of the cessation by Canada at Washington's request of advertisements in the United States of high wages for farm labor with exemption from military service. See also *The Times,* Jan. 21, 1916; Jan. 8, Feb. 7, 1917.

lation of California.[9] They were also the years when high prices justified the introduction of laborsaving machinery which decreased the farmer's dependence on seasonal labor. With the help of increased public and private capital, development was accelerated and expanded in large-scale irrigation enterprises which brought American and Canadian dry lands into production. Only a few keen observers foresaw the mountainous burden of debt to be carried by someone when peace came and prices fell.[10]

The armies had an insatiable appetite for manufactured goods as well as food—ships, guns, munitions, motor vehicles, clothing, boots and shoes, and equipment. At the beginning of the war, American manufacturers rushed in to fill real or imaginary deficiencies in Canada's industrial equipment and capital resources; then Canada systematically adjusted production to the new demands, and, as the war went on, both countries were called upon increasingly to manufacture and to finance manufacture for other countries as well as themselves.[11] North America had never before seen such a feverish expansion of industrial production. Factories and shipyards sprang up like mushrooms. Allied missions stimulated the organization of great industrial combinations to which they rushed plans and specifications across the Atlantic for a mad succession of products in a desperate technological race. Great Britain scoured the world for gold coin and bullion and dispatched it to the mint at Ottawa, where it was standardized before the inevitable rail journey to New York. Gradually both countries discovered to their surprise that in a world of rising prices and currencies divorced from gold their national money incomes had risen to a point where their own peoples could be depended upon to contribute or lend the funds necessary to carry on the war.

The reflections in population movements of these frenzied developments were complicated in the extreme. While the food industries

9. Canadian-born in California: *1910*, 44,647; *1920*, 59,686; *1930*, 101,-677.

10. The Canadian agricultural situation can be seen in convenient summary in *Royal Commission on the Natural Resources, etc.*, cited.

11. The authoritative treatment of the migrations of industry and capital between the United States and Canada is H. Marshall, F. A. Southard, and K. W. Taylor, *Canadian-American Industry*.

laid their demands on the farms, the other industries stimulated the mining and forest producers beyond their accustomed peaks of exploitation to the opening of new mines and timber limits. Since the United States was not at war until 1917, and had much the larger and more capable industrial equipment to start with, the flow of labor was for over two years overwhelmingly from Canada to the United States. Demands for raw materials, however, the oil and gasoline, wood products, copper and other minerals which were being consumed as never before, and the desire or need to share in Canada's expanding industrial economy gradually brought about some return movement. American oilmen revealed that the high plains of Alberta, like those of Texas, lay above oil-bearing sands. The lumbering families which had during the past three generations played leapfrog across the international boundary from the Maritime Provinces and New England to the Pacific coast laid greedy hands on the magnificent forests of British Columbia. American mining engineers poured into British Columbia, Ontario, Quebec, and Nova Scotia bringing some advanced techniques and learning of or helping to develop others.

Yet oddly enough, American labor, except for a relatively small number of specialized technicians, did not follow American dollars. Canadians and Canadian conditions were so like Americans and American conditions that it was not necessary for them to do so, and anyway the United States could use at home all the man power she could rally.[12] The two countries were actually competing for the workers in their factories as well as in their armies, and the agreement of early 1918 referred to above was designed to regulate both kinds of demand. Industry in both countries drew off what the armies left of the transient labor which had found refuge in the cities during the depression of 1912–1914, but industry as well as agriculture was being forced into the adoption of more and more laborsaving machinery and routine.

Perhaps the most important consequence (as affecting population movement) of the great industrial development was the clear emer-

12. The only serious attempt which has been made to investigate the relative attractions for labor in the United States and Canada is by H. A. Logan, "Labor Costs and Labor Standards," in N. J. Ware and H. A. Logan, *Labor in Canadian-American Relations* (New Haven, 1937).

gence of certain international industrial areas where workers developed the habit of disregarding the boundary in their choice of employment. The forest industries of the Pacific coast threw Seattle and Vancouver together; the mining industries of the Rockies tied south central British Columbia to Washington and Idaho; the milling industry embraced Winnipeg and the Twin Cities; the same internal-combustion engines were manufactured on both sides of the Detroit River; Niagara power-transmission lines, lake transportation, and the Welland Canal created another great international industrial region at the western end of Lake Ontario; the upper St. Lawrence, the Montreal region, and northern New York drew farm boys and girls to its mills and factories from the same rural regions; and down at the Atlantic end of the Maine–New Brunswick boundary the population and the local products went to and fro with a freedom which would have appalled the officials of stricter regions, and Calais (Maine) and Milltown and St. Stephen (New Brunswick) pooled their water supply, hospital services, and fire-fighting equipment.[13]

Seen in the large, the war period had on the whole conformed to the clockwise circular exchange of population which had set in with the industrialization of eastern North America and the penetration of the Far West by railways. Canadians moved into the northeastern and central states while Americans moved into the western provinces. The end of the war, however, ushered in a new phase in North American development whose political and economic particularisms were to interfere seriously with the old rhythms.

At the end of 1918, the United States and Canada, still intoxicated beyond the capacity for exact thinking about their domestic economic structures because still under the impetus of their amazing expansion, had to face at the same moment three serious problems— the repatriation and resettlement in civilian pursuits of their very large armies, the contraction of their productivity to the shrunken demands of foreign customers whose impoverishment by war was sharply felt at the end of hostilities, and the reaching of some decision as to policy toward the hundreds of thousands of distressed Europeans who wanted to emigrate to North America. Both coun-

13. See remarks by H. A. Davis in R. L. Morrow (ed.), *Conference on Educational Problems in Canadian-American Relations* (Orono, Me., 1939), 112–114.

tries had grown accustomed to borrowing in what would have seemed in 1913 astronomical proportions, so that both were prepared to carry their populations through the difficult transition from war to peace by further deficit financing in the name of "reconstruction."

The United States suffered severely from 1919 to 1921 in the processes of readjustment, but she enjoyed the advantage of an enormous domestic market whose consumers had grown accustomed during the war years to a high standard of living unique in the world. Immense profits had been reaped from the war, and during it the automobile had, under rationalized production, been brought down to a price where the upper and middle classes, at least, could afford to buy new cars and the less well-to-do take up the second-hand ones. This combination of 105,000,000 consumers, of vast new wealth, and of an expansive new industry had begun to pull the United States out of the depths of depression by the middle of 1920. About the same time, the postwar mold of American thinking began to harden. Not only would the United States withdraw from the iniquities of world politics, but she would set up almost prohibitive tariff barriers against those foreign goods whose equivalents she could produce at home, and she would establish quotas to end mass immigration from abroad, substituting for it the entry of modest numbers in as close a ratio as possible to the existing elements in her population. Characteristically enough and in harmony with past North American history, however, this quota system was not to apply to those born in the neighboring North American countries.

Canada, on the other hand, was far less able to rebound from the postwar deflation because of the great dependence of her standard of living on continued high purchasing power abroad. Her postwar depression, therefore, persisted until 1923. The consequences can easily be guessed. The United States, expanding once more from 1920 onward, and having sharply reduced her usual flow of labor from Europe, began to act like a suction pump on the sections of Canada near her great cities and industrial regions. The result was what Canadians have called the Great Emigration,[14] and, since the industrial center of the United States had moved well into the Middle West, Ontario now began to suffer as well as Quebec and the

14. Thus forgetting the much more debilitating outflow of 1873–1896. See chapters VIII and IX.

Maritimes. Even when world trade began to recover and to lift Canada's exports with it, Canada as an economic internationalist state found it impossible to check the loss of her people to the economic nationalist state next door. In the end, as we shall see, she chose to fight fire with fire.

After the war, as before it, emigrating Europeans often failed to differentiate between the United States and Canada once they had decided to go to "America." Now, with the United States closing her doors against them, they began to pound at the portals of distressed Canada. The Canadian government dealt with the situation by adaptable administrative enactments rather than by a precise statute, sending a large corps of inspectors to European ports of exit to sift out the applicants. None were wanted for the cities except domestic servants, but those who would go to the farms and forests and mines and who carried enough capital beyond costs of transportation to give them a start were still welcome. The emigrant sheds of Europe saw tragic scenes as thousands were turned back, or when, as in December, 1920, the capital requirement was raised from $50 to $250.[15]

It speedily became apparent, however, that many of these Europeans had no intention of staying in Canada. They counted on slipping over the border into the United States as thousands had done before them, and, when American controls were tightened up, they were willing to pay large sums to skilled smugglers who evaded them with relative ease.[16] From the Canadian point of view the most regrettable feature of the situation was its combination with the privileged position of born Canadians as nonquota immigrants to the United States. Since they could always be admitted, they were all the more easily dislodged by newcomers from Europe. Europeans came in and Canadians moved out. National concern over the pros-

15. *Labour Gazette* (Ottawa), Jan., 1921, 2.

16. See *Annual Report of the U.S. Commissioner General of Immigration.* Fiscal year ending June 30, 1923 (Washington), 23, 25, 26. "During the past winter the St. Clair River for practically its entire length was an ice bridge, and at many points down river jitney busses [private cars carrying passengers for hire] were in operation between Michigan and Ontario." Also same *Report* for 1924, 14, 15; and same *Report* for 1925, 14. "When 'rum running' . . . ceased to be as profitable as in previous years . . . it was only a short shift . . . to illegal transportation of aliens."

pective alteration in the component stocks of Canada was continuously reflected in Parliament and periodicals as late as 1929 and was
the subject of earnest statistical inquiry after the census of 1931.[17]

The soaring North American boom which halted in 1929 and dis-
solved in 1930 swept Canada as well as the United States to remarkable economic heights and dropped them both to equally remarkable
depths. During the expansion period the capacity of the United
States to absorb Canadian men and Canadian materials superficially
appeared to be almost limitless. Below the surface, however, an equilibrium in population was being achieved as the indirect consequence
of such conspicuous arrangements as tariffs, and in odd, piecemeal
ways which were comparatively inconspicuous at the time and whose
combined operation was often overlooked during the miseries of 1929
to 1933.

It is out of the question to go into the details here of how, between
1918 and 1938, the United States and Canada hammered out the
compromises between their half rival, half complementary economic
structures, which in turn have gone far to influence their present
sharing of North American population. As might have been expected
in a neomercantilistic world, the most conspicuous landmarks were
the rival tariff walls. Beginning in 1921, the United States proceeded steadily and systematically to protect home industries by
building higher and higher tariff barriers against products from
abroad which competed with them. While a number of important
Canadian products remained on, or nearly on, the free list, many
others were practically excluded and the process reached its peak in
the curiously defiant tariffs set up against Canadian copper and certain wood products just before the British nations were convoked to

17. See note 2, p. 246 above. Also *Dom. Can.: Debates H. of C., 1923,* v. 1,
43, 67, 77, 628, v. 2, 1082, 1093, 1125, 1129, 1165, 1245, 1339, 1341, 1404,
1892, 1975, v. 3, 2400; *1925,* v. 1, 26, 156, 184, 204, 600, v. 2, 1907; *1926,*
v. 3, 2086, 2228, 2290, 2363, 2530, 2693, v. 4, 3402, v. 5, 4182–4183. The debates for succeeding years reflect continued concern down to 1929 in spite of
a substantial return movement of Canadians and a swelling tide of European
and American immigration from 1923 to 1929. Also, "Drain on Canada: The
Drift to the States, from a Canadian Correspondent now in California," *The
Times,* Jan. 27, 1925, 15; D. McArthur, "What Is the Immigration Problem?" *Queen's Quarterly,* XXXV, 603–614 (1928); and A. R. M. Lower,
"The Case against Immigration," *ibid.,* XXXVII, 557–574 (1930).

consider economic reorganization of the empire at Ottawa in the summer of 1932. Great Britain had just adopted protection and was prepared to embark for the first time in a century on the world game of bargaining in tariffs.

As has been noticed, Canada was converted to protectionism late in the 1870's and in spite of changes of government she had accepted it as a regular practice. Because of her vital need of foreign markets, however, she was much less thoroughgoing about it than the United States, and at the end of the nineteenth century she turned to what was to become her characteristic bargaining instrument, the bilateral trade treaty. The main outlines of her trading position came to be that she bought much more from the United States than she sold to her, but made up for this by the opposite relation with free-trading Great Britain. Her principal response to increasing American protectionism was to raise tariffs against American manufactured goods until the manufacturers found it more profitable first to erect assembly plants and then complete manufacturing units on Canadian soil, thus employing Canadian labor, if making profits for American capital. Canadian manufacturers in turn invaded the United States.[18] The net effect during the 'twenties was perceptibly to slow down the loss of population to the United States, both by the greater encouragement to Canadians to stay at home and by inducing some of those who had emigrated to return.[19]

By the various bilateral trade agreements adopted at Ottawa in 1932, Canada took advantage of Imperial sentiment to secure her great market in the British Isles and to expand her sales to Imperial countries by giving British and Imperial goods a moderate preference over American and other foreign goods in the Canadian market. It took some time for Washington to change its habits in response, but the Roosevelt administration finally secured legislation enabling the United States to bargain for tariff reduction in bilateral pacts, and its first great accomplishment under the act was the trade treaty

18. On the whole subject of Canadian response to American tariffs, see J. M. Jones, *Tariff Retaliation* (Philadelphia, 1934). For a comprehensive study of American enterprise and investment in Canada and *vice versa*, see Marshall, Southard, and Taylor, *op. cit.*

19. For estimates of this movement, consult the headings "Elements of Growth" and "Emigration from Canada" in the *Canada Year Book* for the years after 1924.

with Canada of November, 1935. This in turn necessitated a new Anglo-Canadian agreement and the process reached something like a logical conclusion in November, 1938, when the United Kingdom, the United States, and Canada agreed upon regulations governing by far the mightiest triangular exchange of commodities in the world. The three countries as it were "froze" their economic competition and coöperation in an agreed-upon pattern. They had already worked out arrangements which ensured for their currencies a rough parity and a stability which were quite remarkable considering the violent disruptions going on in the world. In effect, the United States had broken inside the British system created at Ottawa in 1932, at the price of reducing her own tariffs and, in particular, of recognizing as normal the flow into the United States of a large number of raw and semimanufactured products from Canada.[20] This great commercial compromise provided the most comprehensive illustration of an economic stabilization, to which migratory North Americans found themselves responding.

Behind this spectacular tariff war a number of other developments had been taking place which helped to determine the distribution of population within North America and the proportions of the flow from abroad. It is impossible to indicate the weight of importance to be attached to each, but mere mention of them will give a broader idea of the complex circumstances which had to be resolved in the achievement of something like economic and migrational equilibrium.

Unquestionably the most noticeable problem was that created by the international industrial areas at various points along the boundary, most notably along the Detroit and Niagara rivers. Here the "border commuters" had emerged as a problem, in the United States almost as soon as American immigration restriction had begun to operate, and in Canada when Americans came over to hold key jobs in branch factories at a time when Canadian unemployment was still serious. Arrangements were soon worked out for identification of the "commuters," but the inevitable friction and suspicion which arose forced the matter into diplomatic channels and carried it before the

20. The economic unity of North America is graphically epitomized by a remarkable map of the Canadian-American railway structure in W. J. Wilgus, *The Railway Interrelations of the United States and Canada,* opp. p. 304.

courts of both countries.[21] The early outcome was agreement in 1928 that properly identifiable Americans and Canadians might freely cross the border, and even hold jobs after fulfilling certain rather expensive formalities, but, when the depression came, both countries by administrative devices practically withdrew from alien commuters or new entrants the privilege of employment.

A Windsor man might go to a ball game or theater in Detroit, or a Buffalo man continue to use his Canadian summer cottage or attend the Toronto Exhibition, but only in narrowly limited circumstances could either obtain or hold a job across the line from his home. The seasonal transborder migrations of lumbermen, potato and beet pickers, cannery workers, and grain harvesters presented less of a problem, for it was simple to set up a bonding arrangement which ensured their return after a brief spell of work in pursuits which had always required temporary labor reinforcements.

The appalling proportions of unemployment in both countries which developed unchecked from 1929 to 1933, and which persisted on a large scale even after both countries had loosened some of their economic fetters by changing the relation to gold of their currencies and their debt structures, meant that central and local authorities began to apply citizenship tests when it came to dispensing relief. Alien public charges were unceremoniously repatriated, and in both countries, but more notably in the United States, this often involved the discovery of European immigrants whose entry had been irregular. In some cases the alien of illegal residence in the United States could show that he had a legal claim on Canada by previous residence or naturalization, but for thousands the depression meant being herded into the immigration buildings at New York, St. John, Halifax, Quebec, or Montreal, to be returned to lands made unfamiliar by years of North American life. This whole field of activity was of course blended with the limited legal migration to and fro between the United States and Canada and with the voluntary return movements which were bound to occur (French-Canadian repa-

21. The materials in public law are conveniently assembled in N. A. M. MacKenzie and L. H. Laing, *Canada and the Law of Nations* (Toronto, 1938), 221–229, 242–247, 251–252, 269–282, 283–286, 479–484, 516–521, 521–527 (the test case in U.S. Supreme Court, 1929, *Karnuth v. United States,* 279 U.S. 231). See also P. E. Corbett, *The Settlement of Canadian-American Disputes* (New Haven, 1937), 100–101, 105–108.

triation organizations were particularly active), but it also had interesting effects on the exchange of population between Canada on the one side and the United States and the British Isles on the other.[22] During the calendar years 1930–1936, inclusive, about 100,000 Canadians returned home from the United States, and until 1936, so far as border officials could record the movements, the balance in the exchange favored Canada. In 1936 the trend was slightly reversed, with a loss to Canada in 1937 of about 8,000 persons. During the same years, some 50,000 immigrants came to Canada from the British Isles, but 103,000 British nationals returned home. The loss by this movement was about 6,000 in 1937.

Another major phenomenon of the postwar period was the disaster which overtook the western grainlands of North America. The acreages were too great, once the World War ended; the debt structure based upon wartime prices was too heavy for average peacetime to bear; the expenditure on expensive laborsaving machinery and on many of the irrigation projects was also out of proportion to the cash return for crops; and, worst of all, the huge region entered upon a drought cycle, intermittent in its effects down to 1928,[23] but settling down in grim earnest in 1929 and persisting till 1937 in the United States and 1938 in Canada. The postwar recovery in agricultural prices which was perceptible by 1924 had held up fairly well until the abrupt descent of 1930 and it gave the West a feverish and irregular prosperity during those years. But during the same years Russia had worked back into production for export, and many of the consuming regions of the world were building up their own agricultural productivity and sternly rationing imports. North American agriculture faced an inevitable decline when prices crumbled and drought set in persistently.

The effects of the twenty postwar years on population movement in the West simply cannot be estimated, largely because the same picture of abandoned farms on subhumid lands greeted the visitor in both countries, but also because no border posts or patrols could pretend to keep track of the populations set adrift. American farm-

22. Prosperity had drawn back 246,000 Canadians from the United States, 1924–1929. For statistics of these movements, see *Canada Year Book* (1938), 210–211.

23. The bad years were 1918–1921 and 1924. *Ibid.* (1929), 230.

ers continued to enter Canada and continued to be purchasers of farms rather than homesteaders, but unquestionably more Americans left Canada than entered and they were accompanied by even more Canadians. Certain distinct trends were detectable, but they were intranational as well as international. The least firmly anchored westerners abandoned everything and made for the cities where relief was available. The better-off stuck to their farms until debt reduction and relief were extended to them there. Seekers for greener pastures farther on loaded up their belongings in carts, or in cars and light trucks which horses sometimes had to haul for want of gasoline, and made for the moist Pacific slope, or for the last watered prairie land in the Peace River district.[24] The principal reasons for believing that the United States gained population at Canada's expense in these migrations are that the United States succeeded somewhat in bolstering up grain prices by protective tariffs for some years before Canada subsidized her grain growers, that there were more and larger cities south of the forty-ninth parallel than north of it, that the large proportion of American settlers in western Canada would be likely to strike for the land of their birth when troubles came, and that there were more and better roads through lower mountains to the Pacific coast in the United States than in Canada.

In spite of there being two depressions to one boom for Canada during the postwar years, her total productivity increased enormously, partly because her population increased, and partly because of the great invasion by American and British manufacturing establishments, but also because she greatly expanded her pulp and paper industry, her mining and oil-extraction industries, and the hydroelectric power industry which normally accompanied the first three of these. The statistics of these expansions are remarkable and explain to a large degree Canada's persistent relative well-being. In particular, the abrupt rise in the dollar value of gold in 1931 stimulated an already swiftly expanding industry and raised the return from $43,000,000 in 1930 to $143,000,000 in 1937. Yet these developments, when set over against American economic expansion, were either so much less attractive to labor or required so little that they accomplished not much more than to diminish the exodus of popula-

24. C. A. Dawson and R. W. Murchie, *The Settlement of the Peace River Country*, covers the years to 1931.

tion to the United States. Only the industrial districts around Montreal and the Niagara peninsula, the forest and mining districts of British Columbia, and the mining industry of Northern Ontario and Quebec, visibly exerted a pull on the northern margin of the neighboring states at all comparable to that of numerous urban and industrial regions in the United States.

One consequence of the relative rise in the importance of industry in postwar Canada was a notable growth in urban as compared with rural population,[25] and this in turn accentuated the effects of an old influence which had always drawn Canadians to the United States. The growth of cities meant the growth and improvement of educational institutions, both the schools and technical schools which fed commerce and industry and the colleges and universities which trained men and women for the higher professions. For many years before 1914, Canada had produced more railroad men, artisans, nurses, teachers, engineers, writers, actors, doctors, and clergymen than she could profitably employ, but for real or imagined reasons there had been a distinct appetite for their services in the United States, so much so that American employers had the habit of sending agents to, or retaining them in, Canada in order to be sure of a Canadian supply. Americans cherished a kind of romantic notion that Canada was unspoiled, and that education, home background, and morals there were more solid and produced more dependable employees than did their counterparts in the United States.

These beliefs and tastes persisted after the war and reinforced the very natural desire on the part of Canada's surplus production of some kinds of technically and professionally trained persons to secure the employment for which they were educated.[26] Canada began to export, if not the cream, at least the top milk of her population in

25. See the figures for city populations, 1911, 1921, 1931, in order of 1931 magnitude, in *Canada Year Book* (1938), 146–148.

26. See J. E. Robbins, *Supply and Demand in the Professions in Canada* (Ottawa, 1937), a study which covers 1920–1936, inclusive. In a study, made by the U.S. Bureau of the Census, of statistics collected in 1910, and to be published for the first time in the companion volume to this one, certain interesting facts about Canadian employment in the United States appear. Dr. L. E. Truesdell, Chief Statistician for Population, believes that the situation is little altered today. English Canadian-born persons were more commonly employed than the general white population as "professional persons," "pro-

very large numbers, at the same time that she was importing, largely from the British Isles but also from the United States, substantial numbers of specially trained professionals.[27] It seems significant that of six groups of professional graduates from Canadian universities, 1920–1936 inclusive, the three which show an absolute increase in number (doctors, clergymen, and engineers) were commonly in demand in the United States, whereas lawyers unfamiliar with American law, dentists confronting the home of modern dental science, and pharmacists facing a profession unnaturally inflated by Prohibition show absolute declines.[28] It is an open question whether the commonly offered explanation for this Canadian exodus, that American salaries and wages[29] were much higher than Canadian, is at all adequate. Canadian emigrants characteristically tended to go to cities, and there American standards and costs of living were higher than at home. Patriotism and sheer inertia would have been enough to keep Canadian technicians and professionals from leaving, had Canada been able to offer enough of the positions for which these emigrants were prepared. The head of the Dominion Bureau of Statistics has said: "As between Canada and the United States the interchange on an occupational basis has been without apparent system,"[30] but the origins of Canada's proportionately greater loss of highly trained persons by the exchange lay in her excellent educational institutions, in her smaller total population, in the special American appetite for Canadian skilled employees, and in the greater economic activity of the southern partner in North America.

The statistics of the period between 1930 and 1938, when read

prietors" other than farm owners and tenants and wholesale and retail dealers, "clerks and kindred workers," "skilled workers and foremen," "semi-skilled workers," and "servant classes." French Canadian-born persons exceeded the proportions of the general white population as "skilled workers and foremen," "semi-skilled workers," and "laborers" other than farm laborers. Comparisons for the states most favored by Canadians are not available, but these would no doubt afford sharper contrasts than the United States as a whole.

27. R. H. Coats, M. C. MacLean, and E. E. Ware contribute interesting information on the employment of Americans in Canada and *vice versa* in R. G. Trotter *et al., op. cit.,* 106–129.

28. Robbins, *op. cit.,* 21.

29. H. A. Logan, *op. cit.,* examines wages, but not professional salaries.

30. R. H. Coats, *op. cit.,* 118.

against the background of politico-economic endeavors by the United States and Canada to hold their own for their own, convey a picture of an immobility among North Americans which contrasts sharply with that of any other time in the continent's history after 1760. The two nations appear to have worked out an artificial economic equilibrium between them with which their peoples seem to be conforming. The last great areas of profitable agricultural lands seem to have been occupied. The day of great migrations seems to have passed. Even the natural increases in the two countries seem at last to distribute themselves within their native boundaries. Yet the legacy from the past remains significant. "If we count all of Canadian stock," reported the Dominion Statistician in 1937, "perhaps a third of us are south of the line, whilst certainly not more than 1 per cent of the Americans are north."[31] North Americans, particularly Canadians, have always refused to be tied down, and they have never really policed their common boundary. Drought cycles have come and gone before. North America has never yet failed to provide new opportunities for exploitation, and it may be that Canada's rapidly expanding mineral and oil production is to be the next opening of the treasure house. If so, Americans will almost surely be found where the economic opportunity invites. Whatever happens, it seems likely that Americans and Canadians will continue to mingle a good deal as they have in the past and as some thousands of them are openly or surreptitiously still changing residence today. Canada shows no signs of wanting a political merger with her powerful neighbor, and the United States no signs of wanting to force one. Even granting the extraordinary unpredictability of international affairs today, it seems reasonable to expect that the governments of the two countries will look on, perhaps with formal disapproval, but actually with comparative equanimity, as their restless peoples distribute themselves in a pattern roughly corresponding to the best chances of making a living which they can find anywhere on the continent which they have hitherto developed in remarkable unison. The American poet Robert Frost reminds his readers of the New England saying that "good fences make good neighbors," but in the case of the United States and Canada, at least, history would seem to justify some very substantial doubts.

31. *Ibid.*, 114.

INDEX

[Names, places, and first citations of authors]